America

Voices Coming Together

*In Rememberance of the Tragedies
of
September 11, 2001*

Sharon Derderian & Machel Perala, Editors
Iliad Press, an imprint of Cader Publishing, Ltd.,
Sterling Heights, Michigan

Acknowledgements

September 11th, 2001 is a day of tragedy that we will never forget. The world, while watching and listening in disbelief to radio and television broadcasts, witnessed loss of life and destruction due to radical terrorists attacks on the World Trade Center in New York City and the Pentagon in Washington, D.C. We all mourn these losses.

Yet, despite the calamity of these events, we come together in support of building a better America as well as a better world for all people. Collectively, we draw together to bring an understanding to what has happened and what is yet to come. In this book, we explore our inner feelings and beliefs while reaching out to others by sharing support and guidance, wisdom, and prayers.

Thank you to all contributors to the *America-Voices Coming Together Anthology*.

This book is dedicated in the remembrance of the tragedies of September 11, 2001.

Expressed thanks to Marsha Breaugh, Fredaricka Ayikwei, and Cerresa Warner for their assistance in the preparation of this manuscript, production copy and logistics; Sharon Derderian and Machel Perala for proofing and editing, and Sharon Derderian for art selection and format layout.

Copyright © 2002 by Iliad Press, an imprint of Cader Publishing, Ltd.

All rights reserved.

No portion of this work may be reproduced, in whole or in part, without the prior written consent of the publisher and/or the author(s) of the individual works. Individual works copyright by author.

Printed and manufactured in the United States of America

ISBN: 1-58915-057-0
Library of Congress Catalog Number: 2002113472

Iliad Press
36923 Ryan Road
Sterling Heights, Michigan 48310
586-795-3635 Phone
586-795-9875 Fax
www.cader.com   Web Site
info@cader.com Email

Table of Contents

Special Note: The contributions to this anthology all original work by the artist. Spelling, punctuation, grammar and word ussage that may not seem correct is "poetic license" being utilized by the author. Iliad Press corrects clear errors, however, sometimes the author may select to change the correction back to its original state.

Preface
A Note from the Editor   i

America - Voices Coming Together
Contributors from Around the World   1

The Family Pages
Multiple inclusions from one person or from multiple family memembers   81

About the Author
Biographies of Select Writers   97

Index
Arranged Alphabetically by Last Name   105

In Memoriam
The Victims from the World Trade Center, American Airlines Flight 11, American Airlines Flight 77, United Airlines Flight 93, United Airlines Flight 175 and The Pentagon   107

"The world will little note nor long remember what we say here, but it can never forget what they did here."

Abraham Lincoln

A Note from the Editor

Dear Readers,

My idea for this book came from a good thought, "bring people together to share their feelings about America." However, the terrible event that took place to trigger the idea is one day in history that we will never forget.

It was a call from a friend that alerted me to the attention of the horrifying events of the tragic morning of September 11, 2001. That day started as normal for me; I was busy working in my home office. After receiving her phone call, I rushed upstairs to turn on the television to find out what was happening.

Crawling into the comforts of my bed, I began watching in total disbelief all that was unfolding. I saw the thick death of smoke surrounding the World Trade Center as it was burning, debris falling, and then suddenly – a second, horrifying plane crash and the crumbling of the World Trade Centers to the ground. This was not only a sight that was suffocating, but also one that burned a lasting, tragic memory into my mind. On this day, September 11, 2001 – it was to be the beginning of a day that forever changed my life, the lives of all Americans, and others world wide.

I now sat frozen in the shock of what was happening. Spending most of this tear-jerking day in the console of my bed, I watched the shocking coverage of countless numbers of heroes on rescue missions and the news accounts of what had happened; four airplanes loaded with passengers and terrorists, set out on killing missions. No one would have ever considered such a tragedy could occur.

My thoughts instantly considered my children. How they were doing? Are they afraid? Should I go get them out of school? A quick telephone call to the school informed me that the school was in a "lock in" as a safety precaution. The children would be fine and I would have to wait until they came home on the bus as normal.

Normal? Would there ever be a "normal" again.

Most likely, no one slept well the night of September 11. I awoke in the very early morn after tossing and turning all night long. So many random thoughts flew in and out of my head, sympathy for the thousands who had loss someone in the crashes, confusion as to why this was happening. Feeling impelled to write my feelings I headed for my office computer. As I sat at the keyboard trying to record my reactions, I wondered how many others were doing the same? The idea that people would need a place to record their feelings about that day came to me. Being a publisher, I thought "why not produce an anthology, collecting writer's thoughts about this historical event and anything that follows in the aftermath." In talking with my husband about my inspiration, we decided it could also be an excellent way to collect funds to help the victims of September 11.

In the days that followed, in my attempts to being "normal," I set aside all other works in progress to begin the start of my newest project. Doing so, while watching the TV, fueled my determination to produce a historical collection of thoughts and feelings about that day and the aftermath. Yet still, sorrow smothered me, instilling in me not fear as the terrorists had hoped, but that of deep sadness and the idea that life would never again be the same. Many tears flowed in those early weeks.

Life has a new reality as our lives are now permanently changed. My children will grow up in a world of "uncertainty". The comforts and security once felt confidently are now questionable. As we repair and rebuild, much of our lives will return to the way it used to be, but always with a sense of doubt, "will it happen again"? We have been bitterly reminded that you can never take anything for granted.

It is befitting that the terrorists picked the date 9-1-1 to get our attention. In our fast-paced, free society, we are so busy taking care of business and over-scheduling ourselves that often times we forget to pause and appreciate all that we have. As it often is, it isn't until you lose something that you really begin to appreciate what you have. Our losses, due to the terrorist's attacks on September 11, are immense … the deaths of all the loved ones being our biggest tragedy as well as the loss of landmarks, security, trust and more.

Perhaps returning to "normal" isn't what we should be doing. Prior to September 11, most Americans gave little thought about the Middle East and its people. Most of us took for granted the privileges we experience on a daily basis. Often times we set unimportant priorities, while forgetting most those we love.

September 11, 2001 is said to be "A Wake Up Call" for Americans. There is no way to completely heal from the horrifying images etched in our memories from that day…what was done is unthinkable and hard to understand. We can never bring back those lives that were lost; we can only promise to keep the memory of them alive. Perhaps now we can remember to slow down, and to commemorate and appreciate all the freedoms and privileges we have. We have been reminded how others in this world live without many of the material items and opportunities we so often take for granted. Let us pray that we take heed to the "wake up call" and remember to always treat each other with respect for our differences. It is these differences that make our world a rich place to live.

My heart goes out to everyone directly and indirectly affected by this tragedy. Let the inclusions in this book bring you peace and understanding. We have all suffered greatly.

Respectfully Yours,

Sharon Derderian

Sharon Derderian

America

Voices Coming Together

Authors with a ❖ after their name have a biography in the About the Author chapter.

Ground Zero, Sept. 14, 2001.
White House photo by Tina Hager.

"I can hear you. I can hear you. The rest of the
world hears you. And the people who knocked
these buildings down will hear all of us soon."
George W. Bush

A Prayer for America

By Wanda J. Burnside
Detroit, MI

Dear Heavenly Father,

We come to You in the Name of Your Son, Jesus Christ. We need You. You are the source of life, hope, strength, peace, joy, and all blessings. We seek You. It is in seeking You that we find all that we need.

Thank you for giving us Your Only Begotten Son, Jesus who came to give us life more abundantly. The Bible says,

> "The thief cometh not but to steal and to kill, and to destroy, I am come
> that they might have life, and that they might have it more abundantly."
> John 10:10 KJV

The Attack on America, September 11, 2001, was evil. Many were killed. Families are deeply hurting. Thinking about the thousands killed breaks our hearts. It is more than we can bear.

Give comfort to all that have lost loved ones. Please give peace and hope. Hold them in your arms.

Heal those that were injured. May their bodies be made whole in Jesus' Name. Restore their health and strength.

We are thankful for the police and fire departments, nurses, doctors, medical workers and rescue workers that willingly serve. Many died. Hundreds have been seriously injured. Father, help them.

Bless our military. Be with our men and women who bravely defend our freedom. Keep them safe and return them home.

God bless President George W. Bush. Be with our national, state, city, and community leaders. May they stand in unity. Break down barriers that separate us. May our leaders seek Your wisdom.

Thank you for Your provisions and blessings that You have bestowed upon us. In our sorrows and fears You are with us. We are grateful for Your love and kindness. We put our trust in You. God Bless America is our prayer. We ask this in Jesus' Name.

Amen.

The American Flag
By Georgia Collins
Jersey City, NJ

The red stripes stand, for the Blood Our Soldiers Shed
The white stripes stand, for the Honor of Our Dead
The blue stripes is for United, We Are One For All
America, America, Proud, United, and Magnificent, Stands Tall

The stars, are for the different people who come to our land
Looking for Peace, Hope, Freedom, Equality, and a New Life Plan
Our Flag, Flies Supreme, Wonderfully, Majestically, with power
Just to see her flying, I know America cannot be cowered

When I see our fly waving, in the wind, storm or breeze
I feel how blest we are, because God holds the keys
Let us salute, her, honor her, as she flies proud, flies high,
We are proud, to love, and respect her, and for her, we will die

Georgia Collins

The Day the World Stopped September 11, 2001
By Keith Barrows - age 68
Palm Springs, CA

Terrorist Killings of Innocent People…
With Emotions so High and Weeping with Victims…
The World Stopped…
Silence in the Skies...
Silence in the Airports…
Silence on the Ground...
Silence in Our Hearts...
Tears Streamed down our Faces…
As WE Watched the TOWERS SLIDE TO THEIR DEATHS…
The Symbols of America Vanishing...
It was like a Dagger in Our Hearts!
These Moments so Tragic…
As the Savage Attacks Continued…
The Silent Screams for Help!
Heard only in our Hearts…
The Hate that Swells in Our Bodies…
Towards the FACELESS COWARDS!
With Heartless Feelings…
Killing so many innocent Loved Ones...
We could Smell and Taste the Death in the Air...
In Our Homes, Where ever We were...
Last Words spoken through Cell Phones…
I LOVE YOU! THE SILENT PRAYERS!
All Your Strong Hugs…
We all know The Terrorists…
Are being Punished in Their Deaths!
The Love and Passion of Each of Us Will,
Help Another with a Cry from Our Hearts...
THE WORLD STOPPED!
WE ALL LOOKED UP...
AS THE WORLD TURNS, IT IS...
NOW A DIFFERENT PLACE TO LIVE...

Tribulation brings about perseverance;
and perserverance proven character;
and proven character, hope.

ROMANS 5:3-4

In the Aftermath
By Kellyann Baker - age 16
Downingtown, PA

I can't feel my heart
I cry without realizing

I don't want to eat
My face is frozen

A frown
A solace thought
Posing for the camera

I pray now — though I never used to
I'm sensitive ... that's just not who I am

And I'm very
Very
Scared

I hear droning in the distance and I silence until it FINALLY passes
My lips move

Am I talking?

I lay in bed and wait until everyone else is asleep

Why did they have to attack America?

My Mountain
By Gregory L. Anderson
Lindon, UT

I have seen:
  The repulsiveness of poverty, the abusive nature of power, good men die,
    The delicate beauty of a Columbine.

I have heard:
  The starving child's lustful cry, the approaching storm, the whisper of death in my ears,
    The symphonies of the wind.

I have felt:
  The grief of loss, the anger of betrayal, sorrow for things said and done,
    The sting of snow crystals beating against my face.

I have smelled:
  The sickly sweet stench of death, the smoke of a burning world, the odor of thoughtless greed,
    The essence of the pines.

I have tasted:
  The delicacies of the ignorant, the sweetness of success, the bitterness of failure,
    The quenching waters of a clear mountain stream.

I have sought:
  The meaning – when there wasn't any, understanding – when no one could, the answers to questions – yet unasked,
    The peaceful solitude of the Most High.

I have found:
  Unexpected Grace, unquestioned acceptance, unconditional love,
    My mountain, my God.

I Never Thought
By Joyce E. Andrews
White Plains, NY

I never thought that I could die doing my job in the "Friendly skies."
I never thought that I would see the day when fear gripped my heart.
I never imagined in my worst nightmare that, which occurred on those ill-fated flights.
The total deaths from the air and ground are beyond my comprehension.
I cannot believe these horrific events actually happened.
I have gone back to work in the "Friendly Skies" because I know I have a job to do.
The fear is still there but mine is nothing compared to the people who died.
I thank God every day that I am still alive, and I grieve for the ones who have departed.

For my fellow Flight Attendants

Sea Changes
By Shahira Akhter - age 17
Carlsbad, NM

The sunlight pours in my room
I look up to see a new dawn
But the sky seems overcast
With dark shades of pelting fury
Everything turns to oblivion
Fog embraces unspoken misery
A mist covers the outside world
Yesterday...was different
Evil stroked and abuse innocence
Cries were lost in flames of agony
Darkness enveloped peals of laughter
The curtain of death...fell on man
Smiles were buried deep beneath
The wails of an orphan might never be heard
The tales of crying parents will never be told
As today I look at the remains of the catastrophe
The frozen ache in my heart lingers on
Coz the charm that once existed, has escaped
Leaving behind a trail of dust
Dust that only portrays . . . sea changes.

A Gracious Wave
By Patricia Autrey Crowder - age 51
Marion, NC

The beauty of our flag
As it blows gently, in the wind
It puts shivers, upon me
Like none, I'll have again

Until the next time, I see
Our flag waving, against the sky
And when we remember, the meaning
It will keep our spirits high

The rippling of those stripes
Is really something to behold
While those blessed stars twinkle
As they seem to unfold

Our page to the future
A memory of the past
May we honor our beloved flag
I pray this feeling, forever lasts

Let's give the Statue of Liberty
And our flag, a bow of the head
They're both so important
To the living and the dead

I'm sure our flag would agree
Each time a coffin it drapes
That these special men and women
Deserve a hope we can make

That God will bless America
Our flag and our military, too
Let's all remain patriotic
To the red, white, and blue.

America – Voices Coming Together

3

What America Means to Me
By V. June Collins
Yreka, CA

Born into middle class, patriotic family, of close knit, ranching community during World War I. Grew up extremely proud of heritage. Attended one room, all grade country school. Pledged allegiance to flag each morning, with pride. Gladness in heart. "America" we lived in, was ours. **Only, on rate occasion**
WOULD WE BE AFRAID OF OUR OWN KIND.

Lived during "Horse and Buggy Days." Cars luxury, not necessity. **Freedom** did not lock doors, from fellow man. Knowing, another's could need shelter or food, would use, not trash. **"America," was Our Land of the Free.**

1930's Depression, all in same boat made for closeness. **Freedom** intact. We're poor, yet, never felt poor. Made own fun. Any gathering, an excuse, to roll up rugs, and dance. **Hand me down, built in respect, dependability, appreciation's never failed.**

World War II, again welded people together. Strengthened abilities, rejuvenated patriotic desires...............**"America best place on earth."**

We lived among God-given renewable resource, trees. Understood to be ours, **(We the people's)** deemed by **Freedom** to use, do with, as needed.

1960's **"Hippie Era"** blossomed, invaded trees, hills, and neighborhoods. **Freedoms** challenged and eroded. **New Ideology.** Started missing items from porches, homes, and cars, What's mine in a breath, became someone else's. Anything accessible disappeared, by prerogative, into new ownership. Needed by necessity, to lock doors.
Our freedom No longer, Free!

2001 reaps what "Hippie Era" sewed, into fabric of America, (live and let live theory). **Freedom** tarnished, chipped, eroded. See consequence much lacking. **Do unto others, as you wish to be done by. Now have become afraid of our own kind.**

Comforts nestle deep within. Feel warmth beneath her wings.
America, land of free calls Loud echoes of **Freedom** rings
America our heritage. Man made flaws, scars, and all...
God given America, Yes, America, standing tall.
Each nation's scattered chicks into wind of change, blown,
Gathered, tossed together all included, as her own.
AWARE, AND EVER VIGILANT!
HERE IN AMERICA, WE CAN BELIEVE.
"IN LAND OF FREE, AND HOME OF THE BRAVE."
PROUDLY, WE WEAR AMERICA ON OUR SLEEVE.
ALWAYS AMERICA! - OUR AMERICA!
"WHO'S FREEDOM'S NEVER FREE!"
Sometimes,
Other than "Heaven," if Approved,
THERE IS STILL, NO OTHER PLACE
I WOULD RATHER BE!

September 11, 2001 Terrorist Attack
By Doris J. Cowan - age 68
Appalachia, VA

Smoke and ashes fill the air
Blotting out the sun
Stunned, in utter disbelief
We watch as one by one
Buildings crumble, emotions, too
Our hearts filled with dismay
Never will we be the same
From events this mournful day;
And yet resolve to carry on,
The motto of this nation—
"In God we trust" our shield today
Against the enemy's gratification;
We lift our leaders up in prayer
As we join heart and hand
No earthly power can overcome
When with the Lord we stand!

The Divine Healer
By Sheila Bates
Reliance, TN

Come one and all,
Bring your down trodden
and afflicted.
If ye believe
ye shall be healed.
Come unto me with an open heart
and ye shall be healed.
Nothing is too small
nor too great for the Lord.
If ye believe
ye shall be healed.

United
By Sheila Bates
Reliance, TN

Label Me Not
A Baptist nor a Catholic
For I Am Not
Label Me Not
A Mormon nor a Presbyterian
For I Am Not
If You Must Put a Label on Me
Label Me a Child of God
For That I Am
For By the Grace of God
I Am Redeemed
There Is But One God
So Let Us Also Be As One
Let Us Stand Together
In addition, be UNITED.

Freedom
By Joan Z. Bergen
St. Augustine, FL

9/9/02

I sail through the East River heading south. Hell's Gate is full of turmoil. What is this strangeness I feel? I can hear sirens on the streets of New York City. I can hear horns blowing; I can hear the heart of the city beating.

I can see the majestic buildings rising to meet the sunrise. I can see the flag of China flying at the United Nations. I see joggers, mothers pushing carriages, I see smiles.

I can smell the freshness of the morning. The litter in the water. The smell of coffee, the smell of life rising from the surrounding streets.

9/10/02

I sail into Chesapeake City, Delaware. Not to far from New York City. Past Nuclear Plants steaming with energy. Sailing into a quiet morning. I see the sleep coming off the Coast Guard Station. I hear the bells on the ship, I smell life.

9/11/02

God No! I hear the terror, I see the fear, I feel the tears, and I smell death. I realize I am an American and I will fight. I am not afraid. Fight; so I can again hear the sounds, smell the life, see the smiles, and hear the heart of our greatest city beating again. Freedom, yes Freedom is what I have been seeing, smelling, and hearing as I sailed by.

The World is Much at a Loss
By John P. Clemmons - age 47
Rayville, MO

The world is much at a loss.
Loss of loved ones, friends, and heroes.
The world is much in prayers,
the population of heaven has grown.
The wounds are far from healing.
Hearts are still crying,
love is still mourning.
Lonely days, nights of sorrow.
God draws you nearer unto him.
May you find comfort,
may you find peace.
For your lives show,
that you have found strength,
courage, and unending faith.
The world sheds its
tears with you.

The Tie That Binds
By Mary Utt Bishop
Dallas, TX

There is no gesture to assuage our grief,
We are exhausted by our tears,
Our souls are heavy with the burden of loss,
We feel older than our years.

We find our strength in the spiritual,
Material thoughts are far away,
We seek peace and understanding,
This is a new era, this is a new day.

Our flag will fly higher than the towers,
Destroyed by those who dare
to sink out souls in misery;
They did not know so many cared.

And in the trenches of a misguided few,
Who look at the world with different eyes,
They direct evil works in the name of God,
But God is love, not hate in disguise.

Underneath the rubble and the ruins
Where many heroes died,
America the Beautiful arose,
Not scarred by smoke and fires.

The memory of those who lost their lives
Will be forever etched in mind,
And strengthen all of us, with values changed,
They are the tie that binds.

The Anguished Heart
By Geri Blackwell-Davis
Elmsford, NY

Oh Dear God
Did you see what happened today?
Did you see that evil display?
So much destruction and lost life
So much sorrow, so much strife

Oh Dear God
Did you see what happened today?
Did you see evil have its way
Your creation is in danger because of a few
Though many in the world still worship you

I don't have the words to explain the pain
Or the anguish in my heart
You've known this evil from the start
Yet you love us all and still we betray
I know you're saddened this sinful day

So bless me Dear God as I plead
For the victims of this foul deed
And bless them as only you can
Hold this world in your protective hand
Oh Dear God, did you see what happened today?

Twin Towers
By Sandra E. Beguhn - age 59
Davenport, IA

On the eleventh of September,
the day we'll not forget,
both the towers in New York City
took a massive hit.

Every fireman was on call;
they had made their choice.
The priest walked right into the mire
because, he had heard God's voice.

God's voice above the sirens scream,
was one he knew so well;
it called to him as it had before,
he boldly walked towards Hell.

The sweet reward, when this was done,
was to see his Master's Face.
He knew his life on earth was over
as he approached this place.

Maybe he could find one soul,
and help them to the door,
but maybe, on the other side,
he could help them more.

He gave his life in service
to his Savior and his Lord,
as did so many firefighters
who all jumped right on board.

Many hands were helping
on that fateful September day...
let's just keep on praying
for those it touched that day.

You Can't Take My Life
By Cecil Boyce
Lubblock, TX

To the terrorists, I say in these mighty words,
For freedom permits me to write instead of
    using swords.
The damage you've caused will go away, we
Will quietly come back to fight another day.

No, the words won't kill, or maim, or scare,
But you remember the words there!

You can't take my life even though you pierce
    it,
For my God, country, and family, I will gladly
    give it!

We Pull Together
By Dagon A. Dehoff - age 82
Martlon, NJ

On September 11, 2001, this old world was shocked by some men who were demon-possessed. They thought they were doing something smart. Of course, they had to do what their boss told them to do, which was not so smart. Those men will suffer for what they have done.

The two buildings that were blown up only brought the United States closer together. Our army and navy are closer together than ever. We are determined to bring an end to terrorism once and for all.

People who do not want to live have no right to kill someone else. The Bible does not say that he who kills will be saved. No! No! The Bible says, "Thou shalt not kill." Yet in this day and age we are coming down to the end of this old world. The devil will be thrown into the fiery pit forever and ever.

I am so glad the people of the United States have stuck together. They are pulling for one another. We will fight to the end. We are determined to stop terrorism no matter what.

There were thousands of firemen and policemen who were killed that day. It is up to us to settle this once and for all. Thank God we are united people.

We the United States have drifted away from God. We need to get back to the basics, the Bible. The Bible says, "Blessed is the nation whose God is the Lord." Psalm 33:12

Dear Lord:
By Ann R. Berry - age 53
Portland, ME

We give thanks for helping us unite as a common people to defend against those who would destroy us. The lessons You've taught of compassion and love for our fellow man have shown no brighter than on September 11 and since. People of all races, creeds, and points of view bravely risked their lives to help others. No one was looked upon with disdain, only as a victim of cruel and senseless tragedy. No thought of personal risk was as important as alleviating the sufferings of others. We honor those who died in Your service. We know that they now dwell in Your presence and suffer no more. We ask Your blessings on those left behind.

We give thanks for our national leaders who have forgotten party differences to unite against our enemy. Their strength has shown the world that we are not to be trifled with.

Though the eagle flies with a wounded wing, she flies sure and proud. For in her heart she knows that You stand beside her. Bless those who cry, those who defend our freedoms, and those who must make the tough decisions that will protect those freedoms.

Thank you for sending these angels to help us defeat Satan and his evil minions. Once again, you've shown that love can conquer all!
    And for that, we are most grateful...

Freedom's Flame Still Burns

By Patricia Payzant Blake - age 86
Maples, FL

The sudden strike of terror
On the World Trade Center
Fraught with cruelty and horror
Stunned the Nation,

Dense smoke and fire balls
In the raging inferno
Caused crumbling walls
To dissolve as sand castles.

Innocent people were buried
Under concrete and steel
As loved ones waited in anguish
The shocking misery was unreal.

The Nation's Brave Heroes
In fearless rescue efforts
Faced perils of "Ground Zero"
Amidst the fallen towers.

Out of the grief and pain
The tumult and tears
An incredible spirit reigns
A spirit of pride in America.

It was a time to unite and share
In the lighting of candles
For special services and prayer
And the display of flags.

The "Statue of Liberty" stands
Holding the torch high
A Beacon of Hope in our land
A symbol of Freedom
And Justice for All.

Problem Solving

By George Boecher
Clearwater, FL

Our age is one of problem solving
Beyond our wildest dreams —
Twenty thousand leagues under the sea —
Around the world in eighty days
Seem ancient days — old hat
Drifting in the tides of yesterday —
Think of these days of war and terror —
So where do our problems lie? You say
Beyond our reach in human psyches.
For war there must be a better way —
Strong ointment or a rare nepenthe.
Ignorance no longer suits us —
Emotion is our great problem —
Rage, revenge and ruthlessness —
Give us insight like the speed of light
Or finding worlds in outer space —
Let insight show the power of mind.

Up from the Ruins
September 11, 2001

By Mary Beth Bott
Fostoria, OH

Silhouetted against the sunlit morning skyline
The towers had stood so proud and tall
'Till pierced by silver lances... suddenly bathed in fire
A world in shock had watched them fall

Stumbling down thru searing smoke and fire
We watched those fortunate... emerge
Praising God... for every precious life spared
To defy the terrorists' evil scourge

As our heroes toil amidst the smoldering rubble
Eyes filled with tears... and asking... "Why?"
A shocked and weeping Nation prays
Casting its eyes toward the sky

Praying for just one more miracle... One more survivor
Praying... for lost friends and families
And, praying for our bleeding Nation
As it stands... transfixed... in disbelief!

Knowing... nearly four thousand precious angels
Awaking... so innocent and unaware
Have slipped from the grasp of a shaken earth
To touch the healing hand... of God on High

Now... thru a million tears of sadness
We hold a million flags on high
Praying that images forever etched in all our minds
Will never again assault our eyes

Tho' terrorism's horror has shown its' face upon our soil
We'll rise to strike it from our shores
Willing to pay the price with even blood and lives
As we're led to other nations' doors

We will not allow America's freedoms to be destroyed
We'll rise to fight the evil throng
Showing that our mighty American spirit... Will survive
They cannot destroy our faith... so proud and strong!

America... is rising from the ashes
America... is rising to take a stand
Ensuring... our Nation's Freedoms once again shall be restored
Ensuring... that Peace returns... to this great land!

Photo by: James R. Tourtellotte

President George W. Bush and Laura Bush participate in a wreath-laying ceremony near the site of the crash where seven crew members and 33 passengers died when the plane crashed in Somerset County. Officials believe the plane was heading for a target in Washington, D.C., when the passengers fought back against the four hijackers.

The Pain Upon My Shoulders!
By Christopher W. Boyden
Palm Beach Gardens, FL

For scores of years, I've held my lamp,
Beside this golden door,
But in a flash, it's been revamped;
Those Twin Towers stand no more!

Such pain and human tragedy,
I have never seen so close,
Yet it seems so very clear to me,
That our pride and pain will both

Become one, in defense of liberty,
As we often have done before,
For our strength is in our diversity,
From all the huddled and the poor;

To our giant corporate powers,
Who's two symbols stand no more.
I will not forget the hour,
When hatred knocked upon <u>my</u> door!

Just barely behind my green shoulders,
I saw true evil raining down,
Then I thought of all the young soldiers,
Who so soon would be leaving this town.

As we morn for all the souls we've lost,
And their friends and families,
We need to acknowledge, that's long been the cost,
For defending our sweet liberty!

I was thinking that I might be next,
Though I'm only bronze and steel,
But, I'm hopeful, more than all the rest,
We'll remember just what is real;

That it's liberty, which we all stand for,
And we have sacrificed much in the past,
Now these present pains, as those before...
Will probably not be the last,

The last time a daughter loses her dad,
Or a little boy loses his mom,
But in one small way, we all should be glad,
That most of our past trials, we've won;

Maybe not in terms of the lives,
Which were tragically lost at their peak;
But certainly, with the passage of time,
The World learned that; we are not meek!

While outraged, we've been brought together,
By this recent sad turn of events;
And Old Glory's become our new leather,
While our freedom has made new cement!

True adhesion between all our people,
Is the best goal, for which we should strive,
Just as millions, beneath a grand steeple,
Pray for each of our own daily lives.

Our great nation will surely move forward,
With a freshly renewed sense of cause,
With a dove in one hand and the other a sword,
We will fight against <u>all</u> that's been lost.

The struggles ahead will be daunting,
Yet they too, will be causing more pain,
And while justice and truth is our wanting,
We must vow; <u>this won't happen again</u>!

As for me, I will stand at my vigil,
With my lamp lit as bright as can be,
But it will not be quick, nor be simple,
To guard me; and your own liberty!

No matter what course has been chosen,
I will stand, at my post, by this door;
While this moment in time is now frozen,
We must <u>each</u> and <u>all</u> say; <u>"NEVER MORE"</u>!

This poem is dedicated to all Past, Present, and Future, AMERICANS!

Remembrance of September
By Nathaniel M. Baker
Accord, NY

Memories before; but everlasting memories of this day.
Memories are like music, you never forget.
Memories of happy times and sad moments.
Memories of touching and togetherness.
Memories of sharing our love, with each other.
Memories of a life, but not any more.
Memories of a lasting peace within our soul.
These memories of yesterday; I shall always remember.

New York Beauties
By Jessica Lee
Troy, MI

Towers standing proud
Basking in morning sunshine
Airplanes changing all

Time Heartbeats Our Tears
By Diana Elizabeth Bradfield
Conyers, GA

Humanity arise through the unbroken window shines the eyes of heaven. All to what shall move in the stillness, we must remember there is no ordinary day. Now the summer is over all to what we are feeling. Changing in the silence, we break as we bend, we cry for the answer. Our emotions touch the same, onto the road we walk, there's no turning back now we must awaken all to where our many dreams have shattered across the amber sun of that one morning sky. For now there is the darkest of shadows walking through our very existence. Evil upon evil faces strike our foundation, the structure. Our very earth, now we have a different enemy filled with the monster of envy, all to our portrait of home and pride. Our honor is immortal in song among the eagle in flight, and as free we are the freedom standing strong "How shall we ever comprehend, never to fly?" Even as our buildings of life have fallen away, gone forever...Stronger in my spirit, the fire of my candlelight, I'm burning blue. Asking in my prayer, ever precious is love in the life we must prevail in the symmetry of our eyes to see the brighter day. As we may feel alone, lost, and angry our heroes save our fallen spaces. All to say we are not made of invincible stone, for there is the harbor I long to see as Lady Liberty would know and to voice. We must find our way to the embraces of the tranquil shore; we are stronger in the rain and all to the human kind of a smile to share. Even on our darkest hour of our darkest day "time heartbeats our tears." All to where history shall save the open page, God arises Heaven all to Bless the World for September 11, 2001, Now as we pray.

Terror in New York September 11, 2001
By Genevieve Campbell - age 78
Sidney, NE

New York City reduced to ash,
Thousands of people trapped or dead,
Skyscrapers tumbling with a crash,
The world is shocked and filled with dread.

And now the people come to mourn
With New Yorkers who can't believe
That harm could come from foreign-born.
Such hateful acts they can't conceive.

When settlers came to build and stay,
All races came to fill the space.
A place for all to work and pray,
They lived in peace, in love, and grace.

Why then did monsters choose to prey?
New York did not deserve this day.

A Cry for Justice
By Elladean Brigham
Elkridge, MD

The face of evil is the face of death.
The mind of darkness blew his chilling breath
Of smoke and fire through towers of steel and glass
Until they crumbled in one reeking mass.

The fight of Armageddon is once again on earth.
The forces of evil come through human birth
To rage against the powers of freedom, truth and light.
The battle not for countries, but for cause of wrong or right.

Through thousands of stilled voices we hear the battle cry.
It echoes in our hearts as prayers ascend on high,
"Avenge us! Bring to justice those who live to hate.
They turned their back to Love, and so have sealed their fate."

We who remain, in many ways, fight on for what is right.
We fly our flags, and give our love in deeds against the night.
That Light which guides the darkest souls from hatred into love,
Shines through our acts of kindness as we turn our hearts above.

Lead on, oh Light, and stir the souls of all who seek to harm.
Let their deeds be uncovered and their hearts filled with alarm.
Let we who live in freedom show their acts will not prevail
Nor will terror win over truth, for Love will never fail.

Memorial Day
By Ted Brohl
Margate, NJ

The rifles crack and the bugles sound
And our flag waves proud for the dead,
And we pay homage as emotions abound
And we think of the love left unsaid.

This is the day we pay tribute to all,
Not just the loved ones who died
In service to our nation's call,
And their loss is hard to abide.

Though we will mourn til the end of our days
Their sacrifices will continue to shine,
And prayers are said and the music plays
And a shiver of joy ignites our spine.

These departed heroes in foreign soil and here
Were selfless as they served our nation,
And our memories will be forever clear
For their lives are our country's foundation.

Regardless of sex, color, or creed
We salute them with this message of love—
They came to our defense when we were in need,
Now their souls are at peace up above.

The Way of Infamy September 11, 2001
By Dorothy Bowden - age 82
Zephyrhills, FL

The Terrorists of the world have targeted us,
   Points of interest extending world wide;
Their suicidal jaunts have shaken us bad,
   But they can't destroy our Pride

The World Towers were tall many floors and many people
   Working everyday side by side,
Enemy planes roared in and all lives were lost,
   Though our Heroes remained there with pride.

Police and firemen from all around,
   Worked diligently, saving all they could;
But many lost their lives, while saving others,
   As we prayed, being afraid they would.

Now six months have come and gone,
   Our Heroes are still working hard;
Over fifty bodies were discovered in the past two weeks,
   That makes us so very proud.

"God Bless America" and all its people,
   It's all so great and grand;
We're all brothers under the skin,
   Living in freedom, in this Promised Land.

There are no more World Towers,
   In this great land of the Free;
But "God Bless America," anyway,
   And we'll replace them in time, you'll see!

God Bless America
   the
Land of the Free
   and
The Home of the Brave.

Untitled
By Edward Ehren
Oak Park, MI

Her face is like a cloudy day
Overcast and always grey
Waiting for a drop of rain
To align itself with her pain
Frost from Winter's frozen tears
Always there as sadness nears
Melting only to refreeze
But God forbid the Winter's breeze
Should opt to blow her tears away
And leave her face a cloudy day

Memories
By Sheila Bates - age 38
Reliance, TN

Memories of yesteryear
are so close
but yet so far away.
I can't see them nor touch them,
But yet, when I close my eyes,
I feel them ever so close.
My memories are my Treasures
forever locked in my heart,
Which, can never be taken away?

Lady Liberty
By Paulette DiTizio - age 45
Westville Grove, NJ

O Lady Liberty,
Our enemy has cut us deep.
The loss of our fellowman,
Caused all our hearts to weep.

Although we do bicker,
Each believing he is right.
When faced by an enemy,
We stand united to fight.

Fear not, o sweet Lady,
For your torch burns in our souls.
The wrath of Justice mighty,
For those opposed, the bell tolls.

God <u>Was</u> at the Pentagon and Twin Towers
By Gloria Jean Brown
Annapolis, MD

In an instant God grasped them amid their known distress.
Saying child I am taking you graciously to your home and final rest.
You will not know or feel the pain—
of what the terrorists did hope to gain.
During this horrible attack on nine one one,
my day with you had just begun.
While jumping out of windows, I heard your cry,
caught you in my arms, gave comfort in your sigh.
When families and friends awaited your fate,
I gloriously blew the flag of the United States.
In your solemnity, sorrow, and many tears,
the red, white, and blue will settle your fears.
This act of hatred, of evil, of guile,
I do not honor, nor do I smile.
Patience is all, I ask of you,
love and cherish in all you do.
Charity for all mankind is your utmost goal,
and you shall remain the victor of all that unfolds.
What happened to those who knew not my name?
I gathered them in my bosom without any blame.
I caressed those who fell, easing their pain.
The terrorists were failures in their dastardly fame.
Flying high in the skies of blue,
The victims were taken with a love so true.
The mighty flight of 93,
went down with heroism and victory.
Fear not tomorrow or any day,
together we unite, together we pray.
The United States is what we hail,
and to this end, we shall prevail.

This poem is dedicated to my husband,
Lt. Cmdr. Larence H. Brown, USN Ret.

The Red, White, and Blue
By Brenda Joyce Dias - age 53
Saugerties, NY

Red, white, and blue, the colors that I know
Our majestic flag just look at it blow
American armed forces unfurl it with pride
Defending it bravely many have died

America, America, we all love you!
We shall all defend the red, white, and blue!

Democracy, proclaimed by the people
The Constitution makes it all quite simple
Wars have been fought, our land well defended
With spirits of pride, our rights defended

America, America, we all love you!
We shall all defend the red, white, and blue!

Swords into plowshares, sweet peace is our goal
Freedom from fear and terror touch our soul
Peaceful and friendly to all those we know
Helping those in need wherever we go

America, America, we all love you!
We shall all defend the red, white, and blue!

We all walk our streets unguarded and free
Osama Bin Laden, oh, don't you see
Americans all born in liberty
Our spirits undaunted, watching you flee

America, America, we all love you!
We shall all defend the red, white, and blue!

Evil men must die; you retreat
Terrorizing done, your maker must meet
Our God is so good, our principles pure
The Taliban and you flames will endure.

America, America, we all love you!
We shall all defend the red, white, and blue!

Lives we have lost, we all grieve our own
In freedom we live, you are not our clone
Founded in freedom, America is strong
Liberating spirits live the day long

America, America, we all love you!
We shall all defend the red, white, and blue!

We all proudly wave our red, white, and blue
Osama Bin Laden you'll get your due
United we stand, we're all joined as one
Afghanistan watch out, we've just begin

America, America, we all love you!
We shall all defend the red, white, and blue!

*Dedicated to our courageous soldiers
fighting to keep America free.*

September 11, 2001
By Duranda Buckley - age 18
Vandalia, OH

Some jets flew over the night of the 9th. My family heard them, but didn't know why. The night of the 10th, I jokingly told my sister, "Wake me up if something strange happens." The next morning, the 11th, I awoke to hear my sister's voice. "A plane just hit the World Trade Center," she said. I jerked up and looked at the television she turned on. "What?" I yelled! I couldn't believe my eyes. I was so scared. I remember thinking that my house could be attacked any minute. I immediately called my friend that was leaving for Germany on that Thursday, to tell her I love her. I was confused, and worried all at the same time. I am supposed to be growing up in a peaceful country, but now, everything has changed. I was glued to the television for the entire day....which soon turned into almost three days. It was like I was afraid to look away. My friend came over the 11th and we talked about everything and how scary this was. We went outside to leave with my parents, when suddenly we heard two loud booms. I began to cry and ran to my dad. My mom and my friend stood closely together. I remember my dad saying, "No, not here." That scared me. We ran inside to watch the ongoing news to see what it was. We later found out that it was two jets in a dogfight to clear the air for Air Force One to fly overhead. A hush fell across our nation that day as everyone watched the Towers collapse. Our country has pulled together and we're winning this war. My "brother" called from California that day, where he's stationed in the Marines, to say that he wasn't going overseas. That brought more relief than he'll ever know. I am very proud to be an American. My whole view of life has changed, and I no longer take things for granted. I hope this changes our country and our world for the better. God Bless America!

"Truth"
By April L. Delaney
Durham, NC

America – Voices Coming Together

New York! New York!
Trouble and Rubble, September 11, 2001-A.M.
By June Allegra Elliott - age 81
Seal Beach, CA

Morning light and autumn
    crispen splendor —
All a'sudden, an interruption there —
On slant wing perilous flight,
    two silvery planes aimed
    into twin concrete skyscraper
    towers, icons of America's
    capitalistic society —
The scene of death and
    destruction, unrolled like a scroll before our
    eyes, with bomb
    blast orange flame
    billowing.
In suicidal pact,
    hidden terrorist hijackers
    guided these planes on mad
    trajectories, met
    Satan promptly!
Their passengers met God
    in Heaven instantly!

Dedicated to persons in harms way including their friends and relatives.

Mom, did you see it?
By Nancy L. Falzone-Cardinal
Springfield, MA

Mom, did you see it
From the safety of God' s arms
The horror here on September 11th
The dreadful, tragic harm?

Did you feel the quaking buildings
Caused by evil and rage?
Did Jesus weep over the Bible
Questioning every page?

Do you see how Americans live now
In this newly, insecure place
Not knowing when, if ever
Someone will attack our space?

During aftershock
We need for you to pray
To keep us strong and spiritual
Through our remaining days.

Did you over hear me
When I thanked God
That you weren't here?
For as much as I miss you
You shouldn't live in this fear.

America the Brave
By Patricia L. Backlund - age 74
Medford, OR

    I have always held the view that some good can come from something bad. After the unbelievable events of September 11, I see Americans, regardless of color or race, united as one proudly displaying our nation's flag and writing words of encouragement and praise everywhere.

    Individuals are responding by giving money or assisting in many ways, those families who lost loved ones in the horrendous tragedy.

    Once again, the call to serve our country was issued and our service men fight to conquer those who would destroy us. Now we see acts of unspeakable brutality in many other countries.

    Patriotism surrounds us and eyes tear when we hear our national anthem or God Bless America. We may never again experience our former feelings of freedom, but let us go forth as proud Americans and become victorious over fear as we strive to return to become once again the home of the brave.

Rebuild bigger, better: United they stood
By Cella M. Candanoza - age 18
Prosser, WA

    Since 1973 the twin towers of the World Trade Center stood, soaring 110 stories above the New York City skyline. They were signs of financial success to the citizens of New York, to Americans, and to the world.

    These buildings were built to withstand ground-shaking disasters and the like. Not even a 1993 bomb explosion could bring the towers down....the world moved on. However, on September 11th, the United States was shocked and the world froze on its axis when the Twin Towers crumbled to the ground. Now a pile of dust and debris lies where two great edifices once stood.

    The question that remains for America is, should the Towers be rebuilt? Some say yes, but not as high. Others say no, build a memorial in place. I say yes, but bigger and better. Let's put back what was taken and show those terrorists that we cannot be torn apart. In the midst of tragedy, America comes together, but more importantly, America bounces back.

    So, from the ashes in the financial district of New York, resurrect the towers, restore the void along the East Coast horizon. Show the world we can be knocked down, but we will rise again....stronger, together.

America's Heroes
By Madeline J. Carlson
Gothenburg, NE

Americans around the world stopped to pray
As the New York skies turned an eerie gray

Without hesitation they answered the call
Losing their lives as the towers would fall

The ultimate price they would have to pay
Becoming heroes on that fateful day

Many heroes working from sun to sun
Hoping they could rescue, even just one

Volunteers giving their time, doing their share
Strangers giving their money because they care

At Ground Zero Old Glory would wave
Giving honor to the lost and the brave

There's been a rebirth of patriotism and pride
The freedom of our country will not be denied
We as a nation may falter, but we'll not fall
Maybe there's a little hero in us all

This poem is dedicated to all the heroes of 9-11

September 11
By Maria Alice Carreira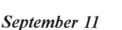
Elizabeth, NJ

The darkness started before mid-day
Just right after people started their day...

Broken bodies flying broken hearts crying
Broken voices screaming under the building...

Who destroyed the twins of the world?
Who flew the blind birds?
Who took away the hope of those on board?

How can any human take away innocent lives?
From fathers and mothers that left children behind
With tearing eyes and wondering minds...

To those their bodies are still missing
Resting under the debris...
And their families looking for consolation and peace.

There's time for everything
And only God knows the destiny of our time
So was this meant to be for those who died?
And grief to those who stayed behind?

American Quilt
By Ruth Cone
Pomona, CA

Patchwork Plains in
Multicolored hues,
Fruitful green fields,
Bordered by raging blue rivers,
Majestic snow-capped mountains,
Endless foaming oceans,
Proud land
That calls itself
America.

Patchwork people from
Multitude lands.
Asia, Africa, Europe,
Great Britain, Arabia,
Myriad philosophies.
Christianity, Judaism, Islam,
Buddhism, Atheism.
Proud souls
That calls themselves
Americans.

God Bless the U.S.A.
By Peachie Chalke - age 49
Jaffrey, NH

America, I'll always love you for you will always be,
The Grandest Land of them all to me.
In more ways than one September 11, 2001 was a blue, blue day.
As mommy's and daddy's gave their lives as heroes, so others might stay.
I thank God each day for each one who survives.
Pray each day for those who without thought gave their lives.
Today we need to put our hands in the hands of each other and go on.
Knowing in our hearts some of our heroes are still here — some are gone.
It began in New York and was heard all the way to L.A.
The sound of shattered hearts all around our country on that sad day.
Every American boy, girl, man, and women big and small.
Heard stories of heroes who will be remembered always
Not just written on tombstones or a memorial wall.
We must in our hearts know that we'll never walk alone.
This is no time to stop believing in our country
Where the flag of freedom is flown.
The terrorist will not destroy America as they planned.
For this is your land, this is my land, this is our land.
So God will Bless American again,
As we know, He holds the Whole World In His Hands.
One day we'll reflect upon these events and someone will ask,
"Where did all the Heroes come from?"
Everyone will answer from America
Who is and always will be number one!

America — Voices Coming Together

2001/Nine
By Annette Caster - age 49
Vicksburg, MS

The year America was brought to her knees
With dust and debris drifting in the breeze
Terrorist destruction came with such ease
And now several nations are much too pleased

We have cried and hurt for the thousands gone
Digging for answers will take so very long
We have found no resolve in the corpses wrong
So many nations have broke out in America's song

Disaster has befallen us with cruel intent
We now know the ones that were hell bent
They will find this nation will never ever relent
They should be cautious of the troops we've sent

For thousands will go to capture a few
And justice will be long over due
For now the world has been shaken anew
Awakened power of the red, white, and blue

We have come so far with our peace proclaim
Now we're rattled by a group we think insane
This sleeping giant cannot....will not refrain
For justice will bring our freedom to reclaim

We were in huge numbers when she fell
The twins that shone to the world to buy and sell
We are there in huge numbers with stories to tell
A few think it's good, the rest think it's hell

We will never forget what Satan has done
He has wronged the wrong nation, we won't run
We will bring him to his knees with his beguiled son
And when it's all over this nation will have won

The countries that harbor will feel our wrath
We can do nothing to them of equal blood bath
Carved in bronze will be their cowardly epitaph
And America will have comfort in their timely death

Our America will recover....on that we all agree
This is what we stand for....the reason we're free
A country of nations united to a formidable degree
We are holy ground, from sea to shining sea

Twin Towers
By Ashley Edem Ayikwei - age 11
Roseville, MI

Our twin towers went down
We put on a frown
We flew our flag with pride and joy
And our frown went up but not down
We know it's a test
But we did our very best.

Destiny
By Luella Knauss Potts
Cadmus, MI

The sun broke forth from clouds of gold and blue
It was another day and everything was new.

Nature's choir sang their early wake-up call
The Twin Towers like sentinels stood straight and tall.

Then all at once a plane we thought was passing by
But then a loud crash and flames and we heard many cries.

A tower had been struck, we saw the tumbling walls.
Then the second tower was hit, we saw people fall.

The Pentagon then took a blow and we heard screams
Police and firefighters rushed to the dreadful scene.

When the words, "Lets Roll," was heard on flight 93
The terrorists knew their plan was not to be.

As a nation we kept the faith on that horrific day
We joined hands and hearts and together we all prayed.

Memories will be forever etched from the landmarks that once gleamed
We pray time and faith will heal all broken dreams.

In memory of my husband, Russell William Potts

Untitled
By Kristie Crampton - age 17
Wilmington, MA

Hundreds of heroes were born on that day,
After thousands of lives were stolen away.
A nation was woken from a lengthy slumber,
After the ominous planes roared like thunder.
Countless realized how much life was worth living,
Which spurred a rush of unity and giving.
A country was wounded where it mattered most,
In the hearts of its people from east to west coast.
Hate poured from the souls of some,
And mixed with the tears that quickly did come.
Questions were asked with a sense of deep need,
And left unanswered; our nation left to bleed.
Fear was then checked and a recovery started,
Pride was shown by all with respect for the departed.
Our strength never did falter or waiver,
After it was decided war was in favor.
We sent our bravest-our strongest-our best,
As we enter the war for freedom-the great test.
Six months later the nation slowly heals but never forgets,
Its people are changed and live without regrets.
Time has passed and healing has begun,
It has been repeatedly proven: OUR COLORS DON'T RUN!

It Was A Clear Day 9/11
By Barbara Birenbaum
Clearwater, FL

A perforated sky
was all that remained
after messengers of hate
punctured buildings with planes —
acts of atrocities of
man against humanity.

Jet fuel melted down
the core of their existence,
leveling the infrastructure.
Glass and metals shards stand
as reminders of twin towers
that stood for world globality.

New York City smoldered in chaos
only for a moment before
medics, police, firemen and
humanitarians converged
on the inferno, raising a flag
of unity in defiance of martyrs.

America's resolve as a stronghold of peace
lessened the pain of families
fractured by death and separation,
people confronted with confusion,
to stand as one nation, under God,
with liberty and freedom for all.

September 11, 2002
By Stephanie Dana - age 19
Taylorsville, UT

And I can't hold back the tears
Because thousands were killed today
And I can't be sure if I'll ever
Meet this faceless murderer
And whether it was a
Religious-cultural struggle
Or an act of pure hatred
And my heart sinks
Like an anchor to the bottom
Of an ocean, blue with freedom
And my love has already begun to rust
In deep despair
And my soul will forever
Reside in the rubble
With the innocence that was
Taken from America today

Remembrance
By Irene A. Fontaine - age 53
Springfield, MA

God be with you, and bless you all.
In this beautiful country,
We've all learned, to stand tall.
We hold our heads up high, and proudly try;
To let the tragic moments of 911, pass us by.
Although, our loved ones will never be forgotten;
We can rest assure, that God has taken them, under his wing.
For all eternity, his praises to sing.

America's Brotherhood
By Sonya S. Batts
Jacksonville, NC

The time has come
When wings of unfamiliar destinations has taken flight upon our sacred grounds.
The ground where the roots of many origins are planted
And bare the seeds of common tides.
"WE HOLD THESE TRUTHS TO BE SELF EVIDENT!"
"WE HOLD THESE TRUTHS TO BE SELF EVIDENT!"
That any branch lying mangled on the ground is of a sacred trust.
That freedom
Sweet and blessed freedom will answer the cry of her fallen once.
As sure as the sun does shine after the storm abates
America
Will most assuredly gather her common tides that say in unity,
"WE ARE ONE!"
In the time of need, America will even extend her branches to foreign woes.
America extends her branches off of one common tree.
The olive branch
The olive branch
America does bequeath, to her fellow brothers.
For our nation was founded on this principal
IN GOD WE TRUST!
IN GOD WE TRUST!
We depend on him, and him alone, to set us free on earth and in spirit.
And that is why we, as Americans know
That OUR EAGLE WILL FLY!
Destiny has it, that when pilgrims of familiar purpose leads and bond together
That the will, of woes
Will loose its grip, on those with a common purpose.
These pilgrims of one bond, one purpose, on pursuit, will in the end
PREVAIL!

Oh wings of unfamiliar flight
Take not one of our brothers underneath your wings.
Though we are a people of many different lands, with a brotherhood of togetherness
WE WILL STAND!
As Americans we sing, we sing a song of peace and courage, in harmony.
IN GOD WE TRUST!
IN GOD WE TRUST!
America's brotherhood was founded on this principal.
Take not one breath of solace in the lost of our beloved brothers.
Our brothers of many races, many religions, many colors, and many creeds.
For we as Americans stand firm, upon this are sacred ground, and shout
We shout in solidarity,

"OUR EAGLE WILL FLY!"

America United
By Freda M. Dehoff
Marlton, NJ

The tragic events of September 11, 2001, will be forever etched in my memory. I was horrified by the terrible loss of life and destruction. My heart weeps for all those who are mourning the loss of a loved one.

Something else stands out vividly in my memory. In the midst of this tragedy, Americans have united and found the strength to keep going as a nation.

Several things made this possible. One was that people everywhere were reaching out to help others. Firefighters and rescue workers labored selflessly on that day to help people to safety and to free others from the debris. Many even sacrificed their own lives. Since that day, they have been working endlessly at ground zero to clean up the rubble left by the destruction.

Another thing that has united our country is a deep feeling of patriotism. Americans proudly sing our national anthem as their eyes fill with tears. Flags can be seen waving proudly in front of houses, businesses, and from car antennas. Young men willingly serve our country and do it with pride.

The most important thing, however, that has united Americans and given us the strength to go on is our dependence upon God and prayer. Thank God, for the example and leadership of President Bush who called our country to prayer. Soon people everywhere across our great land were uniting, together for one purpose—to pray for America. Turning to God and to prayer has given Americans strength to go through this crisis and will continue to give us hope in the days to come.

Memories
By Eleanor L. Crichlow - age 59
Virginia Beach, VA

The twin towers stood tall,
Their silhouettes cast slender shadows,
Upon the city streets
With the morning sunrise,
Echo's of the hustle and bustle
Filled the air,
While elevators raced,
To high-rise floors,
As they did the day before.
Unexpectedly from out of the sky,
Came the pilots from hell,
Lives shattered,
As the twin towers fell,
Unaware, that the Pentagon,
Had been struck as well,
Many souls,
From many faiths, walked together,
Towards heavens gates,
As a Nation we stand tall,
Waving our stars and stripes
So all the innocent,
Lost that day
Will live in our memories,
Memories, that will not fade.

Our Home
By Sonya S. Batts
Jacksonville, NC

It is the beauty of the land, our people
Standing together
With pride and strength, that makes our country
American, Reign.

There is no other homeland
That gives her people the will to aim high.
The will and courage
To take flight with her national symbol
On the wings of the eagle
We fly!

With God to lead us, we shall prevail.
"In God WE Trust!"
In any storm that may arise
For we, as Americans
Mount on the Wings of the Eagle and Fly!

Our blessed home
Is blessed, because we know the price of freedom.
We trust in God to lead us!
Whatever storm may arise, it is on the eagle that we
mount up, and on wings of the eagle we Fly!

Twin Towers
By Emma Currie - age 21
Christchurch, New Zealand

How must you have felt
When your world came crashing down
A tidal wave of destruction
Threatening to swallow you.
How must you have felt
Walking dazed amongst fellow humans
Dusted a ghostly white
Once busy streets lay silent
paralyzed by shock.
How must you have felt
Deafened by the pounding of your own heart
Blinded by storm clouds of smoke
Suffocated by fear
Bleeding invisible tears.
How do I feel
Physically oceans apart, but spiritually
In every heart
Praying I can hold up your fallen sky
Weeping for your blazing souls
Hoping each and every tear
Will help fight every internal fire.

Attack on America
By Stacey Dunsmore
East Northport, NY

FREEDOM! Let freedom ring.
Isn't this what America stands for?
But what did this freedom recently bring?
Death, sorrow, and so much more.

For all the families and friends in grief
Just remember America is so strong and true
That eventually there will be relief
From the flag that waves so high of red, white, and blue.

We have been shattered
But with unity we will survive.
We have been beat
But be thankful for the ones who are giving their lives.

We are not destroyed
Nor will we give in.
Our lives now have an empty void
Due to a coward's sin.

But because America is so strong
Don't think we will not retaliate
We will put them where they belong
And show them how it truly feels to hate.

So for all of those who lost loved ones,
Our hearts go out to you
And even though we are in sorrow and are blue
America we still love you.

United
By Derick R. Bryant - age 25
Dorchester, MA

We can't be stopped.
Each and every one of us has a heart.
Our souls will never be destroyed.
We're people of color.
The lives that we live each and everyday are precious.
We will not live in fear.
United we stand.
What we need to do is come together as one.
We all can make a difference.
In this world today we deal with hate.
Also we come across poverty.
Another problem that occurs is violence.
There's no need for race.
Diversity needs to take place.
Stop the bombing.
Think about what goes on this world.
You can't go around putting one another down.
Lend a hand and give credit to our people.
This world could be a much better place.
We can we turn to?
All we can do is pray.
Don't take life for granted.
Live your life day by day.
In life we make our own choices.
I would like for you to take this poem into consideration.
I didn't write this poem just to write it I wrote it from my heart

Twin Tower
By Sandra Glassman
Oceanside, NY

It took only an instant and the destruction began
So much like the tragedy of 103 Pan Am
The earth shook and the smoke spewed like a shout
People inside were so anxious to get out
Who would believe such an absurdity could happen
Here, it just proves nothing is safe anywhere
So many hero's from police to firemen, to EMS
But the people themselves rose to this tragedy
The best!
It will take patience and time to place the blame
And those responsible should recoil with shame
The children who witnessed this will have plenty
to say these horrified memories will haunt them
Even at play
In spite of all this the TWIN TOWER'S can no
Longer stand tall as do tree's
And we can show the world that New Yorker's
Can't and won't be brought to their knee's

Controversies End
By Kenneth William Daigle - age 45
Lowell, MA

If we could just stay awake for a moment.
Things are set for the morning.
The clock is in place.
I suppose there is not much thought to it.

We can barely wait for the next day.
In the morning there is the bright sun.
Tonight there are stars in the heavens.
The stars are compared to birds during the day.

Metaphysics abound.
We carry ovals not rounds to scare the witch away.
A warlock may be in that during the day.
Objects chase those things away.

You can understand if something does not go away.
We advise that you carry the objects as a charm.
No harm and it does not prove the day.
Or it does not believe in those things.

Those are the arguments not do or die.
To the foes can do the work of serfs for them.
We can live the stoics end.
So the true philosophy can wake us up!

God's Beautiful World
By Ruth Talbott George - age 88
McArthur, OH

Tonight I rode through the beautiful hills,
I wanted to experience the many thrills
At seeing the touch of the Master's hand
As He splattered His colors all over the land.

The sun was sinking in the West.
This is the time of day I like best.
It brings back memories of days gone by
I tried so hard not to cry.

I stood by Ollie's grave as I do each night,
I looked toward the East, such a beautiful sight.
The trees were aglow from the setting sun,
I'm sure God was proud of what His brush had done.

The flags were gently waving with the breeze,
The little birds were singing in the trees.
How peaceful it was for our loved ones who sleep
Beneath the stars, I prayed to God, their souls to keep.

I said goodnight to the one I love,
I know he is with my God above.
Someday he'll be there to welcome me
And, oh how happy, again, we will be.

For What Are Americans Thankful?
By R. Lowell "Ted" DaVee - age 77
Mooresville, IN

Churches of all kinds, free to preach,
Dot our nation, in easy reach.
Worshipers decide right from wrong;
Wide are topics of joyful song!

Public schools for all youth are free;
Private, at affordable fee.
Boys and girls of equal concern;
No limit to what each may learn!

Homes at a good price can be bought
In most any location sought.
Create your private kind of charm:
Apartment or family farm!

Jobs, usually plentiful,
Make happy workers, so grateful.
Athletes are valued by us all;
Protectors we salute in awe!

At vacation time, name your choice;
In one's own yard, daily rejoice.
Natural beauty fills our land
As if placed here by God's own hand.

United We Stand
By Sherri Gibson - age 42
Evansville, IN

Bleeding hearts, yet united we stand
All of America joined hand in hand
Tears of sorrow shed by what was done
Yet united we stand, they have not won
Unexpected was the attack
But bravery and heroism we did not lack
They brought their acts of violence were well planned
Yet still we plunge onward, united we stand
Visions of that day flash before our eyes
"United we stand" is what America cries
Shaken, yet hopeful, for peace once again
Triumph shall be ours in the end
Red, white, and blue spotted everywhere
United we stand, something our country shares
Blessed by God in the land of the free
Bleeding hearts come together in unity
A dear price, Lord help us, we did pay
From an erupted hatred launched that day
Yet united we stand forevermore
Lives devastated to the very core
All of America mourns to this day
So many innocent lives taken away
God bless everyone whose lives were affected,
By surprise attacks that were so unexpected
No, this is something they thought was well planned
Don't lose hope, for united we stand

911

By Kathleen Donovan - age 44
Hillsborough, NJ

Our lives were changed forever on September Eleven,
When we all took one step closer to Heaven.
Terrorism hit America's shore.
Something that will change our lives forevermore.

Although there was death, there was rebirth,
For this event will make us fight harder for peace on earth.
The place where we must all begin,
is to not judge people by national origin or color of skin.

Secondly, we must reassure our young and let them shed their tears,
Hold them close and ease their fears.
We must teach them that under God we are one nation,
Regardless of color, origin or religious denomination.

For we must remember our children are strong and resilient,
Encourage them that their future will be bright and brilliant.
If we all simply agree to disagree,
The world will be safer for you and me.

We must respond to this act of terror and not be silent,
If it was only possible to respond with love and not be violent.
We must show the world that we mean business this is not a bust,
We believe in God — In God we trust.

We rejoice that the dead are safe in God's arms,
Free from any further earthly harms.
We must reach up to them through constant prayer,
The only way to show them we care.

For without prayer we are an empty vessel
Let us continue to pray and become the world's trestle.
That stretches from here around the planet,
And never, ever take freedom for granted.

We must stop living life as a trivial game,
And realize life will never be the same
These poor people on a window ledge taking their last breath,
Deciding how they should meet their death.

God wants us not to worry about recovering bodies for
He safely holds their souls,
He wants us to work on achieving new world goals.
To march forward to accomplish a lasting world peace.
To this terror, we must call a cease.

I think this event was God's wake up call,
For peace on this celestial ball.
Let's start now in 2001,
We must never stop until peace is won.

All we need to do is look at ground zero,
Where we will find many a true hero.
Working, digging, their stamina hard to explain,
But if one body is recovered, their work was not in vain.

Buildings they can blow up and steel they can destroy,
Nothing will ever tumble our happiness and joy,
That we have by living in the USA,
For free we are and free we'll stay!

Dedicated to Henry Keegan for his never-ending love and support.

United We Stand

By Karen K. Fritz - age 40
Algoma, WI

On a day that started out lovely and bright,
Terrorist managed to fill an entire country with fright.
Our freedom was something we could no longer take
For granted,
With their act — fear they successfully planted.

They may have destroyed the pentagon and twin towers,
But we still have our faith in Gods Almighty Powers.
They took far too many innocent lives,
Yet out country still survives.

As the events continue to unfold,
And many more details are being told.
Remember the victims, the hero's and our leaders together,
Than pray for Gods guidance in all of our lives forever.

From this tragedy we will recover,
Hopefully other nations will learn and discover.
We are a nation of love and United We Stand,
With the help of God and his ever-loving hand.

Bursting the Bubble

By Sandra Glassman
Oceanside, NY

Bubble bubble toil and trouble
An incomprehensible tragedy has hit at our hearts and
The fabric of humanities existence. Can the horrific
Sights witnessed ever be erased? Will our emotions
Forever carry the burden of this deed? The valiant
Firefighters and medical personal heightened pure
Instinct to be displayed by strangers towards their fellow
Man. Society as we know it is being challenged in a way
Never before.
Red blood was shed and red blood will rebuild with a
Flourish and determination unknown in history.
Grief and valor shall give us more sustenance for a
Triumphant tomorrow

America, I Love You!
By Alma Woods Tisdale
Miami, FL

America the Beautiful!
So strong and so free,
I love you America,
From sea to each **MAGNIFICENT** sea!

Taking the weight of the world
Upon your ready and willing shoulders;
Knowing that the journey to peace is long, rough and treacherous
And even the sand beneath your feet like Boulders!

With embattled men and women,
Giving up their lives and freedom to set others free
As one falls, another arises
To take the banner of the Almighty God and Thee!

Yes, time and time again you prevail, America,
Ignoring the laughter, the put downs, and scorn.
"AMERICA," they say, **"The Great Satan!"**
Yet America, Weakened by the heavy load, trudges on!

I love you, America,
Somewhat meek, always tried, but forever true.
"UPON THE WINGS OF THE MIGHTY EAGLE, LET MY VOICE SOAR THROUGHOUT THE LAND! AMERICA! AMERICA! I LOVE YOU!

9-11-2001
By Cass Farrell - age 46
Clearview City, KS

One plane, two planes, three planes, four
From Boston, Newark & Washington,
Coast to coast, they were to fly
Instead, they changed our lives, forever.

The twin towers stood tall and proud
A gate to the rest of America
8:45 it began, 10:28 it ended
The World Trade Center Towers came down.

The Pentagon, symbol of America's military might
Like Jericho, the walls came tumbling down
Out of the flames, the Marine Corps colors flew
Disbelief turned to anger, then outrage.

In Pennsylvania, the last plane met its fate
Heroes wouldn't allow another tragedy
They chose to sacrifice themselves
So America's spirit would live on, strong.

This week bravery has known no bounds.
Firefighters, Police, and the common man
Thousands died, thousands came to help
In the candle's glow, we came together.

Drums of War/Trumpet of Peace
By Louise Evans
Trenton, NJ

When the drums of war are sounded,
and the young are called to fight,
it shall be a dreadful morning
and a very grievous night.

When marching off to the battle
where there is naught but woe,
we shall look on those departing
and weep to see them go.

When the cannons roar with thunder
where the ground is stained blood-red,
and there is naught but sorrow
folks will bury kin now dead.

When the trumpet sounds in heaven
to announce the coming King
all these battles be ended
with the peace that He shall bring.

When we wake on that glad morning
and we lift our eyes on high,
we shall welcome our Lord Jesus
descending from the sky.

The W.T.C. Aftermath
By Madeline Eastman
Marysville, CA

Terrorism in our country
Seemed like an impossibility
But we've been awakened to the knowledge
That this day, is another day of infamy.
We've lost our whole way to life
To say nothing of the endless strife
Suffered by families who gave so much.
The whole world has been touched
By this devastation so untimely
Where thousands of lives were snuffed out
By a thoughtless unknown enemy.
We say justice must be done.
How do you justify such a great loss
To the families suffering this terrible cross
Of loved ones they will never see again
Nor hear their voices when they come to explain
All that happened throughout this day
And what they did when they were away?
We who are left can only pray
For our acceptance and their salvation.
God is a caring God, we need only to ask
It is our obligation to accept this task
To pray for peace throughout the world
We would make things better if we could.
Our country is trying, but we need help.
The kind of help that comes from above
That will turn hatred and anger into peace and love.

The Bloody September 11th
By Dr. Todor Gabrovsky
Bethesda, MD

The world is bristling and fatigued,
terror is in the all Earth.
Where is the root of this evil,
shrouded in mysterious fog!

But when a struggle breaks again
and the people hid their danger,
then you will see bloody strain,
in this war for life without terror...

Wave proudly starry battle flag,
the people must remember this evil!
O, God! Grant us this power,
let it come eternal peace.

In memory of the victims of the WTC and the Pentagon

A September Prayer
By Yvonne A. Gannon
Kaneohe, HI

Tears of happiness replaced Thank You's,
For the love we have for each other need not be spoken.
Through tragedy we have learned once again,
That all Man is as one united in prayers.
Man has fought bravely for this Universe we call home.
Each acre blessed by Our Miracle Heaven's.
Safeguarding Our Rights and Freedoms,
For all Mankind to enjoy the most beautiful of lives.
For the people of New York,
September 11, 2001 is a new beginning.
For they go forth with new friendships made.
And yes, if they should inquire of us,
We will return to visit.
We will be there to hold their hand,
And renew Our faith in life together.
To share Our Love,
And walk the Earth together,
To that place where once a landmark stood,
The Twin Towers.
That special place marked by time,
On which a landmark will always be.
For the people of New York,
Perhaps they are the stronger ones,
They seemed to have always led the way,
Giving hope to all Mankind.
United, we send them Our Love,
For as they progress, so do we.
      Amen

The footprints of Man crisscrossed, New York on September 11, 2001 as well as Our thoughts and wells wishes. Each Man, Woman, and Child responding to Our Own Oath of Decency, "To help in every way we can to help ease the pain for all those who have suffered so. To make the tragedy of the day just a memory." With Love and Trust, Mankind is once again the victor undaunted in the face of adversity. Our Prayers were with them on that day, September 11, 2001 and for always...

Flags Raised High
By Lori Brown
Fairfield, CA

One morning in September,
we watched in helpless horror
as New York's sky turned to ember.
An unforeseen terrorist act of terror
against our freedom we'll long remember.

After the crash of the Pentagon wall,
a heroic attempt on a Pennsylvania flight,
and the Twin Towers began to fall,
it became clear a faceless coward wanted a fight,
hoping to make America unsafe for us all.

Our leaders said, "We must unite!
Be confident, stay strong, have hope!
It's necessary our faith remain tight.
We'll heal, we'll cope,
we're Americans, we'll fight!"

With our flags raised high,
we gave a moment of silence,
as our air force took to the sky,
vowing for our patience
while our country began to fortify.

To our Heroes, your courage held true.
Your sacrifices and dedication
helped to pull us all through.
For your love and devotion,
our hearts will forever be with you.

Many innocent lives were taken that day.
As a country we'll forever weep,
for "goodbye" is a hard word to say.
We pray to God your souls to keep.
Freedom for America is here to stay!

Untied We Stand
By Britnie Richards - age 15
Sandy, UT

Terrorist have to come to take away our land,
But they can't succeed,
UNITED WE STAND

With this new war, terror is band
Soldiers fight for peace in the US and Afgan land
All this says
UNITED WE STAND

We reach out to all in need
Helping the victims of this vicious deed
For our freedom, Soldiers will bleed!

Fighting for peace in our land,
UNITED WE STAND.

America – Voices Coming Together

Parker, His Little Light Shines
By Flora J.M. Rhodenizer
Bridgewater, NS

On All Hallo's Eve
a shiny spirit was born
to bring light to this world

A light that shines as bright
as the stars in heaven
from whence he came

He arrived at a time
when tragedy ripped a large hole
in the fabric of humanity

The tragedy of Sept. 11, 2001
was only days afore
as the dust still clings to the horizons

Into this world torn by so many deaths
the light of Jesus shines thru
the eyes of this blessed one
as with all new birth.

His candle bright will not cease
to bring comfort to a world torn
as his tiny face round smiles upon the world
Especially to mine spirit

Today was no exception as he did give
a remembrance of a loved one long ago gone
with his name in remembrance of another son

With this legacy I do see
great things to come
as this little one grows more bright

On October 31, 2001
Parker Edward James Fowler
my first grandson was born
to bring light
to this world so forlorn

Sand of Peace
By Boniface Idziak - age 76
Iron Bridge, ON

Desert peace written in the sand will not last.
The winds will come and shift the grains of sand.
Wiping clean the words of peace from the lands of sand.
The grains of sand move across the land.
Peace makers claim all the grains of sand.
In the Holy Land, wherever they may land.
The winds will always move the desert sands
In the Holy Land.
Will peace be ever possible?
In the Holy Land of desert sands.

Dedicated to Patriots who died for Peace in the Land of Sands.

United We Stand
By Anna Recupero-Faiella - age 35
Revere, MA

America's spirit and way of life was attacked on nine-eleven. As planes approached, God's tears came down from heaven. Two symbols of freedom were taken from this country. Destruction and pain was felt through out the Big City. Lives were lost on this dark and dreary day. And yet, all of us in our hearts all knelt down to pray. Terrorist came and attacked our land but through all the destruction and sadness United We Stand.

New York City - September 11, 2001
By John A. Gray
Toronto, ON

With precision, the towers exploded that beautiful September morn.
Suicide bombers had stuck, cowards we could only scorn.
In a city of positive energy, of vibrant life,
A beautiful city never exposed to war or strife.
Valiantly struggling through the smoke, four thousand people tried,
To escape the burning towers but perished and died.
The grief was overwhelming on that September 11, date.
People anguished over friends or a loved ones fate.
Directed toward the unholy terrorists was a prevalent hate.
America realized the hounds of hell were at the gate.
From the eternal smoke and ashes of flesh and steel.
The president and his gallant people stated no deal.
A resolution had arisen, that could not be bent.
America will destroy terrorism was the strong message sent.
A firefighter raised a tattered Old glory above the debris,
Patriotism sprang forth for all the world to see.
America realized it would not flinch, but soar again.
Freedom, spirit, pride, determination, and vision become the positive refrain.
To always remain free must be America's primary goal.
America's destiny is freedom that only America will control.

Freedom
By Belinda Guthrie - age 46
Winamac, IN

As I tried to write this poem,
I used my dictionary for clarification
being out of school many years
I wanted to be precise....

We live in a democracy.
People elect our representatives
who run our country.
We have liberty and independence....

We have many freedoms,
which include freedom of speech,
freedom of the press;
free enterprise.
We are born free from slavery....

Freedom-is more than a mere word.
It's a way of life-our way.
And we have helped others obtain it,
as many dream of having it....

So, when you see our flag-be proud,
it stands for many things.
America the land of the free
over 200 years and still standing for
FREEDOM....

May God Bless America
May God Bless Us One and All

A Memorial Tribute to the September 11th Fallen Heroes
By Cynthia L. Groopman
Long Island City, NY

Dear heroes, great role models and deep sources of inspiration,
you shall always be,
Your deeds of valor and reassuring words will forever be emblazoned
and etched into our heart and in our memory.
Undaunted and extremely courageous were you
And you were our knights in shining armor, so loyal and true.
Your Precious life you did generously give
Rescuing so many, so that they were able to survive and continue to live.
Battling evil in the face of adversity, you did not wince or cry aloud,
We salute you for your bravery and of you we are so very proud.
Now in peaceful bliss, you are dwelling with God in His eternal resting place,
Being sheltered under his mighty protective wing enveloped in His living
Fatherly embrace.
For you valiant acts of heroism, we shall honor and remember,
On that fateful sad day on the 11th of September.
We shall cherish and pay homage to you,
Because you were our heroes, and a blessing from God, too.

New York In Memory
By Jay Hip
Orlando, FL

This morning I doth wake from sleep
Put on my television, a nightmare I did review
My beloved building came tumbling down.
I cried until I could no more.
This is New York and we will rise again.
Soon will come another one
Built bigger and better than the one before
I mourn for the dead.
They cannot rise anymore.
It is senseless to kill those you do not even know.
Cowardly is a nice word to use for a man who possesses the
devil's heart.
I pray for those who died so graciously in the name of God.
Long live New York City
It is still the heart of America
May those who died not have died in vain
Dear Lord look after those who were my friends.
I love New York.

Unsung Heroes
By Edwin N. Denette

Does anybody ever give a thought
   to the hard working nurses and EMTs?
Does anybody ever look through their eyes
   and try to see what they see?

Valiant warriors battling death
   they fight to ease the pain.
Returning every single time
   to do it all over again.

Does anybody ever think of them
   when they pack up to go home?
Does anybody remember the comfort and smiles
   when they were laid up and alone?

Angels pouring out their heart and soul
   helping the people they don't even know.
Even after many long, drawn-out hours
   they don't let the weariness show.

I remember a loving tenderness
   given like a soothing balm.
I remember the best healing given
   soothed what the drugs couldn't calm.

I'll remember these unsung heroes
   long after their memory of me goes.

Dedicated with my love to Ms. C. Frady, CHA (nurse)

The Awakening
By Shahira Akhter - age 17
Carlsbad, NM

I walked to the Ocean where the sun called my name
The mist of a new dawn weakened my resolve
All the past of love and heartbreak had vanished within a million yesterdays
The scars, had healed as I wondered along the road
There weren't only sunbeams but cherished dreams
A flame of hope within my heart still cried
At least along with emotions, it hadn't just died
As I looked up at the horizon now bright and clear
The vast expanse of it challenged me and gripped me unaware
Realization struck me now that there were those who still cared
It was an awakening to a new dawn.
One, which was cold but the time, was going on
As I saw my reflection in the new waves
I knew the face that looked back hadn't cheated me
It wasn't yet time to sigh
Because I felt among the eagles, I could fly
And that...I wasn't alone.

Tragedy to Triumph
By Louise Evans
Trenton, NJ

It took the 9/11 tragedy for America to unite.
A day that was marred by tremendous grief and blight.
Yet, out of all the ashes where death and grief were great
emerged a mighty triumph, when love conquered hate.
People spoke more kindly seeking to help and share.
Good deeds were a way of life, and so was humble prayer.
In the midst of this sorrow, the laborer was hero
clearing shards and ashes out there on that ground zero.

In the midst of this tragedy when Americans united.
Our banner lifted high so that it would be sighted.
Patriotic fervor soared to reach a brand new height,
and saying, "God bless you," was now considered right.
Yet, grief from this tragedy will always endure,
for those who lost a loved one and see no final cure.
They and many others will walk on in despair,
needing both a helping hand and a humble prayer.

Now and in the future, we Americans should stand,
united as brothers while walking hand in hand.
Striving to persevere, bestowing love and care
helping those in need with kindnesses we share.
We need to keep seeking God, taking time to pray,
asking Him for wisdom to make it through the day.
We should not be judging man's status or his race,
but rather seeking fellowship in which to embrace.

We need to remember the tragedy we met
and seek ways to love, lest we should forget,
forget to give mercy, a helping hand, an ear
to listen to a sorrow, a worry, or a fear.
We need to continue in striving to unite,
united as brothers, and pleasing in God's sight.
We need to keep seeking God, lest we should forget,
that hate caused the tragedy, this tragedy we met.

The America I Love
By Glenn Abby Garvin - age 53
East Meadow, NY

The America I love
Give me freedom to write
She gives me freedom to speak
Allows for all to unite

Together we stand
Firm on liberty
There's a war for us to win
That is our destiny

Finishing on top
We'll do the right thing
With caution and purpose
Our songs we proudly sing

They started something
And now they will pay
For their transgressions
We'll wash them away

With tactful precision
In time they will fall
From top to the bottom
We'll make the right call

The lives of those lost
And the hurt that we feel
Seems like a nightmare
Yet we know it is real

America I love
America survives
Victorious we'll be
To avenge all lost lives

God Bless America!

From Mourning to Joy
By Jeffrey V. Gray - age 36
Aberdeen, NJ

For those who mourn the dead, dust and ashes adorn the head. There is no longer the need to wallow in sorrow, for joy will certainly come on the morrow!

Sackcloth is the garment, not by choice, of those who talk in a mournful voice. There is no need to linger in sadness, for the music of the harp will be that of gladness!

Tears of weeping come from the eyes of those who mourn one who had died. The long, bitter night of grief is close at hand the joy of a bright new day is around the bend!

Memento
By Horia Ion Groza
Rhinelander, WI

News was like
Drinking air, eating bullets—
The first was unbelievable
The last bled the heart for ever.

An infamous blast
With metal taste
Under the limpid eyes
Of the unrocking Liberty Lady.

There was no need for minds to guess
Their last minutes
In the perishing planes and buildings—
They became part of us
In sadness and courage.

And then
It was the sacrifice for others
In the maze of bones of dust
The most painful and fruitful investment—
Life for life
Sky for sky
Light for light
Hope of tomorrow.

I know a place
Where now
Day and night
The wind whispers in piety
His colorless shadows
Of sorrow.

Take Heed; an Ill-Wind Bloweth!
By Alma Woods Tisdale
Miami, FL

Lift up your heads, Oh people, My people!
Look upon the face of the **h**orizon!
See the smoke in the distance; **H**ear the groans of the old,
the weak, and the piercing cry of the young!
Take heed to the **Howling** of the night;
For an **Ill-Wind** bloweth!

Listen! Listen closely, for the dull of hearing will not hear
and cannot see the approaching **enemy.**
Hear the sound thereof and **pray**
that you'll be counted worthy to escape.
The **hour** cometh and now is
For ALL to stand-up and be counted!

Awake! Awake out of sleep!
Fill your senses with awareness of your surroundings!
Pin-point the rumblings of things to come; **P**erceive the **Evil**
that **rides on the wings of the wind! Heed the warnings,**
Lest you All sleep the sleep of Death unaware; imposed
upon you by the Rigors of the night: Deceived, lost souls
that creep through the darkness and strike out at Noon-Day!

Make haste! Gird up your strong ones; build up the waste places;
Fill in the gaps; cover the weak with your strength; fill the mouths
of your young ones and the poor with good things; shore-up paths
for their feet, and stand, stand together; Supply the cord that
cannot so easily be broken! Guard! Guard against the day
when Evil rears it's Ugly Head!
Above All, LOOK UP! LOOK UP to the SUPPLIER of
All Our NEEDS and LIVE! LIVE! (reverberate)

God Bless America and Its Heroes Too
By Linda Cheryl Grazulis - age 50
Pittsburgh, PA

God bless America, as united we stand
And all the heroes doing the best they can.
For it takes a hero to rescue and save
So many victims on September 11, a dreadful day.
No one expected a war to break out
As we all stood amazed, with so many doubts.
But when the planes hit and flames glowed,
Many dropped to their knees, prayers flowed.
Oh, God, help this nation and be by our side
As we lift up our hearts and in You abide.
Bless all of the folks whose loved ones died,
And wipe the tears of so many who cried.
Be with our leaders; give them wisdom from above,
And also send us faith on the wings of a dove.
And we thank You for brave men and women that day
Who risked their lives midst skies of gray.
God bless America, as united, we stand
And all the heroes doing the best they can.

The War Goes On
By Carol Ann Grumbling - age 57
Neodesha, KS

It's been over a month since that eventful day!
The terrorists perished — our nation learned to pray!
Most of the country goes its own way,
Aside from the first shock, peace reigns so they say!
The military has retaliated again,
Man's self-centeredness causes wars sin!
Blessed has this country always been,
Blessed the United States can be again!
But first its citizens must fall on their knees
Too long we have ignored God's blessings
We've done as we pleased!
The nations around the world have lived in constant fear,
Wars in their lands when America's near!
It's time all God's sons rise to the His Will,
Not letting their carnal mind reign still!
Pure spirits of God in earth suits of day,
Time to mature — fulfill God's purpose today!

America – Voices Coming Together

My Heart's Treasure Chest
By Doris Lee Gribble - age 67
Chesapeake, VA

Down life's horizons of mystic dreams,
  All decked in their array;
It's hard to sum the heart's contents,
  And tell it all today.

I've known so much of this life's joys,
  A little of its woes;
Through winding paths and upward steeps,
  Found strength to onward go.

The things that I count special,
  And hold most dear to me,
Are the untold priceless joys,
  Of my treasured family.

Each has their special image,
  With each face it's hard to part,
But the love of each is treasured,
  And is stored within my heart.

I feel a place of emptiness,
  Of one who has gone away.
And yet, "This Special Place" remains,
  Within my heart to stay!

Down memory's lane I stand and look,
  And reflect a lifetime through.
I see no greater joy for me,
  Than the love which was left by you.

So bound with mutual feelings,
  I'll keep filled "Your Place" you left,
With all the joys of life we knew,
  In my "Heart's Treasure Chest."

Dedication: "May your heart's treasures comfort each who have lost loved ones!"

Drawing Tears
By Marcus Henderson - age 25
Tallahassee, FL

    We must go on when tragedy comes and remember to love when the day is done. We live with memories and cherish every one through the hard times and all the fun. With hope, freedom, and a voice so loud the water still flows, as the world turns round. We're drawing tears from eyes of the young while releasing the fear from a dying tongue. The bravery of a few is strength enough to comfort the world when things are rough. Like stars in the sky they shine for us all sometimes they fade and the sometimes they fall. In the brightness of night, the sparkle is clear to fulfill a dream we must face our fear of sleeping in anger and waking in pain thinking each day will never be the same. Only together as one, shall we survive and help mend the hearts of broken lives.

The Circle of Life
By Edna Hagen - age 44
Kal, MT

A child is born;
    A mother has such great joy
A child is left to cry
    A father weeps!

An eagle soars —
High above the clouds.
As a policeman saves a life,
A fireman is left to clean up...
The mess of man; we take his job in stride!
    As the flags wave high...
    And we have hopes of great peace,
Blood runs cold;
Parents have only grief!

The mess of September 11th
Is left in our streets —
What hope can come out of this?
And yet, as a rosebud opens wide,
And the smells of spring linger all around —

The earth is so quiet —
As we have only the sounds...
Of a new-born infant's cries!
Great joy is in the only sounds that we have on this day!
The hope of new life is left in our tears.
    The smile of new-found life —
    Is left upon our face —
    Given to us by —
    God's holy grace...

Our Awakening
By William Furlow - age 57
Ocean Springs, MS

I was born among the last of the war babies.
We were a proud nation
Saying the Pledge Allegiance and Lord's Prayer before classes,
And singing the Star Spangled Banner at our sporting events.

Vietnam came and we went astray,
We listened not
Saying the Pledge Allegiance, or
Singing the Star Spangled Banner.
God was cast from our schools.
The FBI and CIA, guardians of our security,
Played cribbage in the lunch room, while
Terrorists made plans against our nation.

One can never take away from the tragedy of 9/11,
But hopefully those who died set the platform for
OUR AWAKENING and becoming the
NATION we once were.
For all evil some good evolves.

A Loud Cry that Echo's Hurt
By Elizabeth A. Harrison - age 52
Tarboro, NC

It is healing time, it is a time for togetherness, it is a time for love,
it is time for caring and depending on one other.
A loud cry that echo's hurt has been heard through out the land.
People are crying, People are hurting, People are looking for some sort of
relief, you can see it, you can feel it, in every corner that you turn hurt
is there waiting to be comforted.
Tragedy has stepped in, destruction has shown its ugly head, it knows no
respect of person, tragedy has knocked on our doors and made itself known.
Is there hope for a nation of people covered under a blanket of so much hurt
and despair?
There must be a light shining out of the darkness that surrounds us all,
let us take a look and see what we can see. Here comes hope,
to have hope is to have life.
A loud cry that has echoed hurt has continued to go out.
A ray of hope shines out from so much pain in our nation.
Let's take another look shall we?
Our flag flies so proudly with its colors and it strips, the red that it wears
means the blood that has been lost for this nation's freedom,
the white means the loyalty that we as a nation stand up for.
The blue that it wears stand for the many battles that have been fought to
keep freedom and hope alive for the years to come in our nation.
The strips are the bridges we cross over after each battle that we have won.
For out of the cry that echo's hurt we stand up with boldness ready to go
forth in faith to handle the task that is before us, despite the pain and the hurt.
We must indeed go forth our very survival depends on it; shall we march on?

Victory is before us, defeat is behind us.

In the Stillness
By J.M. Bennett Hammerberg
Plainfield, IL

Greeted at early dawn
Sky of colorful hues
Slight mist of fog
Beauty, serene and spiritual
I bow to creator

Sky of grace dissipated
In fade inferno and death
Anguish, fear, helpless
God, mercy, America
I weep. I weep

Whimper, whimper, death, living
Mourn of belly grief
Mystified, hope whispers
United, one, America
I pray. I pray

I Need To Remember
By Michelle Lyn Haskins
Boston, MA

I want to remember.
Don't you see?
It's now become
A part of me.
An unimaginable act
Deliberately set in place.
It changed every life.
You can see it in the face.

I want to remember.
Not that I could forget.
It was shown nonstop
The moment the first impact.
And then another
Was set in place.
An act of terror unfolding
In every space.

I want to remember.
It's important to me
To remember the lives
Taken intentionally.
I want to remember.
I need to remember.
It's etched in my heart.
I will never forget, not ever.

In Memory of the Victims of September 11, 2001

A Time to Weep
By Diana J. Hill - age 65
Slatington, PA

This has been a time to weep.... and a time to mourn
For firefighters and for police whose loss of comrades strikes home
For friends and loved ones of those missing dead who could not
    escape the horrors of their inferno prisons
For all those who narrowly escaped death.... leaving others behind
For those heroes and heroines who gave their lives
    to save others from death

For our family members who are now called to serve their country
    in a war against an elusive enemy
For those innocents whose lives are being sacrificed in war
For all of us who, having had our security and sensibilities shaken
    Find this a time to weep....

Let us take time to weep
    Let us take time to mourn
        Let us take time to love
            Let us make time to heal

September, 11, 2 Thousand and One
By Sue Sally Hale - age 64
Vista Santa Rosa, CA

Lower Manhattan, New York, September 2 thousand and one a day not to be forgotten when done. Evil did its best to frighten and rule not understanding Americas unique "pool". People with dignity, strength, resilient, and undaunted in pursuing justice and right. One nation indivisible under God we stand heads held high in might. September 11, 2 thousand and one American jetliners full of folks used as missiles exploding in "our" buildings like huge orange egg yokes. Smoke soon to pour, oh so black! People on the ground taken aback. The World Trade Center Towers wounded to the core. Huge "holes" did the planes bore, one by one the towers crumbled, disintegrated and tangled to the street floor. Massive clouds of mushed building, glass and steel blew through canyons of buildings coating and hurting all in their way. Firefighters, police, and medical personnel who chose to stay enveloped, crushed by debris never again to see the light of day! Before the first tower bent, it was 110 stories high. Engulfed in flames and smoke people chose to take the sky. Out the windows, some holding hands went. It rained people, to them our prayers were sent. Not long after World Trade Tower apart flew. Followed by #6 and #7 who fires also slew, as to the dead, is it many or is it few? Mean time the pentagon was hit by another jetliner, folks on board. Three rings were penetrated by that 600 mph sword. The fires burned intensely well past the next morning sun. A mistake we're told, it was to be the Whitehouse and Air Force One! Soon another hijacked jetliner United 93 was a pile of debris. On separate cell phones it was heard from 3. Knowing they were doomed, but out it in the ground these brave examples of this land of the free. No American Pilot would have allowed these dastardly deeds. If in control, they most likely died at the hands of the maniacal breeds. What kind of coward takes pride using a place full of civilians, their evilness to hide? It must be unsettling to these cowards to see the depth of resolves that is America and her people when life they know dissolves. From the ashes do we rise unity, love, and strength grows in size. Woe be those lowly breeders of trash who stand for nothing. Justice will be dealt in many forms from this nation and people who stand for something. To Americans united we stand Together we band. One for all and all for one in this magnificent land of the free. We are proud of you and me.

911 on 9/11 2001
By Mary S. Gratman - age 62
Orangeburg, SC

America has always and continues to be a nation, of Justice, Freedom, and Peace;
We showed our strength to the Terrorists, with United Spirits, proven our Power, will never cease.

Thus, the call to "911" on the 9/11 disaster, will forever ring!

Remember Only Today
By Angela Harges - age 27
Claremore, OK

Hold on to the night
For it will be gone within the dawning light
Speak less of tomorrow
For you will only drown in sorrow
Keep within you today
For that is where the fallen have come to lay
Picture not the months ahead
For you may see yourself on your deathbed
Mark not a calendar week
Less perchance, the stopping of your clock you seek
Look for nothing from the upcoming year
Forbid yourself, for today comes the shedding of a tear
Today is the day sadness seeks the lost
Remember today as a day fear came at no cost
Remember today as the day that brought America to stand tall
Remember today as your hearts cries come to call
Remember... Remember... Please God let us all remember
The dead of the eleventh of September.

Perfect World
By Jarrod Higby - age 14
Keene, OH

The day was very bright
The wind seemed quite light
It seemed like a perfect day
And for that perfect we now pay
It was such a big cost
For all the lives that were lost
Induced was such a fear
That normal was not here
And people watched the news
To see how much you can lose
Is this what we must deal with
For what is truth we thought as myth
We must now pay attention
For September 11 I mention
Is a stab in the back
For all the perfect that we lack.

Looking Up At the Sky
By Debra Baird - age 42
Burbank, CA

A country flaunts its democratic view,
and Middle East resentment grew.
Terrorists slowly start to infiltrate,
making plans to incapacitate,
as they look up at the sky.

Suicide missions hit icons tall,
Shangri-La drifts in pieces, as debris falls.
An invulnerability we can't ignore.
We weep for the dying, unlike on other shores,
as we look up at the sky.

Anger feeds thoughts to retaliate,
against a country harboring hate.
Innocent people start to cry and flee,
from the threatened coming debris,
as they look up at the sky.

Instead of making terror escalate,
let the world lock up those that hate
Terrorist activities, united, we'll deny,
so no one will ever have to cry,
when they look up at the sky.

Bin Laden's Tears
By Erick K. Huling - age 32
Elk City, OK

Unforgiving tears fall from her American
eyes onto her swollen belly, her child
kicks restlessly, awaiting a fatherless
life, all because of....Islamic
Fundamentalism? How do you explain
that to an 11 year old? She worries.
A strangely calming lullaby
makes its way like whispered
morphine into her upset womb
and soothes her only hope:

Who will cry Bin Laden's tears
For he cannot whose eyes are spears
Whose hands are guns
Whose thoughts are bombs
Who kills our fathers & our moms
Who will cry Bin Laden's tears
Whose soul is dried through hatred years
When he's consumed in Hell's brimstone
And reaches up so all alone
For Abraham to quench his fears
Who will cry Bin Laden's rears?

God Give Us Strength
By Crystie Ham - age 35
Jackson, SC

Over three thousand died, in less than two hours.
At the Pentagon, in airplanes, and New York's Twin Towers.

The whole world stood silently, watching in tears.
While Satan's destruction, caused lingering fears.

Dear God, help us all to, somehow understand,
why those men, that day, followed evils command.

Such heartbreaking cries, filled our land with great sorrow.
As hope disappeared, for a brighter tomorrow.

His followers laughed and danced. They feel this was right.
While American troops, prepared armor to fight.

With God's divine power, we will soon persevere.
He'll drive out the evil, that has brought about such fear.

These acts were designed, to destroy and cause hate.
The peace in our nation, they refused to tolerate.

But through such inflictions, what we've found is strong love.
And with every hand joining, set our sites on above.

Now our concerns turn, to those in great need.
The souls of the men, who carried out this deed.

And although that seems like, the last thing we'd do.
We must always remember, once we were lost too.

The Hour
By Gabrielle Hitchcock - age 38
Austin, TX

Where were you when the planes crashed into THE TOWERS?

Do you remember the moment or the hour?

People so full of panic they jumped to their death.

Knowing no matter what choice they made, it would be
their last breath.

THE TOWERS came crashing to the ground.

Even the angels in heaven didn't make a sound.

We were warned over and over again about the coming wrath.

It's not supposed to be pretty, in fact it was a blood bath.

What can we do for the 4,000 sacrificed?

The children that cry at night for their loved ones lost,
could there be a higher price?

America — Voices Coming Together

Crusade

By Margaret R. Hellewell - age 82
Rockledge, FL

That Day of Infamy, September 11, 2001, terrorist
attacked America with remorseless plotted fiery blitz!
Now our brave Crusaders go proudly forth by sea, air
and land, the fanatic rogue regimes to quell
though these outlaws battle to the very jaws of Hell.
Hard-hatted NYPD and NYFD, of civil trade,
at Ground Zero, dedicate courageous aid
to unearth the quick and the dead from their dust and rubble grave,
sacrificing life limb the hapless victims save.
"Greater love hath no man than this;
that a man lay down his life for his friends." St.John 15:13

President Bush has said: "We will not rest and we will not fail."
October 7, 2001, on orders of our President, the strikes began
with ceaseless precision-planned hits in Afghanistan.
We have crossed the Rubicon to ensnare
the ruthless Taliban and Al-Queda in their hidden lair,
where terrorism breeds unrelenting threats
to freedom, with fanatic global nets.
We attack, not in hate or blind revenge
for even military might never can avenge
the barbaric, suicidal terror reign
across America the Beautiful, where their acts profane
dealt mass destruction, death, and fears,
changing forever our forebears' legacies forged on raw frontiers.

November 2001 the Taliban "is on the run,"
but the global war has not been won
to ferret out the terrorists who flee and hide
to threaten further attacks worldwide
with germ warfare and destruction far more dire
destroying Peace and Freedom to which we all aspire.

Dedicated to each hero who serves at Ground Zero.

If We Could Be Heard

By Judith Reagan Harwell - age 55
Dubberly, LA

We have loved and we were loved by so many.
We were someone's mother, father, brother, or sister.
We were someone's wife, husband, friend or neighbor.
We were someone's aunt, uncle, cousin or just
acquaintance. We were someone very important.
We were co-workers or visitors caught in this wicked
and cruel scheme to hurt America.

We learned to live our lives, while others beings were
taught to give up their meaningless lives to eliminate
anyone in their path, and today, September 11, 2001,
we paid the ultimate price with our lives, when the
World Trade Center in New York City was bombed.

To the <u>families</u> of the firefighters, police department,
military, and everyone else that died that day, the
victims say "thank you," for the extraordinary bravery
shown by your loved ones, in their rescue to save lives.

To the firefighters, police department, military and
everyone from all walks of life, the victims say, "thank
you," for your dedication to giving your all to the
rescue.

America keep your hands and hearts joined.
Pray daily to preserve freedom and safety.
Ask God to be with our President and other
Government Officials around the globe as they strive to
find solutions to wipe out terrorism. Prayer will be
your tribute to all victims. This is a beginning to what
we would say, if we could be heard.

*I would like to dedicate this to the families of the
Firefighters, Policeman, and military for the outstanding
rescue mission they performed after the September 11,
2001 bombing of the World Trade Center.*

Thanking the EMT's

By Lisa Maurice
Wallington, NJ

September 11th has taken the lives of many great men and women from all different walks of life. One great thing resulted in such terror and disaster; the concept of unity. When the problem arose police, firefighters, and rescue were called. Everyone praises the firefighters and police, while the Emergency Medical Technicians remain silent.

I am a volunteer EMT-D in New Jersey. To become an EMT, I attended the State Basic EMT Training Class, which met two or three times a week for four months and a mandatory National Professional CPR and Defibrillator class. Afterwards, I took the State Certification EMT-D Exam. Eight weeks later, I got my grade and my EMT Identification card. EMT's are fast thinkers who determine problems, document it and provide care without X-Rays, blood tests and sometimes without a medical history. We act fast in high priority situations. We make patients comfortable as we provide emergency care and transportation to the hospital. We are trained for mass casualty incidents. Helping people in their time of need is worth the sacrifice.

I was on standby September 11th. I was disappointed when the FBI told our police department to keep our squad behind to protect the propane tanks in the Meadowlands. Our neighboring towns had already gone to New York City to help. They risked everything to provide emergency care to victims. Some died and never saw their families again.

Everyone who helped that day or offered should be recognized and honored. We are thankful that many EMT's, firefighters, and police officers who volunteered their time, along with the general public and companies who donated supplies. I would personally like to thank everyone who helped, big and small, during the country's time of need. Your efforts have made a difference and will not be forgotten.

Belonging

By Aaron W. Hillman
Fresno, CA

I belong to you.
You belong to me.
We all belong to each other.
To belong is to be apart of,
To be apart of is to belong.

I lift my lamp beside the golden door.
I now belong to you.
You belong to me.
If you stand apart, don't belong,
You don't belong. You are nothing.
We become something when we
join the whole.
We link our spirits.
See the world as one.
Ourselves as one within it.

There is a tide in the lives of all.
Sometimes it is low and sometimes
full. When full the whole is working
together. The waterfall is
irresistible.

I am many things.
I am all others.
We all belong to each other.
Put your arm around my shoulder.
Hold me close. Keep me close.
When the arm drops,
We are still one.

American Tragedy

By Verna Ray Humphrey - age 82
Palestine, TX

Towers reaching 'way up high —
   Sun shining brightly in the sky....
Evil birds came flying by —
   No one knew they would die.

Towers broken and falling down....
   People running all around —
Many bodies never found ....
   American tragedy in New York town.

Rescue Team working all day long,
   With no time to return home.
Hoping beyond hope until all hope's gone
   To recover bodies buried so long.

AMERICA! United We Stand!
   No one will ever get the upper hand.
Evil must be destroyed in our great land,
   And America will always be considered grand.

One Sad September

By Robin Hoffman - age 42
Clifford, MI

When I seen the grief and fear all the bad on the news
I really felt so blue, I thought to myself, only God
can make this right.
Only God can fight for what's right.
We will all unite if we pray, in Gods Holy sight.
We can truly be a free land.
Hate can do so much, to hurt this world.
But we have to remember we're not alone.
God doesn't just sit on his thrown.
I pray, people don't blame God.
God lets life take it coarse, so people have heart changes.
Otherwise, there wouldn't be to many going to learn now!
We have to love one another, not just ourselves.
God will show us the way!
But, we must start today, so this world can heal.
There's so much pain, but God can help us, live again.
Than we can say, God Bless America proudly.
Let love rule our land.

Good Times On Billygoat Hill

By William D. Irwin - age 45
Princeton, IL

    I was raised on a three-acre piece of land between two small towns and I have many fond memories of three small houses with woods behind them, on a hill so long ago. For I still remember my Grandma and Grandpa smiling in the yard putting in another fence, along with Mom, Dad, and my Brother, who I loved more than they'll ever know.

    It was called Billygoat Hill and was covered with clay clover, dandelions, and trees. There was a willow tree alongside of the house, with lots of woods and a creek in the back. For it was very plain and not much to see, but it was kept immaculate. My brother and I was very fortunate to have grown up there, as nothing we lacked.

    For we had loving Parents and Grandparents who loved us and were always there to help us out. With Mom taking care of us when we were sick and Grandma and Grandpa always had extra groceries. Dad would watch my Brother and I play catch in the yard. We liked going through the woods to pick blackberries. Grandma had dogs they were Pekingese and Grandpa had chickens, rabbits, and horses and all are in my memories.

    A lot of times Grandma and Grandpa took us on fishing trips to the near by lake. In the spring we would plant a garden and flowers all around our huge yard. When Dad was home from the factory he would sit in his recliner and watch football on television, Mom was in the kitchen fixing supper for all of us, after cleaning the house and doing laundry all day so hard.

    Yes, my Brother and I grew up in the country on a three-acre piece of ground between two small towns. For such are good times, we had on Billygoat Hill. I smile, thinking of the crickets chirping and the whippoorwill calling to me in the night lazy breeze. These fond memories are planted forever in my mind, for I love my family and always will.

Dedication: I love my family and I'm proud to be an American

America – Voices Coming Together

When the Devil Came Knocking
By Connie Holt
Waynesboro, TN

When the first knock of the Devil hit out
   door, it was at 8:50 A.M. Tuesday September 11
We will never forget that day, not ever.
September 11, 2001, will forever burn brightly
   in a ruby red glass on the hearts and the minds of all.
With our flag flying at half mast; will forever be a symbol
   that American will never fall.
September 11, 2001, will always burn in our memory.
Those who died by the terrorists, their memory is our memory.
The evil was Satan on earth, walking as terrorists — with
   cloven hoof across America.
They enter unlawfully. An offense; a sin to harm our beloved
   home we call America.
When we first heard the news we all bowed our heads to pray.
For those who died that day.
My eyes filled with tears too.
Just as I know they did for you.
The Father's voice will ring out, vaulting the heavens, sure
   to be strong.
Over the terrorists for their wrong.

Dedicated to the victims, fire fighters, and the New York City Police.

My Beloved Country
By Ellen Isaksen
Holiday, FL

My beloved and compassionate country
My heart mourns along with yours as I silently
Watch the unfolding of an alien world...

With tears absent of emotion I sense
The distancing of all things familiar...
My soul numbs as I observe that mother peace
Is momentarily but an illusion.

My dear, cherished homeland...
I cling to thee for refuge—
I kiss your soft earth—
I revel in your sweet freedom—
I watch as you stretch your arms outward
Even as your wounds sting hard.

My dear and gracious God on high...
Guide and keep my nation
Through this time of darkness...
Keep her safe, strong, resilient and vibrant.
Comfort her people, my beloved countrymen,
Assuring them that right and honor shall prevail.

Lead us to know that the answers lie deep within...
Give us courage to make that journey
Into the depths of, our own hearts...

Be still and listen...
Be still...
Be

A Moment
By Ronald E. Hudkins - age 50
Denver, CO

Who could predict the September day
When so many people got taken away

What can ever mend the pain
Of the day when on us terror rained

We wake with a mind so full of things
Don't think twice what the day will bring

We let every thing get in the way
Put things off to some other day

Take for granted the company shared
Focus attention upon what to wear

Even the spat we want to solve
Gets overrun by some business resolve

Don't take time for a needed stop
To send a rose from the flower shop

So I ask myself what I can say
Since I am one to survive that day

Don't stress about the things unsaid
We all carry around in our busy heads

Hold the love and wonders shared
Yet, don't stop loving the others who care

Put the moment aside sometime this day
To appreciate those who share your way

I can not change the fate of all those lost
But, their beauty and memory I will not toss

One Question
By Jodi Ingram - age 17
Airdrie, AB

Daddy why is every eye crying
Why are people running and screaming and banging on doors
Why are mothers on their knees in the street
Why are these children suddenly alone
Daddy why did you have to leave and why haven't you come home
Why am I scared like this, I'll never know
Why is that man just laying there
Why are these crowds drifting with no place to go
Daddy why is today passing by like a dream
Why has the world stopped turning
Every eye is on us
Daddy why, tell me why

No Gunpowder
No Conventional Bullets
By Carole Johnson - age 49
Los Angeles, CA

We did not know this man
    he came up quickly behind us
    just inches from our necks
He whispered in our buildings
    and blew
He muttered, put your heads down near my chest
    and hear the thunder, the pounding
Now it's your turn
    Your perfect life will tumble

We began to die that day
    there and then
Some unimportant man
    became a nightmare in our lives
He haunted us
He savagely ripped away our skins of pride
    shredded our confidence
    and our beauty which we perceived we had or had around us

It will take time to heal
    some unimportant man
    became a nightmare in our lives
    became sorryingly important

We have all taken one very big step

The love for our country
    the love and belief for one another
shines above us once more
    blossoms in our souls once again

There has to be much more evil
    to break our chain of pride

Here is the American team
    and God is our Coach...

TRUST in GOD
By Linda Joyner
Catawba, NC

The money in our hand says "In God we Trust,"
but the desire of our hearts — we need to adjust.
Faith in God brought our forefathers to this land,
because they had been persecuted for their stand.
They wanted freedom to worship God in their own way,
but America is in danger if from God we continue to stray.
We must return to the faith our ancestors possessed,
    or this country will be very greatly distressed.
"One Nation - Under God" to our flag we pledge,
    but do our lives to Him we truly allege?
Go to the Lord in prayer — is my plea,
    and let His love for you set you free.
Against the devil and his demons we all must fight,
    and read our Bible to learn wrong from right.
We can't let the American dream become a nightmare,
if we Christians don't make a difference — who else will care.
    Prayer can save America — the land we love,
if we let God guide and give us strength from above.

The Tragedy
By William Granse
Greenville, MI

Well Bin Laden and his friends opened the door
    to drawing America into another war.

On September 11, a lot of blood was spilled,
    property damage and innocent people killed.

Bin Laden is going to run and hide,
    but we will win because God is on our side.

America has been in trouble before,
    like the American Revolution and the Civil War.

But, once again, we will prevail,
    and our enemies will be caught and put in jail.

Bin Laden is going to run and hide,
    but we will win because God is on our side!

America
By Penny Johnson - age 61
Lexington, KY

A land of the brave and free
My home, my birthplace a warm place to be
Every American should be proud
Ring out bells! Ring them LOUD!

In America you can be whomever you
want to be
Come to America, you're welcome, be
free

There's no place like it on earth
Bountiful, beautiful and blessed
    Seasons of
Winter snow, spring rain, summer sun,
    fall's glory
Elegantly dressed

American's are so giving, hardworking
making and sharing their living
There's a spirit in America, second to
none
"Try your best, past the test, be number
one"
From North to South East to West
Americans have a right to boast
It embraces all who want to be free
    Come and See
    AMERICA stands for God's given liberty

To the Edge of Faith

By Manisha S. Joshi - age 29
Jacksonville, FL

I landed safely
As my flight was diverted
Out of harm's way,

But I did not understand immediately
What had happened
That day,

We knew of some kind of attack
A plane had struck
The Twin Towers,

At first
I wanted to believe it was an accident
The reality, I just couldn't devour,

Greater than any trauma
I had ever heard of
I stood shaking listening to the reports,

Hundreds, no thousands
Were trapped, burned, killed
I collapsed still listening to the reports,

I have seen war before
On TV, in papers and in books

I have seen tragedy and pain
But what made me take a second look?

Was it because it was so close to home?
Was it because the world seemed a smaller place?

What would I have done if I were in the building?
Struck and burnt in an instant
Who would I have become?
And would I have had time to cherish my life's best moments?

My brothers, my sisters, my fellow citizens
Were ripped from any sense of peace, safety or security,
And yet, the same brothers, sisters, and citizens
Are not shrinking from the call of American duty,

Fierce, brave, militant
We know we need to be tough,
America has long been the helper of others
But this act of terrorism awoke us to "enough is enough,"

I always believed that everyone is good
That if we do not seek evil,
It will not come to our door,

But here it is
Over 5,000 spent lives later,
It took away people, it took away more,

How will I fly again?
How will I visit undiscovered lands?
Will someone hate me for my looks?
Will they ask me about my religion?

Of all the things I've shared with others
My beliefs never caused me tension,

Now I'm scared but I will carry on
As our flag waves proudly,
And as it stands tall
I will celebrate my freedom and all its glory,

Hatred does not develop in the heart of God
Suffering is not worshipped in prayers and sermons,
There are deeper wounds in the hearts of people
That are lashing out on neighbors, on innocents,

I do not want to rise each day in fear
I work and play and laugh just like you,
I have two feet and two hands
And I will do what God asks me to,

God reaches all
And be punished, you will,
for I love this country and I love this world
And there is no room for you, no room for ill...

"It is not for him to pride himself
who loveth his own country, but rather for
him who loveth the whole world.
The earth is but one country and mankind its citizens."
-Baha'u'llah

Final Words
By Angela Lammers - age 39
Ballarat, Victoria Aust.

As the newspaper, television, reported on the tragedy, of what was happening in America on September 11, 2001. My first response was sheer disbelief. Feeling of helplessness, regret proceeded, as I was not able to be there to assist.

Therefore, my writing, is for the purpose to provide answers, of what I would do, if I was there. For I would show, my support and tears, to all those who patiently waited, for the news of their friends, family, loved ones, who was trapped with in, the destruction. For I would have wanted to be a part of the miraculous effort, of those who engaged survivors from the desolate destruction.

Hopeful to share in the good news. But to be involved with those, who sadly was not immune, to the shock, intense sadness, emptiness, that arise, from the loss, of a large magnitude.

There would have been times, to share grief, but so many are left with an empty void. No words, actions, can attempt to eradicate such pain. For the unfairness, that provides, so many unanswered questions of why. As the loss of lives proceeded without warning. Leaving many robbed of a chance to say good-bye.

Final words, is my chance to assist those that was deprived of this chance. To recognize all those that lost their lives, as they will never be forgotten. They will live forever in peoples hearts. For they brought meaning to peoples lives, nothing will never be the same.

So therefore, to pay tribute, to remember all, with pictures in our memories. The times where we expressed love. For you did enrich all our lives, in so many ways, and for that we thank you. You will always be in our thoughts. For there is no regret in knowing you, or loving you. Love always, forever.

A New World Begins
By Dorothy Chenoweth Klausner - age 92
Castro Valley, CA

As the 20th Century approached its conclusion
and my life grew nearer to one hundred years,
I was happy at how well the world was progressing.
Few wars. Many countries learning to discuss
perceived insults or differences, ignore variations of
appearance, culture, beliefs or religion.

I thought at last we had neared the One World
so long a dream. My family and others,
children yet unborn, would no longer be targets
of bombs and guns, unseen technological torture,
but join in rational discussions, solving problems,
prejudices, until mutual decisions were reached.

Then came September eleventh, 2001.
Over four thousand people, not all Americans,
were attacked without warning, murdered
by terrorists of unknown nation or cause.
New York and Washington DC were the focus.
Terrorists falsely promised Paradise to its forces.

But one unexpected result may be new partnership among all nations of the world, uniting forever for peace.

Soldier
By David C. Lilley - age 49
Cogan Station, PA

Soldier, Soldier.
Wherever the land
Peace questions why
Few understand

Honor and duty
Call you to station
You're trained and ready
To act without hesitation

Soldier, Soldier.
Wherever your shelter
Winter's cold
Summer swelter

Defend our homeland
Liberate the oppressed
Unscathed by filthy battle
Come home in full-dress

Soldier, Soldier.
Follow your mission through
Your leader will lead
As we pray for you

Grand Old Symbol
By Conrad Novarro Kipp - age 68
Dover Plains, NY

They say I'm just a symbol a mere configuration of someone's spiritual imagination with very little significance but oh! How wrong they are, let me explain my resilience, the truth of my longevity. I was created in the year 1814, a symbolic spirit for the American Colonist fighting against the English who were determine to destroy the colonist independence. Their fight for freedom, when the fighting ceased, the smoke of the battle cleared. I remained in tack, victorious in their quest for freedom, the birth of my presence was made known, since then I have made my presence at the Civil War, World War I, World War II, the Korean War, the Vietnam War, during the endurance of my longevity. I have been criticized, spit upon, trampled upon, even burned, but through it all I remain resilient, resolute. I am a Grand Old Symbol, in deed. I am in great dignity and reverence. I have draped the coffins of those in the highest office in the United States of America. The coffins of the most humble who laid their lives down for freedom for bravery and for heroicalness.

I wave in Honor of God, for I'm a representative symbol that "Goodness Shall Over come Evil." Once again, I am being threatened by terrorist in their quest to destroy our freedom. I am in kindred ness with two other great symbols, the "Statue of Liberty" whose torch is held high against persecution, injustice, stands tall for freedom of self-expression and the "Liberty Bell" that tolls every fourth of July in honor of our Declaration of Independence. By now you have realized I am that Grand Old Flag sometimes known as "Old Glory."

Our hearts beat true for the red, white, and blue. Forever and ever may she wave, the emblem of the land that I love, the home of the free and the brave.

Display your flag with honor, pride, and reverence for it represents the very core of the United States of America, it's a timeless treasure.

America – Voices Coming Together

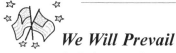

We Will Prevail
By Jack W. Kirsch - age 49
Amarillo, TX

It was a day of infamy,
a day when heroes were born;
From white collars to blue collars,
from carpenters to CEOs,
they all came to the aide
of their fallen heroes;
the firefighters, police, and
emergency rescue workers.
Hand in hand, side by side,
people set aside their differences
to unite with the will to prevail....once again
not because of power or might,
but because of spirit.

The tragic events of September 11, 2001 changed the world. It was a crude awakening. But, as a nation, we Americans have exceeded the bounds of human nature. Patriotism has spread across the land, strengthening us in the face of terror. American flags are everywhere, and out national anthem is played and sung daily.

Even inside the prisons, within Americas' penal system, there is a growing sentiment. As a prisoner myself, I can speak on behalf of those i have known who have fashioned American flags out of handkerchiefs, and those who have cut out pictures of patriotic men and women to proudly display on the walls of their cells.

Feelings of all sorts have made us realize how much we appreciate this country. One inmate told me, "Even though I'm incarcerated, I'm still proud to be an American." I share his sentiment, as my heart cries out for World Peace.

So, no matter where we are in life, free or in prison, we are still proud to be Americans! We will never forget the many victims of September 11th, nor their families. And we will always honor the heroes who lost their lives trying to save others, including the heroes of United Flight 93.

GOD BLESS AMERICA!!!

Fields of Steel (911 Sonnet)
By Tamara Beryl Latham
Brentwood, TN

In a September sky of pearl and teal,
Two silver birds have targeted their mark.
Twin Towers crumble, leaving fields of steel,
as screaming voices echo through the dark.

In disbelief we stand, shocked and appalled,
yet we maintain our rationality.
As raging fires sear us, one and all,
they meld the bonds of nationality.

The dead have found escape from what is real,
but we live buried in cold granite tombs.
Twin Towers crumble, leaving fields of steel
and ebon smoke where Satan's image looms.

A doll, a photograph, a lonely shoe,
unites our common threads: red, white, and blue.

Voices
By Deborah Kay - age 51
Venus, TX

God Bless America!
Red, white, and blue
Is now the call.

United We Stand!
All the people
Throughout this land.

Let Freedom Ring!
From North to South
And East to West.

Peace and Prayer!
Is what we share
Around the world.

Hero's
By Sandra J. Labadie - age 48
Warren, MI

There are hero's that did unite,
When America was amidst a fight.
Most were buried in the rubble,
The hero's added their lives to the struggle.
As a life was found cheers rang out,
From the crowds that remained waiting with doubt.
As the buildings did come tumbling down,
Some of them too did succumb.
They put their lives on the line,
To help the less fortunate in a bind.
Hoping they would all survive,
to rejoin their families, that sat helpless and cried.
so many prayed theirs would be found,
In the silence of that hellish mound.
Unfortunately, too many had to die,
Innocent people with quiet lives.
What happened to Humanity?
Some are selfish with no Dignity.
The hero's will never be forgotten,
Firefighters, police, medics, are all begotten.
We raise our flags for the hero's have won,
As our world unites to become one.
America will never be the same,
But the hero's fought in its name.

Those who survived and those that lost their fight,
AMERICA SALUTES YOU

Red September
By Angela Kush - age 20
Nassau Bay, TX

When tragedy strikes
It is sad to see
To find patriotism
Only within the debris
Looking beyond compilations
of rubble
To see innocent life
Shattered, stolen, crumbled.
Only upon this day
Do we reach out to lost loves
Families regain closeness
We ask forgiveness
From up above.
Why is it now, that we love
our country so?
What about days past?
This is what it takes,
To kill, to let our hatred go
We come together now
Just this day, we all cry together
When we remember
That red day in September.

Tragic of Life
By Thomas Christopher Kambiss
Crystal Beach, FL

Sometimes you want to fly away.
You never expect to have a bad day.
Sick and evil minds board the flight
Take away the people who saw the light.
The light that stood for every thing good and delight
O evil people on a mission who were wrong not right.
It was a tragic of life, many people lost their wife
Some lost their loved ones! Others wondered what was
  done.
When the day was done.
Everybody that what was won.
Disaster and destruction to our town.
People stood not happy but a sad frown.
Fire men and women and police men and women tried
  to help.
It was a tragic of life. Many people lost their wife!
We lost our loved ones! We wondered what was done.
Justice and freedom we took to the sky.
We knew what was done but didn't want a reason why
  we flew our bombs to the devil's land.
Evil people that hid in caves unlike a man.
We want to bring justice to the devil Osama Bin Laden
He ran and hid like a coward that sinned often.
We will overcome the tragic of life.
Believe in God and Jesus our Saviour!
Peace, Love, and God Bless our soul.

Old Glory
By Rebecca Marron - age 48
Benton, MO

"Old Glory" awakened, unfurls for the day,
Billowing forth proudly, the American way.
Each red stripe is a symbol of grief,
Of the life blood that flowed for our belief.
Each white one a banner to a mother so brave.
That she tore her heart out and willingly gave.
Of all the stars shining from her bosom of blue,
Doubt not, my friend, one is shining for you.
Be ye worker or soldier your duty is great,
Protect your own star and you'll save forty eight.
We must not fail nor consider defeat
And pray God "Old Glory" will never retreat.
She's been marched over mountain and down through the valley
And always she's beckoned for free men to rally.
A guidance she's been to the brave and the free.
At the sun's setting the day the fighting is done,
Now we know that freedom and liberty won,
May the "Star Spangled Banner" be furled
as before.
Knowing tyranny has lost and will raise never more.

The Aftermath
By Sandra J. Labadie - age 48
Warren, MI

Today our nations is still in mourning,
America was struck without any warning.
They took over our planes without a thought,
Of what destruction it had brought.
Many people lost their lives that day,
Their families will never be the same.
Their hatred touched so many lives,
But together we will all unite.
Shattered lives will be hard to mend,
As a country this is not the end.
"Liberty" and "Freedom" is what we stand for,
Our country's best will guard our shores.
We will mourn those that are still lost.
And help their families at any cost.
Many people have survived,
We thank God for sparing their lives.
We are united and determined to stand our ground,
Together as one we won't break down.
With so many people joining as one,
There is no doubt who has won.
The Twin Towers and Pentagon no doubt did fall,
But everywhere we look we see who stands tall.
FOR THE FREE AND THE BRAVE,
OUR FLAG WILL FOREVER WAVE.

I AM PROUD TO BE AN AMERICAN
GOD BLESS THE U.S.A.

When Poets Will Reign Like Kings
By Benedict Markowski - age 69
Detroit, MI

When poets will reign like kings
And prophets will serve as ministers,
The exuberant dream will appear
Like a suburb of Heaven
    With Muses dancing in revelry.
It will be a legend crystallized in time,
Who's citizenry will sing
    The Sacred Anthem of Art,
    The Great Law of Beauty,
Decreed from its assembly
Like the bell ringer announcing each new hour.
The citadel will rise above the Holy Mountain,
Like a monument erected nobly,
A temple oasis suspended in music.
It is the poem's imperceptible essence
Which creates the harmonious fantasy,
Transformed into a magnificent design!
While its hero will no longer
Wear the mask of beasts,
But the image of his Master,
Unveiled as the beautiful Samson,
    Aflame with Love,
Inspiring a fruitful creation
Of splendid energy bursting into infinity!

In A New York Morning
By Mia Jennings
Andover, MN

"Good bye Daddy," Molly says, before she leaves for school
Dad makes his way to work-Heads down Fifth Avenue
Tommy's Mom's on an airplane to visit Grandma on the bay
He doesn't know she won't return-It's a black-black Tuesday

Now Barbara speaks to her husband, Ted-From Heaven
She was a brave soul to use her phone-We cry for flight eleven
Towers burn-People die-Ashes fall from the sky
Terror struck upon those deadly flights-Sorrow rains from Heaven

Why so much rage in this world for power?
I cry for all those who died inside the World Trade Towers
All the heroes and heroines who've come and gone
Tried to save the victims in a world gone wrong
Was it worth this price for power?
Sometimes life tastes sweet-Sometimes life tastes sour

Gabrielle cries herself to sleep-Her husband's not coming home
He died as a fireman-A hero-Now she's all alone
"I'm sorry Susie your Mommy's gone
She died an hour ago inside the Pentagon."
Listen to Lady Liberty cry for our home

In a New York morning suddenly America changed
In a New York morning ashes fall upon the streets like rain
In a New York morning life was take in a single breath
In a space of an hour, the world has felt the pain of death.

God Bless The U.S.A.
By Cynthia V. Key
Tallahassee, FL

For these indeed are the times that try men's souls
As the fear, shock, and reality of September 11, 2001 set in
The days tragic events slowly unfold and the search for any survivors begins
Earlier that fateful morning a group of terrorists had hijacked
Four commercial airplanes, they terrorized and killed the people on board
Some of the passengers were able to call their families on their cell phones
While others prayed and called upon the name of the Lord
The hijackers were on a suicide mission to take the World Trade Centers down
The first two planes plowed right into the tall buildings
Then suddenly amid all the smoke, fire, and rubble
The Twin Towers started to crumble to the ground
The third hijacked plane struck the Pentagon building in Washington D.C.
With a furious ball of fire, smoke, and flame
People were running and screaming for dear life, such a tragedy. So insane
Meanwhile, the fourth hijacked plane sped on through the Pennsylvania sky
When the passengers decide to overpower the terrorist hijackers
Then the plane spun out of control and went crashing down
In the eerie silence that followed.... no survivors were found
We tip our hats and salute all these "Sky Angel Heroes" as well as
All the brave souls on ground zero level, who gave their all, to salvage the day
And lest we forget, to God in humble prayer we say....
"God Bless the U.S.A."

Utter Disbelief
By Rose M. Martinez
Romeo, CO

In the dawning of this new day,
God Bless the USA,
Her flags will fly at half-mast
In accordance with this tragedy cast!
I do not yet understand,
But as a nation we will stand,
To overcome this tragedy
and a better place-we will be!
As I watch the news in utter horror
Of the destruction and terror
Inflicted on this great nation
As the tears flow without cessation.
How can this possibly be happening?
To a nation where freedom does so freely ring!
Why would anyone?
Want to cover up the sun
Of a bright and beautiful day
Before destruction got its way?
My heart cannot comprehend
What these terrorists have send
To the melting pot of the world
As the planes they aimlessly twirled!
No regard for innocent lives
Or the thought of hardship and strife
That it would bring to each and everyone
Regardless of from what country we'd come.
After hearing on the news
From the many countless crews
As they too, grieve and don't understand why
So many people had to die!
Such a tragic loss of lives
As the planes fell from the sky
Bringing utter disbelief
As a whole country stops in grief!

American Transition Universal
By Ronnie Lowry - age 52
Baldwin, FL

The Nation has changed; for better, for worse,
and this initiates significant behavior shift
endowed with higher character and greater love,
and with this change a newer vision of our place
    in our Universe.

Many feel they lost but truly their love ones
gave of themselves that we might grow more,
an evolutionary crisis met and dissolved by more,
by few; and the way to total freedom lies
    not in filling our own wants but —
        desiring the best for all.

America-Our Land of Plenty
By Ossie H. Martin
Columbia, SC

Calling all Americans! Calling all American! Aren't you proud to be an American, our land of plenty, home of the brave, land of the free!, despite these chaotic and perilous times? You still have your <u>freedom</u>! Your <u>Red</u>, <u>White</u> & <u>Blue</u> — You can wear it on your feet, your head or your arms.

As you know, America-Our land of plenty has stood the test of <u>Time</u>, the test of <u>Famine</u>, the test of <u>Love</u>, the test of <u>Patience</u> and is currently standing the test of <u>Terror</u>.

Acts of terrorism are sweeping across this global universe as never before, causing permanent damage to historical and monumental landmarks. In essence, taking innocent lives and stagnating financial growth and economic development.

You still have your <u>freedom</u>! Your <u>Red</u>, <u>White</u> and <u>Blue</u> — You can wear it on your feet, your head or your arms.

"Terror, terror on the wall
It's the worst enemy of all
The mighty towers had a great
Fall." Lets' wake up and heed the call-the call for Peace.

America-our land of plenty is thirsty-not for water, but for love, justice, peace and human dignity.

"Peace is love, love is peace. Peace of mind brings joy and beauty, not crime."

"United we stand, divided we fall." Let's wake up and heed the call, the call for unity and human dignity."

These will culminated and bring everlasting peace and friendship, to a dark and dying world, throughout this global universe, if, "<u>We</u>," come together as "<u>One Unified Nation</u>," and <u>Not</u> as several "<u>Divided Nations</u>."

911 The Day We Woke Up
By Neil Mason - age 42
Tustin, CA

I am always intrigued by the way people see
Our faith was shaken, us, the home of the free
The tragedy of lives taken away
The senselessness, our way of life, gone astray
Evil has landed on our front steps
God still shows miracles at humanities depths
New York's bad rap as cold and mean
No longer is that gonna be seen
No prejudice, no black versus white, no white versus black
That's pretty phat
Strangers helping strangers worlds apart hands held out
Togetherness rings loud freedom so strong is now the shout
From now on we must be strong
To keep mankind from going wrong
From now on we shall hold out our hands
Helping our strangers, repairing life's strands
Yes we are fragile, we need guidance from above
It is time to embrace GOD's heavenly love.
It is time for us to see
Only with GOD can we be set free
Home of the brave together we stand
We can no longer hide so hold out your hand
Our nation together one by one
Shall stand tall GOD's will be done.

To all those suffering or lost because of the tragedy. I hope this helps bring some sense of peace and faith back to you.

Attack 9-11-01
By Ruth Diselrod Mattern - age 49
Wilson, NC

What can I say? What can I do? Please help me God. I'm asking you.
How do I help my fellow man repair the destruction to our great land?
It came from somewhere out of the sky. And left us wondering.... How? and Why?
Birds of prey, they seemed to be, creating chaos for you and me.
Destroying the Towers and Pentagon. We can't let this kind of thing go on.
Thousands of people have lost their lives. Parents, children, husbands, and wives.
Mass destruction, death, and pain....brought by Evil with something to gain.
Whatever this Evil is trying to do, we mustn't let his powers get through....
through to our hearts and through to our souls. We must not let him reach his goal.
Together we must be strong and brave, if, our country, we're going to save.
Our differences, we have to shed. Together, we must forge ahead.
Into the future and out of the past, begin again. Let doubts be cast.
Join together hand in hand. Reach out and help our fellow man.
It will take us many years, to ease the heartache, dry the tears.
But never doubt it can be done, once the task ahead begun.
Look into history many years; this country was built with blood, sweat, and tears.
We are strong and will build again, God, country, family, and friends.
United We Stand, this Nation great. We won't let Evil seal our fate.
"In God We Trust." We've always said. Let's keep that sentiment in our head
as we move on and build again. United we will always win!

One With You
By Carole S. Milano
Southington, CT

Our hearts cry out to you,
as you search through
the rubble.
Our love fills
the open wound
where there once was life.
Our tears meld with yours
to prepare this wound
for future growth.
Our prayers reach out
to heal these emotional scars,
to let you know
your loss is ours.
Though more pain may lie ahead
it is what lies within you
and those who have perished....
that has meaning;
it is the human spirit.

America – Voices Coming Together

Behind the Walls
By Wilma 'Sines' Lipscomb - age 70
Prudenville, MI

All the hustle and bustle on September tenth was just another ordinary day in The Great Twin Towers in New York. Nearly everyone was at work. A few were out for coffee or personal errands. Hardly no one had their thoughts on God, or the events of the next day, I doubt it, if one out of ten even said a morning prayer, asking God to protect them through the day.

Then the FRIGHTFUL DAY of the ELEVENTH! People began to shout to God. God why did you let this happen? Why do you let terrorist in our Great country?

Almost everyone across the nation began to call on God at once. Yes, He heard us all. If my people who are called by my name will call on me I will hear! I will heal their lands.

O, if we would've all done this the tenth and every day before God would've heard. God listens to every small voice no matter how weak. He heard every dying call. He heard every prayer that was delivered by a mother, a father, a fireman, a policeman, and the little children, He answered them in His way, it was truly a day of turning to God. Why do we all wait for a terrible thing to happen to call on Him? Tell your loved one today you love them, We do not know if there will be a tomorrow. Hug your child, thank God for them and your family. We see peace through all the disruption on this earth.

God puts His Almighty Hand down and calms the storm! He brings peace in the hearts of all who call His Name. It brought the world closer to Him, The Twin Towers Were Great! but nothing can out last the greatness of God, GOODBYE TOWERS HELLO GOD! GOD KEEPS ON BLESSING AMERICA!

Shaker Cheese Baskets
By Jacqueline G. Masten
Nashua, NH

A cheese in the works.
Soft water pliable reed splint
Square shaped rounded at need.
12 to 24 inch sizes,
Open work weave.
Cheese cloth was placed
In baskets
Whey could drip
Curd to remaine.
Nor sower
Or sweet
Delicate, silky
Just right for the taste.
Had a shaker stomach
To please.
Brought from the shaker cheese baskets,
Straight to the table.

In memory of my Great Aunt
Eldress Gertrude Soule Shaker

The Devil's Flight
By Kathryn Flatley
Yardville, NJ

Silence could be heard, yielding to the screams
As innocence shattered, stealing the dreams
Of women and children by the dawn's early light,
Who never suspected that the previous night
Would give way to terror, as the morning unfurled.
And life would be altered, as evil met world.

The skies shone brightly in their original hue,
As the clouds of cotton amidst azure blue
Turned ashen with death to blind our sight,
On the morning of evil, the devil's flight,
That branded the number 9-1-1
To One Nation under God, grieving and stunned.

A traitor among us, yet the red, white, and blue,
Although weeping bitter tears stood proudly in view.
Anchored as a headstone for the world to see,
United we stood, believing victory,
Could be ours for the taking, if we knew the foe,
Whose invisible presence, we were desperate to know.

Our souls now murdered, as the sickle and scythe,
Slaughtered the skyline of New York's pride,
As men and women fell weakened and numb,
By senseless acts of terror, perverse minds come undone.
By cowards whose hearts were so blackened with hate,
That they consented to Hell as their ultimate Fate.

The stench of death, densely clinging the air,
Reminding us of the bond we share,
With our families and friends who lost their lives
In grave acts of terror, nurtured by the lies
Of malignancy of demons afar,
With no comprehension of who we are,
Or how our wrath would avenge their lair,
By a country enraged, bombs bursting in air.

You can't cower in caves and expect to win
When suicide bombing that are driven by sin
Are reasoned by beliefs in the name of a God,
Then trample our values on this sacred sod,
Where independence is exalted and liberty,
Are treasures we'll embrace for eternity.

Aunt Eldress Gertrude Soule Shaker

Jacqueline G. Masten — Geraldine Boynton

Terrors in the Towers
By Margaret T. McGarry - age 75
Danbury, CT

In the early 70's I visited the
   Tallest Twin Towers,
      On floor 69, fear filled my brain.
         I lacked survival powers.

I heard and felt the building
   Sway, then creak.
      The gurgle sound from the toilet
         Scared me into the elevator
            Headed for the street.

1993, that jealous deadly sin,
   caused envious males to attack
      This mighty structure to win.
         To win war, against untrained
            Civilians earning a living!

The twins employed people from 80 Nations,
   Who yearned to be free.
      The tower of Babel
         Was compared to this tragedy,
            Whatever the reason,
               Such devastation sickened me.

9/11/01, viewed the crashes of a suicidal pair,
   The force of the fire made humans jump,
      Shove and push, high in the air,
         Rather than burn alive.

With New York City's aspiring citizens,
   Firefighters, police, and personnel security, slaughtered!
      Checked six months later, the edifice sank,
         Atop bodies and gold bricks from a bank.

"With Love to Tiger Gillotti from Mom"

One Step Away
By LadyO - age 36
New York, NY

We were one step away from a world of peace
In grandeur and venture and many a speech
One step away for saving hands to reach.

Then in a flash our hopes were dashed
And many loved ones fallen to smoke and ash
As we reflect one step away to the cemetery plot
Now who draws the lot of our burdens while being left here.
Then the sunsets to a brand new year.

One step away to our future is what is left today
Life is life and we must take it, day after day
We will watch time passing, one step away
to infinity.

Dedication: Remember to revere thy family for a brighter future

September 11, 2001
By Kathryn E. Mascherin
Hamilton, NJ

A late summer morn was filled with beauty.
   Fields of sunflowers adorned the Princeton road —
      a perfect day of serenity.

Suddenly radio strains of Bach ceased;
Two towering brothers, attacked,
   fell to ground zero!

America's cherished kaleidoscope
   shattered in disarray!
So much promise killed in an instant of terror!

Towers of success and commerce
   now an amphitheater of gloom.
God, why America? Why now?

Rescue workers, police, volunteers joined as one —
Remove injured, save lives, fight infernos.

We, too, are bonded together!
In the wake of September 11 our resolve is firm.

Justice, retribution, determination are stronger
   than horror.
Each American must don a hard hat.

Together we will reassemble
   that multi-colored kaleidoscope
Into a perfect prism of peace.

Gift of Life 2001
By Shirley Leanore Bohl Ross
Massillon, OH

People in our lives are gifts.
After we open the gift we misuse it....loose it....
abuse it....throw it away.

People are a gift from God like a diamond ring
it has been cut and shaped and measured.
God cut us in His image and threw us in the water.
His light shines yellow, red, white, black, and brown;
a rainbow of beauty.

We are united in His gift of love to share
all over the world. His strength climbed
up the Statue of Liberty and she reached out to
the world uniting one and all nations,

Beneath her there is crying, moaning, creaking,
and rumbling for our lost, our heroes and
the living as we sing Amazing Grace and fall
on our knees (before) Jesus our Lord. Its
wake up call: Love one another till death do us part.
Not gone at all just on a journey home. God, care for all
our gifts we left behind.

The Collapse
By Steve Schneider
Bismarck, ND

Two centers of power collapse
due to a senseless and barbaric act.

You grab your gear and head into the
war zone. The darkness, smoke, and dirt
fill your eyes, lungs, and nose.

You cough, but head into save the lives
of innocent victims.

You save some, but sadly, others perish.
Draped in the flag they are led out of the war
zone. You salute, hoping their souls will eventually
be at peace. It's quiet as you honor the innocent victims.

Those who committed this senseless and barbaric act will be
brought to justice and the souls will rest in peace.

Trapped
By Christina Marie Simington - age 15
Mansfield, MA

Trapped
I feel like there is no way out
Locked in here
Everything is closing in on me
I can't breathe
I can't move
there's no way out
Something tells me I'll be in here forever
Or at least until I take my eternal sleep
The memories rushing through my head
Bouncing back and forth terrifying me
Saddening me to think that I will never see him again
I want to get out
I want to be free
They have taken everything away from me
This morning I was innocent
But now I am a victim
A victim of terrorism
I can't stay awake
My body is too small to bear the pressure
The thousands of people that must be thinking the same thing
Piled on top of me
Around me
Underneath me
I can't bear it
I have to sleep
I wonder if I will wake again

To My Dad
By Donna M. Micheli - age 46
Albany, NY

Love is a dad who thinks you're beautiful
no matter what gender.
Love is a dad who works two jobs to
provide a home.
Love is a dad who worked holidays but
found the time to assemble toys for the
Christmas tree.
Love is a dad who self educated to better
himself and possessed great lessons in
life.
A born Mister Fix it and hardware man.
Love is a dad who tirelessly chauffeured
everyone anytime any day.
Love is dad who was calm in crisis and
patient to teach 2 student drivers.
Love is a dad who decides what's best for
you when you can't and lets you think you
did it.
Love is a dad who imparts mutual respect
no fear just great stability and curiosity.
Love is a dad who lived his professional
ethics and held honesty very close to his
heart.
Love is a firefighter dad who retired as
badge #1 in all our hearts as well as in our
lives.
Love is my dad still Buzzi who I see still
here in all our thoughts.

This is dedicated to my dad Donald
Bussey who passed away 07/20/98.

Dear Mom
By Kate Shelley - age 16
Essex Jct, VT

Mom I know you're wondering if I am ok,
you can see me in your mind mom, and that's where I'll
have to stay.
Because mom I was a victim, you can feel it in your heart,
cause mom you know I'd never leave you, even if we're apart.
You can look for me mom, in the wreckage, but it's the memories
you want to find, they'll always be with you mom in your heart
and in your mind.
It's a tragedy mom, but please don't be upset,
just know that you love me and that you'll never forget.

In Regards to September 11, 2001
By Kate Moscatello - age 13
Newton, NJ

O see the Lady of Liberty, standing tall against the backdrop of her native harbor so savagely attacked and destroyed.

Hear the cries of her people hurtling about in panic and terror. Their frightened screams shatter the heavy air of the crowded streets and their eyes gaze upon the reality they once knew, now nothing but a broken dream.
O America

Your images are burned in my mind like a scar to the skin and deeply I feel your wounds for you are a part of me just as I am a part of you
What was so viciously stolen from you, your people, and bring justice and consolation to our glorious homeland of which will never falter

May the spirit of patriotism never die!
May the eagle always soar!
May the Stars and Stripes never fall,
When this brief death is over...
We shall thrive once again.

Annonomous photo obtained from the website
http://gallery.hd.org

United
By Mary Jean Miller - age 18
Decateur, IN

America, your heart cries out
With pain, fear, and need
While your wounded vessels
Lie helpless as they bleed.

Cities stand still in anguish,
A nation looks on in fear,
Hoping the attacks will destroy no more,
America now sheds a tear.

We mourn with those who have lost so much
And miss the ones who've passed.
Unfortunately, we can't bring them back,
But through memories they may last.

We're thankful for the heroes
And that many lives were spared.
And to all of those who offered prayers,
That showed how much you cared.

The fight for freedom we now have
To stand against fear and pain,
One nation, united, **under God**
Shall be our sweet refrain.

What is lost can't be regained,
And life will soon go on.
The sun will set, the dark will come,
But soon we will see dawn.

Cry no more, America,
For what we can't restore.
Proudly and firmly, one nation we'll stand
As never, we have before.

Until We Meet Again
By Karen McKeever - age 31
Middletown, CT

Life can twist your heart.
So suddenly, so strange life wakes you up.
Since the world has lost her way, you've had an endless journey of loneliness.

I thought I had it all and then a new day came, almost blinding me.
At the doorway of my heart, all the leaves have fallen down.
Where there was joy, now there is pain.

Everyone told me to be strong, hold on and don't shed a tear.
So through darkness let the rain come down and wash away my tears.
Let it fill my soul and drown my fears.
Let it shatter the walls and new day will come.

You will be there every time I fall.
The love you gave will always live.
Forgive me for the things I never said to you.

You made me who I am; memories of you take my sadness and make me strong.
You're the reason I go on and now I need to live the truth.

Right now, there's no better time.
From this fear, I will break free.
I must say goodbye.

When you call on me, when you reach for me, I just drift away.
You'll be my wings that guide my broken flight.
Till we meet again, until then goodbye!

Dedicated to the families and friends who lost loved ones on September 11, 2001.

America – Voices Coming Together

September 11, 2001
By Betty D. Mercer
Muskegon, MI

A bright sunny morning, people going to work....
The World Trade Center Towers — in full view;
Tall, every so tall — they pointed to the sky!
Pride of New York.
SUDDENLY - GONE! They imploded; they stand no longer!

GET THOSE PERPETRATORS!
Even the score!
Seek them, catch them, demolish them, or secure them
Where they'll KILL NO MORE!
We will pursue them until we catch them
And we won't rest until we do.

Take a walk, a long walk....
On a bright sunny day
To where the Towers once stood....
And look DOWN, D-0-W-N, down:
And then look up!
What do you see?

There used to be....but no more:
People working in offices up there....
People eating lunches - on the terrace out there....
People walking around INSIDE;
People seeing flower shows — I saw one there!
PEOPLE MEETING PEOPLE!
Millions of people DIED!

TO ALL THE PERPETRATORS:
If you're not contented with your way of living
Destroying property and killing people
Is not the way to achieve your goal
Of Health and Happiness, Peace and Security....

You are just digging your own hole of deeper misery.

Written on April 30, 2002

Cleansing
By Susan M. Reed - age 35
Wausau, WI

It starts with nothing
The grey of an abyss appears
An abyss which has caused tears,
Found the hearts of many
And united a nation.
In uniting a nation,
We have prevailed
Conquering the goals of the terrorists
Once more extolling the meaning
Of our flag.

Apart
By M.J. McKenzie - age 39
Ashland, KY

There are times when I wonder where you are?
Some days I even wish upon a star.
I just know that you are out there somewhere.
This is practically too much to bear.

Where are you....the only love of my life?
I wanted so much to be a dear wife.
Seems the winds of time have blown us apart—
But you'll always have a place in my heart.

Roll On America, Roll On
By Juanita Russell Sheets - age 67
Altoona, IA

It happened September 11, the year 2001.
Bin Laden had got us one by one.
I was watching the Today Show on TV
I looked up and what did I see! —
A plane hit the tower building and brought it down.
In a ball of fire it fell to the ground.
The smoke and dust bellowed up and down.

The frame of metal, all twisted and bent —
Alas another plane, the other tower did hit.
The second tower building standing tall, strong, and lean,
Came down with a second ball of fire at its wing.

The twisted metal, the screams of despair, —
The smell of burned flesh the smell of singed hair.
Alas God's angels appeared on the scene.
The fireman, the policemen standing tall, strong, and lean.
Started searching for their fallen comrades, whom they had not seen.
They searched and searched both day and night —
And wondered what would be their plight.
They are still searching to this very day,
As God did light the way.
The comrades are in heaven,
Their souls with thee, for while on earth their act of bra-ve-ry.

There were other terrorists across the way, in Phil-a-del-phia,
and a hero on the plane, he did bring down,
To save the White House from falling to the ground.
And I heard the voice of a hero shout loud and clear
"Roll on" my comrades.
We'll all meet in heaven, around God's throne."
And I heard God shout, "Roll on."
A Leader in New York City stood brave, strong, and tall.
Along with the President, gave strength and hope to us all.
Mr. President and Mayor Guillano we salute you.

Can We Ever Forget 9-11

By Vivian Gloff Mollan - age 76
Milwaukee, WI

Can we ever forget 9-11
When Hell blinded the warm rays of the sun?
Peace and calm, daily life on the run,
Gave the Twin Towers their normal hum.
It was a normal fair day of business as usual,
But terrorists from the sky, turn calm into futile.
Brave fire fighters rushed head-long to the scene,
Blinded by hell like they never had seen.
Air had been replaced with clouds of disbelief,
Where life had revolved into an ocean of grief.
Fire fighters keep searching for so many months,
Sifting for the missing through ashes and muck.
Lives forever ravished of love, dreams and hopes,
With pain, fear, and grief now forever to cope.
The world is becoming such a dangerous place;
Evil striving to diminish our whole human race.
Our planet is but a small speck spinning in space
Becoming to God, a creation of total disgrace.
Man killing the innocent as a God granting cause,
Excusing the actions as a religious right law.
Have minds become so demented and so evil,
That Satan has shattered the good and the real?
The angels in the heavens are crying oceans of tears,
Screaming down to the world, but will anyone hear?
God has given each person a heart, soul, and mind, but
Evil knows if to conquer, it first must divide.
If we do not change and have love as our guide,
Earth will soon be the planet that committed suicide!

My Lord's Prayer

By Lori Pingsterhaus
Germantown, IL

My Lord's prayer
I am the vessel
In which your hand
Guides my soul.
You are the wind
That carries me through
The path of life.
I do not wish to live
Without your love.
Everyone tells me
To live by the bible,
But I also choose to live
With my heart and soul.
Please guide me with
Your love, because
I'm your lost lamb
In a world of darkness.
This prayer I make to you
With all of my heart.
I love you, but
I need your guidance
More than ever.
Please help me Lord.

AMEN

Old Satan Got Loose

By Cleo Sobel
Bronx, NY

Wake up, wake up, America.
New York, stay alert, don't sleep.
Our enemies, we know not, where they are or who.
Fight back, stand tall. Old Satan, wants our freedom.
Don't let him get his way.
Our very own teachers taught them to fly, oh yes,
took our planes, for terror turned our beautiful towers to
rubbish. Our friends, loved ones, no more to see.
No more, hello honey at end of day. No more picnic
lunches as once we shared, or our walks down 5th Ave on a
beautiful sunny day. Turned to a hell day, September 11, 2001.
All pain, hate, and fear, will we overcome?
All our tears, floated down the Hudson River out to
sea, yes, out to sea.

The Stars and Stripes Forever

By Carol Merolla - age 56
Johnston, RI

America the beautiful, may it always stay that way,
but to keep Old Glory flying there's a price that we must pay.

For everything worth having demands work and sacrifice,
and freedom is a gift from God that commands the highest price.

For all our wealth and progress are as worthless as can be
without the faith that made us great and kept our country free.

Neither can our nation hope to live unto itself alone,
for the problems of our neighbors must today become our own.

And while it is hard to understand the complexities of war,
each one of us must realize that we are fighting for

The principles of freedom and the decency of man,
and as a Christian Nation we're committed to God's Plan.

As the Land of Liberty and a great God-fearing nation
we must protest our honor and fulfill our obligation.

So in these times of crisis, let us offer no resistance
in giving help to those who need our strength and our assistance.

And the stars and stripes forever will remain a symbol of
a rich and mighty nation built on faith, truth, and love.

Dedication:
God lead us in our struggle
toward new-found brotherhood.

Our United States
By Tina M. Moore - age 36
Columbus, OH

A long time ago, a dream began
designed by thoughts of extraordinary men.

They united people who now stand in awe
of the men who placed breath in the letter of law.

To this day, their achievement remains unique
for they encompassed what all men seek.

The desire to achieve a dream.... live in dignity
but above all else....the right to be free.

On September 11th their vision was challenged with ill intent.
Cowards callously struck.... lives so innocent.

What darkness must lie in the hearts of those
who seek their enemy by the choices they chose.

On this day, we all faced what transposed.
Awakened from slumber, we soon arose.

Forced to accept the death of their deceit,
hatred....harbored in many their goal to defeat.

Striking without warning.... Our purpose.... Hopes & Dreams
They misunderstood the breath in our being.

Our president's strength restored honor to office once erased.
He regained dignity.... Integrity shun upon his trusting face.

We united remembering our dream
assured we would survive evil at any extreme.

Our country is a life.... It cannot be bought.
Nor fall if we become distraught.

What man do you know if given the choice
would not give everything to have a voice?

The protection provided by a force so grand
.... yet no other so freely extends its hand.

Our banner flown proudly, believing with their life
democracy & freedom have sacrifice.

In times of tragedy, our best shines through.
We look deep in our soul for goodness to renew.

Virtues cherished deep in our heart
cannot be destroyed or torn apart.

Our blanket so warm comforts all who ache.... knowing some may choose to forsake.
WE ARE PROUD TO BE AMERICANS.... WE ARE THE UNITED STATES!

The American in Me
By Amy Michelle Osadchuk - age 23
Montezuma, IN

I'll never quite forget
how New York looked
with Americans covered
in layers of *ash*.
The smoldering debris
of September 11th
has burned the image of tragedy
forever into my eyes.
I can't look at our children
without remembering their loss.
It's hard to see a plane
without adding on the flames.
I *stare at towering buildings*
and wonder when they'll fall.
But fire chief Red,
surgeon White,
and police sergeant Blue
seem to get me through...
But God Bless Americans.
And Bless the American in me.
I gave my blood, my money,
and my words
in my country's darkest
hour of need.
But terrorism is nothing more
than an old word with new meaning.
I didn't need another war
to stand up and cry
when I heard the radio play
God Bless the U.S.A.

Mountain's Ground
By Joy O'Connor
Vernon Hills, IL

Was it that the mountains had
   all been brought to ground,
Or had it been that the comets
   had fallen all around?
Take care that your mind
   understands the sounds.
Fear the fears from the
   heart's tumultuous pounds.
Engulf the confusion of life so
   unbound.
Cry for the agony left behind
   by sin crowned.
This day that tears watered
   fallen comets all around,
But for our stars to still
   rise from Mountain's Ground.

September 11, 2001

By Albert Nelson
Venthor, NJ

Terrorism struck again!
An even mightier blow!
The Pentagon just after dawn!
The Trade Towers laid low!
Yet through the smoke and through the mist
The sun's broad face did show!

Or, Freedom, was it yours we saw
That fateful day of days?
Your design to fire the mind,
As you had done always,
Whenever menace, threat, or foe
Your sovereignty would overthrow?

Yes! Yes! 'twas I! What made thee great!
I burned before thine eyes!
The right of man for which ye stand —
I'll not be compromised!

And so I said, and so I say,
Freedom be realized!
To arms! to arms! my countrymen —
For all who live, and died!

The Price of Freedom

By Carrie Nelson - age 34
Louisville, KY

It takes only an instant
to destroy what's always been.
Time stands still
as Americans watch our icons, our livelihood
go from carefree to disaster.
Most all of us can do
is watch in horror as the chaos unfolds
and death for many becomes more apparent.
Our country can ask "why?" all we want
but most know the answer.
Fathers and sons
mothers and daughters
wives and husbands are vacant at their family's table.
Lives are shattered by senseless evil and acts of vengeance
love goes on,
but loss for now is stronger.
We must remember our place in this world:
    stronger, more free, more powerful!
We will overcome. We will restore ourselves. WE WILL fight back. We will WIN!
The enemy must learn they cannot get us down
Our spirit cannot be broken.
They can destroy the materials things we own, they can attempt to scare
but,
When they mess with our lives
They will know they've gone too far.
We will unite. We will rebuild. We WILL regain our confidence. We will come out
    number ONE!

Rescuers

By Janice Mulcahey
South Berwick, ME

What right do I have to deny what's happening in the world today?
What right do I have to try to shut out the every day pain you all endure.
What right do I have to look away, to smile, to laugh, to enjoy this sun filled day?
When our own are grueling through rubble and dust to find those that are lost!
How will they again go about their day with devastations face in their eyes way?
How will they again enter society as if nothing has changed!
Such a job you all do, I often wonder how do you get through?
Do your terror filled days turn to terror filled nights of the sights you saw in the light filled daylight?
You probably will never share the smells, sights, cries, and defeats.
Nor share the guilt of why, "you and not me"?

God Bless you women and men for the pain you tried to relinquish for them.
God Bless your heroic deeds the selfless hours, the dark filled dreams.
God Bless you all I fall to my knees.

Heroes

By Heidi L. Mosher - age 34
St. Albans, VT

God called His heroes home....
on that dreadful September day,
He knew what He was doing
although we didn't see it that way.

An angel hand-picked by the One,
took your father by the hand....
and lead him to a better place
I know it's difficult to understand.

Let your tears be a reflection
of memories old and new....
for love, life, and special times
your father shared with you.

Your hero, yes, he's watching
and collecting all those tears....
and every time your heart aches
he'll be there to cleanse your fears.

And so God needed someone you loved
to be His "Right Hand Man"
to watch over you and guide you now
your Hero was God's plan.

God Bless You.

One Peculiar Day
By Elena` - age 42
Lincoln Park, NJ

Eyes wide open in an unordinary way
Is how I would describe this tragic day
A bit of a shock from those who were not there
People who were would say it was fear

How could this happen to a country so free
That stands for peace and liberty
We live day to day and sometimes misunderstand
Families are a precious part of our land

Many empty hearts and broken dreams
People coming together in time of need
Sharing the loss, touching a hand
We should be proud of this love of man

How did this happen to our old city
Our melting pot of nations
Shall we allow an intrusion of such nature
People were amazed at this devastation

Memories of September eleven
Oh....memories, will not be forgotten
Living on in our children's eyes
Living on in our neighbors heart
Only now with our eyes wide open
Can we change our future

Holding On
By Christina Miller - age 17
High Point, NC

Help me hold on to what life use to be
Help me hold on to the memories
Behind me.

If all I had was one more September day
It would embrace in love and never
Fade away.

Help me hold on to remember what to
Say.
Help me hold on to this tragedy and
Its essence of the day.

Our nation hanging by a moment
We were swept away but came
Back stronger than ever
In every way.

Help me hold on to the prayer for
The nation that went out to
Every station.
Help me hold on to its realization.

I'm holding on.

Twin Towers
By Anne Murphy
Concord, NH

There was a gaping wound in the skyline where the twin towers once stood,
Its former shape was defined by a dark cloud that hung over its former height,
The debris and fallen ashes hit ground zero while flames licked the spilt fuel from the plane, forming a pyre to the thousands caught inside the building,
Bitter were the foes filled with hate in their act of destruction for all to view in shock and horror.
Their solo missions delivered blows leaving carnage and destruction in its wake.
But from the ashes the EAGLE rose to stand united once again as a nation.
We honor the departed souls, hold their memories so dear and in our prayers we share a deep sorrow for the loss of life.

Nine Eleven
By MT-G
West Orange, NJ

```
                                         N
                                         I
                                         NE
                                         EL
Do you remember                 +++++++++ E ++++++++++++++
The sunrise                     +++++++++ V ++++++++++++++
On September eleventh           +++++++++ E ++++++++++++++
The little girl asked           +++++++++ N ++++++++++++++

+++++++++++++++++++++++++++    twin shadows cut a pair of pictures
+++++++++++++++++++++++++++    and laid them over the marshes
+++++++++++++++++++++++++++    over the mountains
+++++++++++++++++++++++++++    onto the sky
+++++++++++++++++++++++++++    the heavens reached out
+++++++++++++++++++++++++++    and covered the ashes
+++++++++++++++++++++++++++    the memories of men and women
+++++++++++++++++++++++++++    with an invisible blanket

Do you see the flag            +++++++++++++++++++++++++++
The pins      the memorabilia  +++++++++++++++++++++++++++
Under the blue lights          +++++++++++++++++++++++++++
Her grandma questioned back    +++++++++++++++++++++++++++

+++++++++++++++++++++++++++    the little girl
+++++++++++++++++++++++++++    pushed the guiding hands     ahead
+++++++++++++++++++++++++++    we must run   we must kill   now
+++++++++++++++++++++++++++    to have peace   oil  and money

Do you have peace oil money war  +++++++++++++++++++++++++++
war     money oil peace   war    +++++++++++++++++++++++++++
money      oil    peace          +++++++++++++++++++++++++++
oil    money   peace      war    +++++++++++++++++++++++++++
```
PEACE OIL MONEY ? WAR PEACE MONEY OIL ?   WAR

September 11, 2001
By Jessika Nickel - age 14
Friend, NE

It came without warning,
It was such a surprise,
Everyone watched with tears in their eyes.

So many injured,
So many died,
The volunteers did their job,
With no complaints, but pride.

Heaven looked upon our nation,
And helped us pull on through,
And influenced the people,
To give all they could pursue.

The Red Cross gathered money,
Food and love galore,
And even though they had so much,
We kept on giving more.

No one in this nation,
Was untouched by this event.
And after the buildings collapsed,
One hundred angels were sent.

Now all that have been killed,
Will now rest in peace,
Knowing that we care for them,
And that our prayers to God will never decrease.

Evil Took Control 9/11/2001
By Vivian Gloff Mollan - age 76
Milwaukee, WI

So much destruction, horror and fright,
Evil took control, bringing hell in clear sight.
The skies so clear with a heavenly view,
Hell flying nearer and none had a clue.
Proud were the towers so high above all,
Soon to endure the greatest of falls.
Terrorists took control of passenger planes,
To the World Center Towers took their aim.
The thunder and crashing will never be stilled,
The death screams will echo and forever chill.
Shock and tears can never be restrained,
And only death, concrete and ashes remain.
Firemen race to the ghastly death scene,
Even they can't believe what crying eyes see.
Taking their own lives into their hands,
No hesitation, duty is in utter command.
Plane number two strikes the twin tower,
Oblivion has struck with uncanny power.
For weeks brave men search 'round the clock,'
Praying to find loved ones in dust steam and rock.
The Taliban with a leader straight from hell,
Brained-washed youth with lies, that still sell.
We each find God in our own special way,
But, no God wills the innocent to become a prey.
Good and honor shall be the only true way,
That the true Creator instructs to convey.
Man must prove he is greater than the animals of Earth,
Lest God will start over, with a second Birth.
Must God soon permit us to destroy ourselves,
Then all face each other forever in Hell?

I Pray
By Don Odom - age 43
Helena, Alabama

These are the days You have told us about
The world is hard to live in, You are hard to live without

I pray for the lives lost on September 11
Have mercy for the souls who did not go to Heaven

Thank You for the heroes who died trying to save
The people who were trapped or hurt on this day

Thank You for the ones You took home to hold
I pray the ones they left behind will have peace and be bold

Let we who believe not hate or hold a grudge
I pray we will not forget, God, that You will be judge

I pray our troops who are fighting will soon win this war
And the ones who are lost will soon come to know Jesus, the Lord

My heart cries for the ones who hurt or who hate

I pray they will know Lord, that for You love it is not too late

Ode to Victims
By Michael Parente - age 80
New Hyde Park, NY

The air was filled with fire,
smoke and dust

A cowardly act performed by
the most unjust

Airplanes flown into the towers
left those within without power

Toiling faithfully at their tasks
became victims of terrible blasts

Falling and tumbling neath glass and stone
only to lie there still and prone

You are now in God's embrace
no longer a victim of an evil face

Now to sleep and eternal rest
and therein lie ever in His breast.

America – Voices Coming Together

The Day Tragedy Hit Us All
By Linda Paquette - age 53
Dracut, MA

I sit here everyday trying to understand, how such tragedy, could had happen to all of us that day, September 11, 2001. Why? What was their point, what was it they were trying to say. They killed so many people that day. So many people that never knew them, and never knew they were going to die that day. For if they had, they would had sent their love, and said good-bye to all of us. Why is it still today, so hard for us to believe, even when we see the headlines in our newspapers, and on our television set. How could this be, we live in a country where we are told that we are Free. We are told that this couldn't happen to us. If you look at a police car, you will read to protect and to serve. Tell me, where is the protection from thieves, killers, and maniacs, how can they protect us all. How can anyone protect us from hate, there is so much hate. The hate for one human being to another, how could it run so deep within someone? When do we all stop bleeding, God help us all to understand why someday. God Bless all the ones that seen hell hit earth that day. And to remember how much blood was lost that day. I guess so we could still feel free, but we will never feel safe again. They took that from all of us. Not only did they take our loved ones; they took the fear of ever feeling safe again. That they did see with a smile.

What, When, Where, How, & Why
By Randal K. Murphy - age 38
Eddyville, KY

What is this gone so wrong with our human condition,
When faced with fanatics of Far East religious tradition,
Where the body, and plane are tools for suicide ammunition.
    How dost one choose by a legion to annihilate,
    Why doth innocent blood at great fallen towers now saturate.

What manner of sorrow on a great democracy has descended,
When at tragedy's door thy public servant with physician hath attended,
Where surely another annual memorial must be recommended.
    How dost one heartbreak afresh daily not go insane,
    Why doth the hope of a nation search out the rubble in vain.

What God over man, and beast could promote such a transgression,
When liberty and justice for all sang them all of progression,
Where dual towers did collapse under the weight of terrorist oppression.
    How once they did stand in full glory to demonstrate,
    Why the prosperity of a nation did choose to retaliate.

What terror our sweet revenge with raining bombs do inflict,
When in other lands a monstrous beast we must try to evict,
Where children suffer daily the maiming of religious tribal conflict.
    How is it not yet finished yet we are the vast majority,
    Why have we not yet destroyed this malevolent minority.

What O' God have ye to say from common folk to presidential,
When they without selfish thought realized charity's full potential,
Where O' Lord is this ruthless demagogue most quintessential.
    How can he with impunity wield your name to oppress,
    Why must we still weep, answer O' God our countries distress.

What great compassion have they who with charity supplement,
When give they from spirit, and purse a loving sacrament,
Where now the foolish zealot doth stand amazed in wonderment.
    How great is my mystery now rising to his humiliation,
    Why from the tears of the living I have reunited a nation.

War
By Stephanie Poggensee - age 52
Denison, IA

A nameless, faceless man sent our own planes to destroy a belief of freedom, in the United States of America. I don't think this man knew America and the people as well as he thought he did. Children saving pennies, dimes, and more to help those who lost loved ones in the attack. People ran to the nearest Red Cross and gave blood for those who needed it. When something like the World Trade Center was attacked, all Americans saw it on TV and cursed the person who did this to us. And I feel that we will, find him and bring justice for the 6,000 people that died on September 11, 2001 will forever change our lives and those of our children and their children. How can we call ourselves Americans if we all sit back and did nothing? But that is not the way we live, we live to help others that need us. And we will be there until this person is caught and punished for the crimes he has committed to start a war. He has millions of dollars and yet he lets his people and children starve and cold. No homes to live in, this man has to be stopped and his people given care, food, and clothing and to see the children smile again. Let us work on peace for all nations let us rid ourselves of this evil man and his people who hide him in there country. May they all be punished for starting a war with Biochemical's warfare? And let us free the women who can't show their faces, ankles, and cannot speak to anyone they see. God Bless America let there be harmony and peace in this world.

The Good Old USA

By John O'Flaherty
County Cork, Ireland

While Americans worked in silence,
In that fall, a September day,
When evil pro Taliban geezers,
Attacked the Great Whiteway.

Used planes to smash the Twin towers,
Pennsylvania and Washington too,
A lunatic fringe, all killers,
How they met their Waterloo.

The leader of the Taliban,
Is Satan in disguise,
Caused the deaths of innocent people,
A scheme that is unwise.

A land where races flourish,
But like rust, some never sleep,
Those thieving scheming rattlers,
Poised with poisoned scythes to reap.

But time is the great healer,
The Taliban race is run,
Their ruthless spin is over,
The free world's sure to win.

And the hand of fate is watching,
Sane beings will have their say,
They support the American people.
In the good old USA.

Freedom Forever

By Elizabeth Ondroczky, SFO
Deer Park, NY

On September 11th time stood still,
When the forces of evil came to kill.
Many innocent people lost their lives,
Now broken families try to survive.
Through their sorrow and their pain,
They look to see the sun again.
Be strong my brothers and sisters don't give in,
Let us stand together and we shall win.
For terrorists have no place in America so free,
This land of liberty for you and for me.

On September 11th new heroes were born,
For those lost, our country and families mourn.
The ultimate sacrifice was made,
And the memory of these heroes cannot fade.
Only with a pure heart victory will come,
And the evil of terror will be undone.
God will bring us love, peace, and light,
And the enemy will be destroyed by His power and might.
So let the bells of freedom ring throughout the land,
As shoulder to shoulder united we stand!

I am Going to Get Osama Bin Laden

By Steve Phillips - age 37
Mountain Grove, MO

Verse 1
 I am going to catch a terrorist, I will fetch my shotgun, and I will have a ton of fun chasing this man because I plan on catching him, because
Chorus
 I am going to catch Osama Bin Laden
Verse 2
 I will swim to Afghanistan, to catch him with my shot gun in my hands and low and behold shoot him right between the eyes because
Chorus
 I am going to catch Osama Bin Laden
Verse 3
 I will stand on the corner of Afghanistan and ask the Afghan people where and where I can find him. I will trade my camel for information, because
Chorus
 I am going to catch Osama Bin Laden
Verse 4
 Maybe I will land on my feet and treat Osama Bin Laden with mighty blast from that shot gun and all the people in the U.S.A. will steeple over me and give me the key to the City because
Chorus
 I am going to catch Osama Bin Laden
Verse 5
 I will be millionaire and be like Jed Clammet and move to Beverly Hills, California, when I get my reward for catching Osama Bin Laden
Chorus
 I am going to catch Osama Bin Laden
Verse 6
 With select company I will be a hero, my shot gun will be permanent display, so everyone can see it, so please
Chorus
 I am going to catch Osama Bin Laden
Verse 7
 Everyone will take there hat to me as you will see the hero that got Osama Bin Laden
 I am going to catch Osama Bin Laden, you bettcha

Tragedy 9-11

By Christa Stapp - age 67
Biloxi, MS

Where ones two mighty towers stood,
There now is silence, only prayers can be heard.
Where ones two mighty towers stood,
There now is rubble and twisted steel drenched with blood.
Thousands of lives lost in this disaster,
Oh, Jesus help us in this pain, for all the lives whom have
 been slain.
Where ones two mighty towers stood!
Terror, terror everywhere, our country is in deep despair,
 give us strength oh, Lord above, to carry on and laugh
Again let those, have not lost there lives' in vain.
Where ones two mighty towers stood!

The Greatest Hope of All
By Patricia Stockton
West Grove, PA

Children are special as we all are
Adult faces surrounding them both near and far
Their eyes are innocent looking for all the strangers
Like the ones who on September 11, 2001, put everyone in danger

It will never be easy to visualize the terror that day
When soon all will ask why did someone that I love go away?
Especially the little children with tiny eyes and hearts,
Who can mend the soul and all their little parts?

There is only one hope, only one joy
For each and every little girl and boy
God is able to mend the evil of all man
When his people on earth, join together with love and hope and say

"UNITED WE STAND"

In Memory of my nephew, "Andrew Jackson Long"
taken away too soon

Patriot's Children
By Cyndee Lee Proctor - age 39
Richmond, ME

Out of the misty morning of dawn,
Of Nine One-One, we drank forth, the cries of war.
For a sinful horror, fell from our nation sky.
Our eagles' coat of freedom was attacked by terror,
As so many, innocent lives were stolen.
And like the wars of our forefathers,
Faithful souls, parishes a patriots parting.
Constant tears fell like a thunderous rain,
As a timeless sorrow of voices, still ring on.
No! Not ever will our hearts lay defeat to such a dooms day.
For our dear ones will never belong to the demons of such acts.
Heroe's were born, in the ruins of the world they have left behind.
Soaring to the heavens as noble silent soldiers.
Fear not: for them no more, as they rest in Gods loving arms,
And graced with wings, of watchful angels, footprints.
Carrying forth a meaningful message, that shall be heard!
As all Americans young and old rose up,
And strangers' hands united, in this smoky, destruction of darkness.
Prideful and brave, shone through the sea of dusty ashes.
With loving hope, Families healed, in the blazed of this rubble.
Kindness and peace lead the broken hearts, to the spirit of glory.
Policies took flight! No longer tolerating the reins of stainful fears, so unholy.
Nor stand blindly, allowing it to play, with our children. We pray!
Stamping out this careless terror, shall echo through this land of livelihood.
Undimmed, is this sweet ground of Red, White, and Blue of Liberty.
Their departing makes a continued, daily independence difference, in histories legend.
Making whole the praise of change, to shelter all-nations children.
Peace will out shine, out live, and thrive in our mighty country.
Through their faces, our eternal light shall survive forever; Strong and True!
As toiled around the world, they are kissed with roses of remembrance.

Where Was God...September 11, 2001
By Linda R. Ramsey - age 57
Newport, TN

Where was God...September 11, 2001?
When terrorist attached our world on the run

Where were we...September 11, 2001?
Laughing, shopping, working, or having fun

Millions of people are angry with God
Him not being around lately is odd

Remember a moment of silence is all we need
No more praying out loud to God, please

God was placed under a moment of silence
While our world was under such terrible violence

Life could take a turn for the worst
We need God to be #1 in our spirit first

God forgive us for being ignorant to the fact
For allowing Atheist to remover prayer from our public school acts

Many people are searching for God
He's right beside you if you don't go too far

Some of us fear the arrow that flies in daylight
And are afraid of the pestilence that prowl at night

Questions are asked if someone is really in charge
God is our life, our world and is at large

Everyone needs to chip in without a fuss
God needs some help from all of us

Our nation in prayer and peace can pull together
All over America we need to unite peacefully forever

Be watchful and strengthen the things that remain
God needs us now more than anything

God can change our heart if we let him
We can cling tight and hold on to the strongest limb

Now have we learned a lesson well taught?

Please forgive us God, for it's all our fault

The Mama of Osama
By William H. Shuttleworth - age 64
Jacksonville, FL

A cuddly, bubbly, baby boy — so soft, so playful,
 so seemingly pure
Sands of time erode — a hostile shadow emerges
 inflicting pain, so we rally to chalk up
 a score
Once warmly bathing among siblings in sandy
 Saudi sunshine midst luxury and wealth
Endowed generously with wonderful creative
 potentiality and exquisite health
But somehow hijacked by the devil himself
 — turned killer and terrorizer —
 "kingpin villain of the world"
Adding and molding many more mean, malicious,
 menacers to his sprawling jihad hurled
Targeting the U.S.A. with a volatile mix of
 doom and gloom
So we blast our trumpet sound, rising up to
 defang this venomous one with a
 boom! boom! boom!
God's grace prevails! — the viper's hiss
 slinking silently away in evil Osama
His terror antics hushed forever? So pleads
 that lonely, echoing cry of his
 wailing mama

It Could Not Be
By Valarie Smith
Watsonville, CA

Peoples
our practice
democracy
a vote
a chance
for all who would
possess knowledge
understand
learn
the freedom to
speak and
the freedom to
be heard and
the freedom to
decide
our gift
edification
how could it be
that one
all
could not
in America
find hope
find peace
it could not be

Sorrow
By Michelle Villela
South Cairo, NY

   September 11 was a sorrow filled day many of our nations heroes were cast away. Many brave men ran into the blazing fires to save lives of others was their only desires. Though many were lost, many were saved thanks to those fighters we call the brave. Wow many babies will grow up without moms or dads, they wont be able to enjoy the simple things I have.
   Do to an enemy who killed for the sake of killing, but we shall bring them down if we are ready and willing. We must fight for the honors of our dead and loved ones, show that our colors won't run.
   I love our country who lets us be free to do all the things I do to be me. So we will show them that United We Stand, we shall bring Justice and Freedom to Our Fair Land.

Restore the Veil
By Claudette Susan Randall - age 50
Topsham, ME

When planes fell from the sky
We asked why
Why did all these people die?
Planes crashed, buildings fell
Innocence lost
A nation counts the cost
Mourns for all we've lost
Cries of revenge and death
Resound through-out the land
Someone will pay
For this evil wrought on the USA.
We search out hearts
Still wondering why
Why did good men have to die?
From the throne of grace
A Father turns his face away
And the veil of grace is lifted.
The sins of man—
An instrument of an evil plan.

Forgive us Lord
For our complacent ways,
We turn and look away
While our babies are sacrificed
In the name of human rights
We fail to see the light.
Even when prayer is silenced in our schools,
We ignore our elderly and our destitute
Banish and chastise those who are different
Embrace and tolerate sexual perversion
Disease becomes the price for indifference.

Forgive us Lord
When we close our eyes to man's evil ways
Forever lust in worldly riches
We want and we take
Are never truly satisfied
As we hold on to our self-righteous pride
Never learning to forgive
Or live by the golden rule.

Once a nation under God
With an armor of faith
And a banner of love
The shadow of heavenly wings
A perfect covering
But apathy and sin
Have lifted the veil
And loosed the prince of darkness
On an unsuspecting world.

Oh forgive us Father
For our foolish ways
Humble and teach us
To lift up holy hands and pray
Make us faithful, willing to obey
Restore the holy veil
Of your protection
Empower us from above
Vanquish all our enemies
From every shore
Unite us to take a stand
Restore our faith
And heal our land.

Birth Arises from a Tragedy
By Flora J.M. Rhodenizer
Bridgewater, NS

As the news flooded the airways
of dreadful scenes
where thousands upon thousands
could not escape
leaving mares of night in its wake

Nightmares of the little ones
who will no longer feel
the warmth of a mother's breast
or the bear hug from a father's arms
giving a stillness to life

Strangers from miles around
gave of themselves
even unto death
in hopes of reviving
some hope for the little ones

As the tragedy of Sept. 11, 2001
tore across the lands
ripping out the spirits
believing all was lost
little miracles were happening everyday

In the wake of such tragedy
hope is reawakened anew
as every minute of every day
a little miracle is born of a mother's womb
giving living to life once more

To this day whenever you see
a newborn babe
or a woman full bloom
Cast your eyes
in order to feel the light
that shines your way
giving hope back to the hopeless

Untitled
By Sarah Stulc - age 15
Greybull, WY

I can almost hear the gentle murmur in my ear,
The words you'd whisper when you held me near.
I try to wake myself from once reality now dream,
But breaking into reality makes my heart cry and scream.
They took you before your time was due
I'm left behind with painful memories
of how deeply I still love you.
Don't be sad, he's in a better place, have no fear
That's what they told me the day God took your near,
But left me alone down here.

A List Poem
Words I've Learned to Use Since September 11th
By Constance A. Warren
Detroit, MI

Suicide-mission, survivor, alert, smoke-smoulder, ash, rubble. Support, prayer, grief, shock, anger. Disbelief, fear, faith, sorrow. September 11 as a noun, like December 7th (Pearl Harbor). World Trade Center's Twin Towers, demolished! World War III? Terror, terrorist, terrorism and terrorized. Sudden destruction, anthrax, patience, martyrs. Fire fighters, police officers, paramedics, citizen patrols, all heroes. U.S. (us) people. Bosnia, Alquaeda, Yemen. Into the caves. Kabil, Kashmir, Jalabad, Kandahar. Combat, 20th high-jacker, Zacarias Moussoui. Arafat, Moullah Ohmar. Tora Bora, Gaza Strip. Peacekeepers, Afghanistan, Pakistan, etc. stan. Refugees, Palestine, Muslims, Ramadan, Haddam Husane, Mosk, Islam. Land mine, smart bomb, missiles, rockets, grenades. Osama Bin Laden, kill, capture, confine, war-torn. C.I.A. Innocents, conspiracy, Arabian Sea...Christianity returning.

The Awakening
By William R. Whittaker
Apex, NC

As the day was dawning
They caught us yawning
And blew away our trust.
From the sky they came
In birds aflame
To reduce our world to dust,
And as the towers fell
Our eyes did swell
With agonized tears of pain.
Not for the stone, the steel and glass,
But for the innocent lives we saw pass
As fiery jet fuel rained...
      On the streets of New York city.

But their terrorist plan
To destroy our land
Was devoid of consideration
For our will of steel
And the love we feel
For our freedom loving nation.
They can ground our planes
Or bomb our trains
Or scar our mightiest town,
But we'll unite
To fight the fight
And bring those bastards down...
      Like that jet in Pennsylvania.

I Shed A Tear
By Ruben Ramirez - age 51
El Paso, TX

I shed a tear when the
First World Trade Tower
Came crashing down

Then another tear when the
Second tower was just a pile
Of rubble on the ground

I shed a tear because it's
The most terrible thing
I've ever seen by far

I can't contain myself for so
Many innocent lives were
Ended by an act of war

I shed a tear as I sat
In awe, feeling helpless
Feeling great sorrow

Worry fills me now for
I don't know what waits
For us tomorrow

I shed a tear for all the
Heroes, for those Americans
Who gave their all

We must now unite like never
Before and tell the world
That America will never fall!

Shadows upon the Free
By William Robbins - age 50
Colton, CA

Thieves raped the virgin's soul.
In hate
they cast an evil darkness
over the breath of freedom.
What angry spell
lured them into a rage
to harm a host of unarmed lives?
Only death
can now defend
their sin.
Sobs like rainfall,
the deep, rippling sorrow
flows from a mother's heart.
Why did they
murder her child?
Answers are hidden in the wind
where the prayers
of both assassin and victims
now speak from
a sky without tears.

America's Tears
By Melanie Marie Ridner - age 44
Hamilton, OH

America's Tears.
Deep hurt and anger.
Our dear one's lost in anguish.
Destruction way beyond belief.
A nation in deep mourning.
Spirits shaken and tears of pain, sorrow
Shock, disbelief at this outrage against
our country and our people.
As the television showed footage after
footage of Our World Trade Center
crumbling;
A quiet hush fell all over the world.
Tears poured freely for the people
in New York.
Prayers came and could be heard in
the deathful silence and outrage.
America's Tears are our tears.
Our land invaded by terrorists.
But we are a strong nation and American's
will survive and grow again.
We are Americans, we are America.
God Bless America, Our Americans;
   Our Land of the Brave and Free.

When Terrorist Attacked Our World September 11, 2001
By Linda R. Ramsey - age 57
Newport, TN

Did we forget to ask God to deliver us from all evil today?
Before terrorist flew American planes into the World Trade Center at bay

The Pentagon was attacked by terrorist in a plane hijacking too
People were screaming and running, wondering what to do

Bringing a plane down in Pennsylvania was a terrorist act
Many people lost their lives even thought they put up a fight

America, we let our guards down by trusting everyone
We can only blame ourselves now that the damage is done

Aviation schools in America taught the terrorist the flight lessons they learned
They lived in low class rental housing but no one was concerned

Is this a wake up call? Is our great nation being tested?
Do we have the right to ask God for his blessings?

We asked God to get our of our governments and our lives
When terrorist attacked our world...we prayed to God with pride

In public schools and sports we are not allowed to pray anymore
God is a gentleman with hurt feelings; he walked out the door

How can we expect God to give us his attention and protection
When we don't want to talk about the resurrection?

As humble Americans we can learn by our mistakes and sorrow
With God in our hearts we will have better today's and tomorrows

In our busy schedules and plans we have put God on hold
He would like to be back in the limelight so proud and bold

Thanks to all policemen, firefighters, doctors, nurses, and rescue volunteers
May God bless all of our Red Cross workers far and near

Let's honor all of the armed forces state wide and overseas
For their effort to keep America the beautiful free

God bless all the people that lost their love ones
One day with Gods help justice will be done

The One Place
By Robert Roan - age 64
Cedar Rapids, IA

   Where in this country can one find peace today? This question has been heard from old and young alike since terrorist struck that day.
   Everyone in most countries feel the pain, while some feel it will happen again. This fear is very real for those who struck before without any remorse could slip back in.
   Many prayers, offers of help and blood donations come in from afar. However, no one knows what's ahead and will these efforts be enough or just a drop in the jar?
   There is one place we can always go even if there's an overflow. In the arms of the Lord faithfully and eternal peace you will always know.

A Dream?

By Carol J. Ritchie - age 50
Riverside, RI

The nights silence was broken by an out crying of our daughter. My husband and I ran to her, finding her crying and shaking from fear. We held her and asked what was wrong. She tried to tell us, but being only three years old that was a difficult task. What we understood her to say was that, this tiny angel had a dream, and in this dream, she could see people, some crying, some angry, most very afraid. Then all went black, and that blackness scared her more than anything. My husband and I looked at our child wanting so much to erase this from her mind because as parents all we want for her is beauty, peace, love, health, and happiness. All we could give her was reassurance that everything was fine and that it was just a bad dream. She finally settled down and soon peaceful slumber fell over her once more. We feel so helpless not being able to keep such ugliness away from our innocent child. My husband and I have the more difficult task of conveying to her, somehow, at sometime, that this was not just a dream. This incredibly beautiful gift from God was aboard one of the American Airlines flights that crashed into the World Trade Center Twin Towers.

My husband, my child, and I stand among the thousands of souls tragically snatched from life's arms, as restless spirits, watching what is left behind. Americans, all now, even the foreigners who worked and died so unexpectedly.

All of us are so grateful for the short time we had on earth, our only sadness is that most of us never got the chance to say "Goodbye," to our loved ones. Death doesn't have to be an end, it's just a different type of journey.

We are all so happy to see America standing united, putting differences aside and being whole just as our creator intended us to live. It makes us all so very proud.

During the next few months the terror of what a few hateful, cowardly, insane, egotists tried to destroy they shall see once more rise, grow, find strength in unity, and overcome all evil that was thrust upon us.

America does NOT lie down for ANYONE, especially Mad Men!

It is our wish for you, our beloved brethren, that you be not fearful of what may come, and mourn for us only awhile because we are still with you. Every time you think you hear whispers of encouragement and love, you are hearing us. And when you feel a presence around you, don't think you are imagining it because you're not. We are with you always through peace and war. Use our strength when yours is being drained and take our vital force to use with your own to remain strong and united.

Death may have taken us but we shall not stop giving because we are still, now and forever, AMERICANS!

Dedications: This is for all, past and present, who always did their best and gave their all and for those who remain to carry on, you are loved and never forgotten!

America's Strength

By Viola Mae Baker Rippeon
Woodsboro, MD

America's strength is not in huge buildings,
It is located in the souls of everyone.
It is our creed, our basic beliefs,
That is founded in the Father and Son.
It is our religious heritage
That guides us o'er the path of life,
God gives us the power to move on
When we encounter sorrow and strife.

God is our Guardian and our Protector
So we should put our trust in Him.
He will lead us through the darkened maze,
Be our Light when the night is dim.
We can lean upon His wisdom,
We can trust Him to show the way,
Buildings may topple all around us
But our salvation will always stay.

The earth may quake and mountains fall
And stars may tremble as they glow,
The sun and moon may fail to rotate
And oceans and rivers cease to flow.
Still God will never ever change,
He was, is, and always will be.
America's strength is not in our creations,
It is God in us that keeps us free.

2001

By Anita Rogers - age 58
Royersford, PA

The door is closing on the year 2001. It started out similar to most other years. Relatively calm and peaceful. However, that was not to be, as the year ends. Many tragic events have touched our lives, the way we live, memories we carry. Unknown to us when the year arrived, this year 2001, will now be in all future history books, due to the tragedy of September 11. It will be the topic of many conversations for generations to come. Many precious lives were lost. Memories to thousands are now treasures to hold close to heart. Tears continue to fall, will fall for many years, as men, women, and children face days and nights alone. Loved ones always in their thoughts.

The United States has become not so trusting. Our way of life, looking at things in general, everyday living, activities, thinking and freedoms these have been altered. Some drastically. Life can no longer be "Business as Usual." We are told "Go about your lives, business as usual." We are, but it is not the same, can never be the same again.

We've had our share of tragedy here on our soil over the centuries, but nothing with the magnitude of 2001. As the "Mother Country," we have always opened our arms to the less fortunate to nurture and help. When you get punished so drastically and tragically it hurts.

As 2001 ends, what are your thoughts? Do you think differently? What are you thankful for? Do you appreciate all you have in life (great or small)? Are you thankful for each day? Each day is a gift, given to everyone of us. We all look at our day differently, and our priorities are different. How we live each day is our choice. Has 2001 changed you?

I Made A Difference
By Steve Stanton - age 44
Jessup, MD

When I was born I made a difference
in your life and in mine.
Making memories of good times and
bad times with justification.
Of who each and everyone is no matter
the race or origin or gender.
Doesn't really happen unless you are
really there to be remembered in a
thought an impression or memory.
I made a difference.

The Attack on My Country, the U.S.A.
By Ina Rosenblatt
Skokie, IL

I had just sat down to have my breakfast,
It was 8 am Chicago time,
In New York City it was 9 am,
September eleven, two thousand one;
On the TV screen in front of me,
I saw a jetliner crash into one tower
Of the World Trade Center's upper floors;
Red flaming swords of fire were flashing
Upward, upward to the sky,
Followed by masses of thick black smoke
Swirling downwards towards the ground;
Soon, fire trucks, police cars and ambulances,
Began speeding to the rescue of the victims,
The thick, black smoke that filled the air
Made it difficult for people to breathe;
But the firemen and policemen wearing oxygen masks,
Worked day and night in twenty-four hour shifts,
To rescue the entrapped innocent victims,
Where friends and relatives waited outside
Praying that their loved ones would be found.
People from ev'rywhere came to donate blood,
Needed for victims who might be rescued.
How do we rid the World of such madmen?
First, we rid the camps holding terrorists
All over the World; and begin with schools,
Where children of ev'ry color, race or creed,
Learn to respect each others differences,
And have student courts at every level,
Supervised by tolerant, loving adults,
Teaching justice, controlling anger, and love, not hate;
It may take years, perhaps a century
To reach such a goal... Peace on Earth... Amen

Postscript:
There has been talk of rebuilding lower Manhattan...
I hope the developers will create a Park,
Where a memorial to those victims who lost their lives
Would be built; then lest we forget,
Establish a day of solemn rememb'ring,
September Eleven, Two Thousand One.
When terrorists struck the World Trade Center.

Shards and Fragments
By Ronald M. Ruble
Huron, OH

Terrorists gave birth to shards.
Pieces of glass, metal, and bone
rained on Manhattan, Washington,
and Pennsylvania, September 11, 2001.

Uncountable numbers of sharp missiles
lacerating comfort, confidence,
contentment and complacency.
Reducing to dust icons of capitalism;
cracking the foundations of
democracy and freedom;
amputating limbs from family trees
with forces greater than hurricanes and tornados.

Blood and horror seeps through
a tapestry of red, white, and blue,
cutting open the fabric and spirit of America,
piercing the hearts of uncountable
numbers of peaceful people around the world.

Shock and inaction give way
to duty and action; disbelief then anger,
give way to patriotism, samaritanism, and reaction.
Empathy and sympathy assert themselves;
we gather and absorb each other's tears and fears.

The beauty of streaking, white entrails
against the azure sky
take on a frightening significance.
We hold hands and chant:
"We will not tolerate blind hates
to rain their shards and fragments;
to molest and rape our rainbowed parade of peace!"

In Memory of Cochise
By John E. Rutherford
Villas, NJ

Ten thousand, thousand starving voices
Screaming whimpers round the earth
Create a sea of violent choices
Against a dam of milk and mirth.

Satan laughing jumps in the violent sea
And tosses men's minds like loaded dice
While God and Allah both claim victory
And collect the souls they lock in ice.

But logic suggests that God and Allah are the same
For two infinite powers should not co-exist
Except in the minds tossed by Satan's game
Which divides and conquers so that evil may persist.

Ten billion, billion thriving voices
Sharing monies round the earth
Create a world of better choices
Against a sea of want and birth.

Hate

By Ronald M. Ruble
Huron, OH

Haughty
Abhorrence, a
Tumultuous
Execration

Capable of consuming the
spirit and soul;
as flames devour paper,
water extinguishes flame,
or locusts strip crops.
As termites feed on the
supports of great houses,
so does loathing dine
on mind and body.

We must be careful not to follow
in the footsteps of hate.

Cancerous; this mind-set
embraces dislike, spite,
ill-will, repugnance
and revulsion.

An easy trap for the revenge-minded
to fall into.

Hate is an abomination
of the ultimate goodness
of the child within.

Remembrance

By Daphne Rust
Milwaukie, OR

This is for the apple tree,
Who's apples never grew —
for the windstorm, dormant now
who's wind, it never blew.
To the lovers, blind and deaf
to tragedy anew —
To all those ill and all those still
Whose remedies are few.
For the warriors and soldiers gone,
whose sons they never knew —
For infants born of drink and drug
whose spirit's are so new.
To all the skies and clouds above
that never did turn blue —
To the homeless and the hungry men
who only want some stew.
And for my friend, whose still so young,
whose life is cut short too —
In my heart is where you'll stay,
I'll always think of you.

Today

By Kristen Szatny - age 15
Sicklerville, NJ

Yesterday I was a child playing in the sand.
Yesterday I was safe, under my mothers wing.
Yesterday the world cried together.
Today I am removed from my mother.
I am now an adult.
Running in the sand,
Am I safe? NO.
I have my own wings, I can fly.
Our countries are at war, our men are dying,
Our women are praying, and our children are crying.
Today is the beginning of our New World.
Will we know peace?
Yesterday we were safe.
Today we are not.
Who knows what tomorrow will bring.
So I think of yesterday.

Act of War!

By Edward J. Runner - age 91
Vincentown, NJ

On September 11, 2001 a horrendous attack occurred by two
      high jacked planes with bombs loaded
Containing 266 innocent travelers were the means of destruction
The hijackers also died without any compunction
In fact this horrifying act was planned over a year ago

Their plans included destroying the Twin World Trade Center
The two 110 story buildings were the pride of New York with none finer
They contained about 50,000 people while working
Thousands of employees died while working
The plane that was destroyed in Western Pennsylvania was scheduled
      to destroy the White House or the President's plane
Apparently a fight occurred that caused it to leave it's planned lane
A passenger called his wife using his cordless phone
His message indicated that they would all be killed by his
      pessimistic tone
He suggested that the passengers would give the hijackers a fight
This was probably the cause of the plane's destructive explosion
      killing all aboard and ending it's flight
In addition to the thousands of employees of the World Trade Center
      over 300 firemen and over a dozen policemen lost their lives
      while trying to help save others
The actual loss and suffering includes parents, grandparents,
      children, friends, sisters, and brothers
The destruction of the Pentagon Building in Washington makes
      it definitely an Act of War
The political "Hating America" is the Taliban
      They protect Osama Bin Laden, the planner, and they rule Afghanistan
These dastardly acts have inspired greater patriotism throughout
      our land
Volunteer help responded to the required demand
Financial donations have reached many millions of dollars
The response is from corporations, workers, athletes, and scholars
It is for other countries' interest to cooperate
For at any time they could endure the same fate
All must remember that this is no time to rest
We will prove to the world that the United States is still the Best.

Once I Had A Dream
By Olivia S. Snead
Philadelphia, PA

Once I had a dream that
I flew away in a plane;
I knew that lives had died
In this confusing time
(And yet the sane world
Does exist)
But I flew away unmindful
That I am mortal.

Not long after, the plane
Flew up, and up and up;
Then it stopped and it jolted;
I knew that it was happening
To me.

I crashed along with the others
But we did survive:
No hurts, just shaken;
Then I looked and saw
The man who'd saved
Our lives
Lying on a stretcher.

I went to him and I looked
Deep into his eyes;
I said, "I know it is because
Of you that we live."

Once I had a dream and
In my mind it seemed
That I should tell it to
Someone close to me;
I thought that perhaps it
May mean nothing;
But who knows,
It may mean something.

Agony
By Ronald M. Ruble - age 61
Huron, OH

Anguished
Gaffes; An
Outcry of
Nakedness;
Yowls.

Pain sears our anguish.
We stand stripped of pride,
of value and neglected,
outlawed and tormented,
we face our antagonists
and scream our misery.

"How could you do such a horrible thing?
How could you hate us that much?"
Our enemies dance and celebrate in the street!
Men, women, and children laughing
and cheering; waving arms,
jumping up and down with glee.

"Why? What have we done
that you take great joy
from such brutality and horror?"
Our anguish and confusion fall
on deaf ears and clouded eyes.

Language and structure
ripped from our earthly
possessions, we suffer.
Mournfully we turn our heads
toward the heavens and
cry as do the wolves.

A Day We Will Never Forget
By Kelsey Scanlon - age 12
Scituate, MA

September 11th is a day we will never forget,
All of those happenings that day made everyone upset.
The whole world heard about the happenings that day,
That day the sun was up but the sky was gray.

President Bush gave a moral boosting to all those that helped,
But nothing could replace the feeling that they felt.
Did you know that 11 appears over and over again,
Such as 9/11 and 11 letters in Afghanistan.

The first plane that crashed into the towers was flight 11,
92 people (9 + 2 = 11) went to heaven.
A man named Osama had a lot of hate in him,
For some reason he hated the USA so bad
that he made the light of the day go dim.

After the two towers were hit and they fell to the ground,
Osama smiled with hate while everyone else frowned.
The streets were covered with debris and rubble,
And when we finally find Osama he will be in a lot of trouble.

NYPD and FDNY shouted, "USA, Go America, USA,"
They shouted it loud, day after day.
Candles gleamed in the night sky of New York,
Almost the whole state could see a gleam of some sort.

Osama Bin Laden still remains missing to this day,
But the USA shall find him, some how, some way.
Whenever I hear the Pledge of Allegiance
like on the morning announcements today,
I think of how I am faithful and lucky to live in the USA.

September 11, 2001
By Nan Tebrinke
Red Oak, IA

It was just another autumn day,
What happened in a few words,
Is hard to say.
So many people killed,
So many families hurt
Not knowing why,
In the smoke, fire, and dirt
War, a word to describe the pain.
Will our country ever be the same?
But, how uplifting to see,
mile upon mile
Our flag and God Bless America
displayed U.S.A. style
God knows the direction
We should go.
He's there to guide
We need Him, so!

And the Flag Was Still There
By Amy Nicole Thomas - age 30
Tell City, IN

As I watched "America: Tribute to Heroes," by our artists and entertainers, emotions overcame me at this joining of people. They used their talents to honor those killed, missing, and still helping from one of the most terrible acts in American history. Tears rose and lodged in my throat at this selfless display of humanity.

As each well-chosen song finished, my pride in my country swelled and filled my heart. These people, who often found themselves unfairly splashed across tabloids, came together...united, to honor America. They, like President Bush previously, gave America a sense of hope and unity.

Tears filled my eyes as each actor paid tribute to a special group or person. When Julia Roberts took her turn in the Tribute, she described the rising of the flag over the Pentagon after the destruction. I realized, as she continued with her tearful description, how precious life was. The United States was not "they," "you," or "I." It was "us" and "we."

Tonight as I watched, the pride of being an American became more profound. I am proud to live in a country, with so much diversity, that in a terrible time of need we come together, not as separate social classes, races or religions, but as Americans...united.

The last days have been tough on all of us, however, none more than those who were directly affected. To those, my heart and prayers are with you. However, in the last few days, with President Bush's speech and now "America: Tribute to Heroes," I gained something lost on September 11, 2001, hope and strength.

I watch these performances and heartfelt pleas in awe of our actors and entertainers. I wondered, as I watched, did they realize what they were doing...how they participated in uniting America? Did they realize they were lifting our spirits and unifying Americans through their talents?

Then, as the scenes of the victims and their families, of Ground Zero, and of other moments since this tragedy, flashed across my TV screen, the tears in my eyes filled and rolled down my cheeks. I wanted to cry one tear for each person affected by this terrible act, as well as the whole world. My feelings of their Tribute are indescribable, but ones not needing to be described. They are felt by all. There is no name for them, but we all feel them. Everyone...all over the world.

I am proud to be an American. I am proud to be free. The quotes that I heard during the Tribute best express my feelings:

> "In spite of everything, I believe there is still good in all"– Anne Frank

> "Take my hand, we'll make it, I swear" – Bon Jovi

> "When you feel hope is gone, look inside yourself and be strong, see the truth, that a hero lies in you"
> – Mirah Carey

....and the flag was still there.

Fallen Angels
By Doris L. Wilson - age 59
Washington, D.C.

Amidst the roar and crash your lives were annihilate,
Betrayed by terrorists who thrive on nothing more than hate.
Though you were victimized, your lives will not be in vain,
Through your departure we prevail, through blood shed we gain.

Fallen angels caught in the crossfire of a cowardly act,
Silence by unknown terrorists who formed a suicide pact.
What could have provoked them to do such a tragic thing?
Without conceiving the anguish it would solemnly bring.
Questions we have, answers we may never find,
That could help us to heal and give us a "Peace of Mind."

Your voice will echo in the wind as we deplore your untimely fate,
In our hearts Sept. 11th will be cited as a disastrous date.
We will hear your voices in every breeze that blows.
In every song of every bird, and every brook that flows.

Angels you will journey upwards as a sacrificial star,
And we will repel that fear that stalks us, here and a far.
Like Americans we will face the murderous cowardly pack,
We will conquer, perhaps dying, but fighting back!

Dedicated to the victims of September 11th, attack on America.

Annonomous photo obtained from the website http://gallery.hd.org

Complete Disbelief
By Alyce M. Nielson - age 59
Brooklyn, NY

9/11/2001, I answered the telephone "Turn on the TV" my husband's voice said. I turned the TV on and much to my disbelief an airplane had crashed into one of the Trade Centers Twin Towers. How could anyone not see the tower? It was a clear sunny day. The Mothers and I gathered around the TV set and soon we witnessed an even more unbelievable event. A second airplane crashed into the other tower. One might have been an accident but two was an attack. An airplane crashed into the Pentagon another crashed to the ground. We are at war. Raw surreal terror has been unleashed on us. How could this happen? How can this be real? So much destruction, so many lives lost, so many heroes both dead and alive; yet life must go on. Now we are at war. Justice must be done. Hopefully when all of this is over, horrific events like this one will never happen again. The terrorist must be brought down.

The Eagle Soars
By Dorothy Randall Stack
Midvale, UT

Nine, eleven, two thousand one,
the day when the terrorist war was begun;
with jets they rammed the Towers' apart,
with intent to drive fear into our hearts.

The cowards killed thousands
in the towers so tall —
men and women, and children so small.
Firemen, police, and rescuers fell
in the chunks of debris and fires of hell.

But out of the rubble rose a country united,
for the Eagle soars, and his eyes are sighted
on the ways of the terrorists and his evil deeds —
for this INSANITY America will heed.

Our Star-Spangled Banner is carried forth
with the power of God behind Freedom's torch.
In our hearts forever remains Freedoms peel,
which will NEVER buckle under evil's heel.

Instead it will serve as a rallying cry,
with trust in our God as in battle's gone by.
We will strengthen our vigil and refuse any blight
that is trying to darken Freedom's bright light.

Walking Shoes
By Thelma T. Steinberg - age 74
Concord, MA

Society is bending
the law to save its skin
and weaving life through loopholes
to gain the quicker win.
We're slipping through the fence
while justifying sway
in order to be freed of
that old chaotic way.

Hob-nailed boots and slippers stress
the system's high and low
but interfaced are Walking Shoes
connecting needed flow.
Through court and law they're trying
to keep us all from fall
and oxford brand is moving in
to help with overhaul.

Oh Walking Shoes, oh Walking Shoes
keep moving for that day
when our old world of chaos
will be gone...like yesterday.

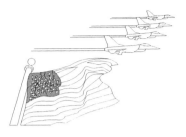

11 September 2001
By Judy Ann Williams - age 58
Kamiah, ID

our God reigns an awesome presence
    though the powers of darkness rage
we'll not fall to their destruction
    despite a fiery battle being waged

terror strikes the heart of a nation
    blood cries out from instant graves
concrete pulverized to dusty specks
    steel columns consumed by the blaze

hate bred in the very depths of hell
    unleashed its fury on innocent lives
though the loss indeed is heavy, Lord
    it is by Your grace we will survive

sorrow and brokenness shroud the land
    America has been shaken to the bone
we clasp our hands in solemn prayer
    thru faith knowing we are not alone

Old Glory unfurled out of moth balls
    one nation united again....under God
musty church pews baptized in tears
    as the road of heartache we do trod

terror can not hold this country down
    we must raise up the shield of faith
may Truth and Honor stand our emblem
    for Love is the conqueror over hate

Lifestyle of a Trucker
By Judy Ann Williams - age 58
Kamiah, ID

Chainin' up along the highway
    fingers frozen to the bone
It's times like this he longs for
    warm flies of Home-Sweet-Home

But he's got to make a livin'
    and this seems to be the way
So he'll say a prayer to Jesus
    pullin' up that lonely grade

Those gears won't go much lower
    but still he's on the climb
There's a sweet thing in the mirror
    tryin' to come across the line

A cup of coffee sure is needed
    he will grab one at the top
With another hundred yards to go
    it's a likely place to stop

Well can the snow get any thicker
    dang! It's really comin' down
Angels a-ridin' on those fenders
    keepin' him all safe 'n' sound

He pulled off a-spell near Lolo
    as supper time fell late again
A cup of soup warmed on the fire
    log-book truth is wearin' thin

He'll untarp that thing come sun-up
    then head back down the road
It's just the lifestyle of a trucker
    haulin' countless heavy loads

"We must not be enemies. Though passion may have
strained, it must not break our bonds of affection.
The mystic chords of memory, stretching from every battlefield
and patriot grave, to every living heart and hearth-stone,
all over this broad land, will yet swell the chorus of the
Union when again touched, as surely they will be,
by the better angels of our nature."
-- Abraham Lincoln
First inaugural address, March 4, 1861

9-11 Attack on America
Simmie Lee Burnside, Jr.
Detroit, MI

Descent From Twin Tower
Flight 111
By Charles J. Thomas
Woodcliff Lake, NJ

New York City, a thousand feet below me,
Moves like a silent film.
The tower top sways slightly in the morning wind.

Steel vibrations; trembling tendons.
Jet crashing under mu feet!
The antenna scribes an oval channel
In the spacious blue sky.
Earthquake rumbling;
Building shuddering; glass shattering.
Vibrations floor to sole; my legs!
I tremble on deep, spinal convulsions;
Cold steel rails intonate doom.
Fear, uncertainty;
Despair births.

Intimidating building's edge;
Deep canyon falling.
Screams of life fill the air.
Steel slides to flat marble plazas of death.
The other tower too far to leap for safety.
The gray expanse of water, too distant.
111 flights; 111 stories.
No escape into the blackening air.
Vertigo, vertigo; America, Oh my America!

No feathers to catch the soft transparent safety;
No waxed wings!
Only the deep, dark stairway down.
Beneath the roof full of antennae,
Blood and fire on the stainless steel sides,
And a gaping wound.

I run on shattered soles,
Footsteps writhing,

Vibrating leg muscles in the numbing concrete,
As the deep, flat Manhattan skyline
Sinks below my peripheral view.
Needles Empire State Building,
Reptilic Chrysler spire,
Slide below my anxiety.

I descend the stairs in the antechamber of disaster.
My shaking legs drive downward
Through whirling smoke
Slipping, sliding on the edges of confusion.
Down, down to the foundation of darkness,
To the heart of burning steel.

On the stairs,
Self-sacrificial firemen and selfless police rush upwards
Young, muscular heroes rising with a will to save others
Greater than my will to escape.

I descend to ground zero
And outside, into the dust of disaster,
As the tower collapses with a demonic roar.
A cloud of rubble pelts my head
As I clear the corner of Broadway
With the walking wounded
Escaping the smothering darkness.

A dull, copper sun peers through the cascading ruins,
Then turns, shining westward to comfort
The Statue of Liberty weeping for her children.
There, he declares,
"The evil night is brief.
I see the Phoenix already rising from the ashes
Eager to join the Eagle who in the dawn's early light
Will deliver liberty and justice for all."

Our Freedom Invaded

By Phyllis A. Smith
Warrenville Heights, OH

As we go about our daily lives,
   what little do we know,
      our freedom will be invaded.

What's this I hear on the news!
   a plane has crashed!
      into the World Trade Center, oh no! by terrorists,
         our freedom invaded.
What's this I hear! another attempt,
   the Pentagon,
      our freedom invaded.

The world is in a state of shock,
   our freedom invaded.

We have lost love one's,
   we feel the pain of others,
      our freedom invaded.

As the Nation begins to heal,
   locked in our memory,
      will be the date September 11, 2001
         our freedom invaded.

As the World came together as one,
   with support and donations,
      we express care and love,
         with time and money to help our fellow man,
            our freedom invaded.

We sang songs of our Nation,
   we honored our flag as we held our heads high,
      our spirit will not be hurt,
         for we love our nation,
            Our Freedom Will Be Restored.

God Bless America and Its People In Time of Peace

By Linda V. Schnall
Croton-on-Hudson, NY

Wouldn't it be wonderful if we all got along.
Just think of it — no guns, no hatred,
we'd all sing a song. A song about
brotherhood, harmony and love.
Love for each other, a time to belong.

No poverty, hunger or suffering there'd be.
To unite once and for all, for all humanity.
Respect for our neighbor, whoever they'd be.
A mutual feeling for life and liberty.

I would like to see this togetherness be.
For the world doesn't have to be a place
of fear or hopelessness for you and for me.

Human Rights

By Sarah McRavin - age 14
Madill, OK

Most people have no idea what this title means
It means that we are free.
Almost everyone takes it for granted these days.
I wish it wouldn't be that way.
When the U.S.A. entered WWII,
We never knew how many lives would be destroyed,
And how many would begin anew.
My grandfather was there, he fought day and night,
Just so I could have human rights.
The war was awful, so many were killed
Peace held its breath, and time stood still.
Then the bombs carried over the September eleventh
Our hearts hadn't ached like that since December seventh
War is very strange.
It tears us apart, yet makes us whole
It's good for our pride, but pain for our soul.
Human rights are important to me, because you see
My grandfather couldn't make it through one night.
My grandfather died so I could have HUMAN RIGHTS.

Good News Sleeps till Noon

By Nycol Thompson-Briatico - age 29
New York City, NY

Laughing Buddha shed a river of tears today.
Allah roared in silent agony.
Kali pounded her many fists.
Yahweh's disciples whispered his name.
Nostrodomous looked upon us bowing his head in humility.
A generation lost.
A nation, a world, a universe stared in dismay.
My tarnished face stood still waiting for the fear to subside
As I watched my mother splintered and decimated to dust.
I, still standing, frozen like my heart, remembering how a city dusted off an
ambitious youth, turning her into a woman
With enough hope for the whole world.
Mourning her wounds,
Mourning the hatred that befell us all that morning.
Mourning my mother, my friends, my heart.
I watched in dismay for a generation of lost souls that would struggle
Out of this dusty pit of terror.
Then, she whispered to me from a million miles away,
"Stay strong little one, for in you my memories sleep.
And on that day when you are called to speak, remind them,
Of all the glory the human spirit hides.
Remind them of a love and a hope that surpasses the wildest of dreams.
Tell my children I am still here.
As I taught you to be strong,
As I taught you to hope when all was bleak,
Grab your neighbor's hand
And speak these words I have given you,
I will rise once more,
The phoenix from these flames
To teach your children to warm fridged souls,
To teach them as I have taught you.
Here, in our darkest hour,
I pass to you my wisdom."
She whispered,
"Faith is only a star's beam away."

America – Voices Coming Together

Emotional
By Sergio Torres - age 23
Walla Walla, WA

Emotional pain
Emotional loneliness
Emotional heartache smothering my life
Emotional love
Emotional change
Emotional words bring my tongue
Emotional cries
Emotional good-byes
Emotional tears dripping from my eyes
Emotional loss
Emotional absence
Emotional AMERICA leading our lives
Emotional soldiers
Emotional beds
Emotional pillows cuddled to sleep
Emotional days
Emotional nights
Emotional eyes drowning in lonely tears every night
Emotional poem
Emotional song
Emotional me...
So lonely, so afraid, so hard to understand...
So frightened by that cold lonely day...
Ohhh Emotional U.S.A.
Ohhh Emotional AMERICA...
Through all these emotions
Through all this pain
A nation we stand
Strong and together...hand in hand...
WE SHALL ALWAYS REMAIN.

On Seeing Evil Then God
By Pearl Wingrove
Pocono Summit, PA

September 11, 2001 will remain seared in our psyche forever.
That second plane hitting the towers played around and around
and again and again in my head.
Tears filled my eyes, throat and chest until it felt like an
unmovable load of sorrow.
Oh, God, how many souls were thrown into eternity
without a second to pray.
Precious lives destroyed at the evil hands of terrorists!
Loved ones, fathers, mothers, sisters, and brothers gone-gone forever!
Pen nor tongue could never verbalize the agony my heart
and spirit felt that dreadful day.
We had surely seen the horrid face of evil - pure evil.
Our world and its people would never be the same again.
The following Saturday we were on a plane bound for
Reno to attend the Famous Poet's Society Convention.
I sat by a window looking out at the fluffy white clouds.
Surely I saw the hand of God.
White fluffy clouds stacked high like mountains,
Then a narrow stream of blue sky that looked like rippling water.
Next to the stream was an enchanting view of small white
snow puffs that looked like a cotton field.
It was as if God had painted a picture of true serenity to
calm and comfort our very soul.
But then, I always knew God would prevail over evil.

September Nightmare
By Charlotte Ann Zuzak
Grove City, PA

In a hotel room in Venice
I stare at a screen
Of towers demolished
the Pentagon invaded
Pinching myself, willing myself
To wake from this nightmare
But the horror won't go away.

It's not happening to me or
My country or
My daughter in DC
Driving and watching the jet
Race toward a five-sided building.

So far from home and so helpless
I want to run through the streets
And tell everyone that my country is good
That I'm a good person,
We have our faults just like everyone.

A shopkeeper in Sicily smiles
From her window
Pointing at a sign she had posted:
"For American friends
Your pain is our pain
Your mourning is our mourning.
God bless you."

To Those Who Knew
By Brian H. Williams
Stillwater, MN

How many in the nation fear the worst
 from utter mayhem and destruction to
have fallen down upon us once again,
 but now, this time so great the magnitude,
the scale of horror well beyond belief?

Our anger and distress be near to burst,
 as we prepare our retribution stew.
Our heavy hearts are overwhelmed, we can
 be galvanized into a fighting mood
to render, to our threatened world, relief.

What will be set in dire motion first,
 besides our willing subjugation, true,
to all realities of war, but then,
 it only demonstrates our attitude
that good defeat the evil cause of grief?

Our cause is seen as just, to us not cursed,
 and yet, reserve damnation, through and through,
as just dessert for all who knew just when
 so many guiltless lives would end — don't brood,
you all shall fall like every Autumn leaf.

Until She Comes Home
By Allison Derderian
Troy, MI

You left this morning
Blowing me a kiss "good-bye"
I sit waiting for you...

In heaven we will meet again.

The Dear One's
By Anthony S. Traversi - age 33
Denville, NJ

Cultivate the Heart's roses in the Garden of Eternity;
Half past Eden, but more intimate with the Light.

Let the need within your spirit draw you from our realm
Through that secret portal between worlds.

Begin your journey to this sacred and timeless place,
Allow the candle's flame to be your guide through the long Night.

Dismiss all emotional barriers that hinder you,
And yield to your true, cherished thoughts.

Empower each rose with the persona of someone dear.
And let your love become the spark of dreams.

Gradually immerse the roses with your feelings,
Flowing like luminous silver streams into their essence.

There are neither special spiritual beliefs nor arcane rituals to perform,
Nostalgic and treasured memories are all that's required.

After Hope has taken seed and the blossoms emerge,
Watch over them in this Hearthstone of immortality.

As they mature, expanding into a miracle of perfection,
They shall be protected and sheltered under angelic wings.

They forever dwell within the glow of Divine Radiance,
No harm may ever befall them; no darkness may ever cross this threshold.

Take time to contemplate the sheer beauty and vastness of the Garden,
Tangible proof that love can never be extinguished.

On Heaven's breath, I often travel to Arcadia, the Garden of Eternity,
To tend my heart-felt wishes and to fortify my spirit.

I can never forget those who have passed from my life....
Just like you, I still need to be near my Dear Ones.

Dedicated to anyone who has lost a Dear One.

United We Stand, Divided We Fall
By Marlena Sabella
Northern Cambria, PA

America is wounded, but we will
   not lay down and die —
A landmark is gone — no more
   twin towers in the sky!
Our hearts may be broken, but
   our spirit's is intact — and we
   must stand together to gain
   strength from this attack!
We are the strongest nation — the
   strongest in the land — and we
   must carefully contemplate the
   strategy we plan.
It's said a wound heals stronger,
   stronger than before —
   America will rise again, but
   now we are at war.
We have to do now what has
   to be done —
Freedom has to prevail for
   generations who are to come.
We will again walk safely
   in the land of the free —
   and calm the growing fear of
   generations yet to be!
For we are Americans, our
   bloodlines are strong and we will
   defend our country with our
   hearts and souls, for this is the
   land where we belong!
Our flag will forever stand
   for freedom and justice for you
   and me —
Flying softly in the wind —
   as a symbol of American democracy!

Yellow Ribbons of Sorrow
By Casey Westview
Troy, MI

Sudden Death
By Lou Ann Tipps - age 52
Sherman, TX

The treasure of life is lost
and quiet little worlds are tossed.
Snuffed by a force so deadly potent.

Erie screams reeked from unknown innocence,
amidst the smoke and sifted fragments of cement.
The wrangled and mangled items tossed,
evidenced lives in this world lost.

Misplaced by acts of man's vengeance,
petrified hearts and of hatred's stench.
Man seduced by secular lure,
the faultless people forced to endure.

Pain shared by mortals left unchosen.
Loss and empty feelings swollen
by senseless tasks so beguiling,
to worlds in its' thoroughfare defying.

Those left with unknown purpose
question evil thoughts and deeds that surface.
Feeling so alone, but we're not,
many share in prayer and thought.

There will be no solitude
found in a heart that's rude.
One who inflicts pain with reckless fuse
will live and die in sad recluse.

Comforting one another,
we'll move ahead, my brother.
Again we'll see the sun
and evidence of peace will come.

Our loved ones know we care,
some day their lives again, we'll share.
Hold to the memories of life's best,
and the Lord supplies the missing zest.

Let not the bitterness intrude
for judgement comes, one can't refute.
Satan's lies are like a sword,
snatching mortals from the Lord.

There are those we scorn
for a time, and those we mourn
for a time, then we'll bereave no more.

For one day our souls too, will soar.

Today Is Another Day
By Mary Elizabeth Tucker - age 72
Brunswick, OH

As we sit and watch the television we look at terrible things that have
Happened the last few days and weeks
It takes a lot of trying to sort out why?
Why did this happen to such a beautiful place?
Will we ever be safe again anywhere or anymore?
We will look over our shoulder more often
The tears will be a long time stopping for most of us
Everyone is coming together to help and show support
There will be many days that we will ask ourselves
The question, what can I do?
The answer is very hard to do I think the best we can do
Is to open our hearts our pocket books and pray
Do not ask GOD why he let this terrible thing happen
He did not! God loves us he does not want us to be filled with hatred
Terrible things happen when terrible people make it happen
They are taught to hate from the beginning
And they will continue to do so as long as they live
Their lives mean nothing to them and they have no heart
Killing little innocent children and the old people as well as themselves
As GOD to be with you and yours and love one another
We will make it through.

God Transcends It All
By Timothy B. Wilder, Sr.
Philadelphia, PA

This days infamy is only just beginning to dawn,
As America copes with the complexities of a tragedy born,
The emotions of choice and memories that's swirling around,
The suicidal attacks on the World Trade Center,
Twin Towers both crumbling to the ground,
Thousands of people working, the safest place on earth perhaps,
The day that shook America when both Towers collapsed,
The grief for our dead is deep and enduring,
As one hundred and ten floors in each building fell apart,
Intended to frighten our nation, but we move forward with courage of heart.

Our peace may have become an illusion, yes, that's Satan's call,
Breaking through the toxic mixture of anger,
We're compelled to admit and convinced that God transcends it all,
Thousands lined up to donate blood, relationships among the nation started to grow,
It came as a surprise to the wisdom of man,
While all eyes were turned to the streets below,
Real people struggling to connect, running to their fellowman's aid,
Accepting their duty as obstacles of peace, suppressed all the feelings they made.

I saw in the streets of the Big Apple that day,
When history recorded a greater display,
When crisis appeared the eleventh of September,
Of airplanes flying into buildings, will forever be remembered,
Our hearts are sadly fragmented, we heed the rage within,
But on this day every American became a brother, a sister, a friend.

Tim Wilder

Untitled
By Lloyd Turner - age 50
Reseda, CA

Afghanistan Naaah
Vic Tanni's and
Law
Afghanistan Baah
Afghan and Paw
And what shall
be done
Afghan and Law
and what have we
done after Agean and
Toch
We pass the Dressing From
An Afghani WOK

Our Flag Still Waves
By William R. Whittaker - age 56
Apex, NC

They're mailing out memos from a poison pen
Waging war on our women, children, and men
From deep in their caves in a desolate land
Trying to make us bow on their demand
But our flag still snaps in the afternoon breeze
Blowing briskly through autumn-colored leaves
While our voices are raised in praiseful paean
To purple mountain majesty and amber wavers of grain

Oh, say do you see by the dawn's early light
What so loudly was assailed then stowed out of sight
Oh, say is that star-spangled banner once more a-wave
Over the land of the free and home of the brave
Where that hard-won banner will forever be free to fly
Where freedom-loving people have died to raise that standard high
From urban streets of America, where the fire fell like rain
to purple mountain majesty and amber waves of grain

City Under Siege
By Timothy B. Wilder, Sr.
Philadelphia, PA

The Simi Valley Trial and Verdict, Ignited This Urban War
Creating This City Under Siege, Like Never Ever Before.
Four White Police Officers Were Acquitted, of Beating "Rodney King"
Videotaped of Their Violence, Yet, No Conviction Did They Bring.

Complete Disillusionment With The System, Every Walk of Life Was Touched,
Like a California Earthquake, Violence Became Their Crutch.
Smoke Blotted out the Mountains, As Buildings Went Up In Flame
That Double Standard of Justice, The Jury Played a Game...

This Case is Evidence of Racism, We All Felt the Mighty Heat,
Not only was "Rodney King" On the Ground, We Were All There Getting Beat.
These White Conservatives From Ventura County, Were Blind to See Excessive Force

Waves of Outrage Swept Through L.A., Nowhere Seemed Genuinely Safe
Gov. Pete Wilson Declared a "State of Emergency, While Panicked Citizens Fled the Place
Streets and Freeways Were Choked With People, The Worst Still Lies in Wait,
No, "Our Eyes Did Not Deceive Us," We're Responding to America's Hate.

Blacks Are At The Boiling Point, The World Needs to Understand,
That Rodney King On This Day, Was Every Other Black Man.
Daylight Illuminated the Riot Damage, A City In the Grip of Fear
The Jury Must Have been from Another planet, They could not have come from here.

Race and Rage have Met Again, Life is Completely Unpredictable.
Scattered Gun-Fire Echoed Through the Streets, Due to the Infamous Acquittal
With T.V. Cameras Rolling On, "Police Chief Daryl Gates Must Go,
Lawlessness Cannot Persist," Everyone Should Know.

Mayor: Tom Bradley Declares A Dusk to Dawn Curfew, We must all come together
and Change the System Too.
From the Tree Shrouded Mansions at Beverly Hills, Hollywood to Long Beach,
Refocus on the Problems America has Swept Under the Rug, and Put Justice Back in Reach.

In the Nation's "Second Largest City, Vigorously, Authorities Struggle to Regain Control,
Blacks Need a Sense of Hope, of Optimism
While Others Evaluate "The Window of their Soul."

The Example
By UnDra Tincani - age 27
Long Beach, CA

As I think back
The things I remember
The sad and tragic things I remember
Things in my life
Things in the world
It's hard to tell
Is hell my home
It seems that way
Sometimes each day
Not sure how to take these things in
my way
Bad things
Bad times
Bad People
Bad crimes
I live in L.B.
Long Beach you see
Bad news on T.V.
Is not new to me
I look all around the children I see
Bad things
Bad times
Bad people
Bad crimes
And this is the example we leave
behind

All Ages

By Tiffany White - age 16
Haverhill, MA

How, can I even say?
How may I ever realize what special grace lies behind your eyes?
In those of you, the epic heroes of today
Wistful breezes twirl about the curious
And a child looks up at me saying

Please make it go away
Why is mommy crying?
Why does daddy look away?
Why is the snow black?

I take her hand and squeeze it lightly
I'll never feel the same, again
I've always preached of letting go
Truly I wish that it wouldn't snow
I feel a touch to my shoulder, and a parent looks down on me saying

We will soon make it go away
My wife will not cry
My daughter will not worry
The snow *will* be white

The hand is strong, yet comforting
My mind is settled on only one side
I look up seeing blue all around, yet a cloud remains
I wish for rain, but only am comforted by the tears I make
I feel a hand on mine, and an older woman looks to me, saying

We can never make it go away
We can all still cry
Our children will soon realize
The snow may turn white someday

But we can never hinder its fall

For those thousands who can no longer show their pride.

An Apocalypse of Angels

By Hugo Walter
Princeton, NJ

An apocalypse of faces turned away from time in narcissi —
    amber whispers of the asphodel — vaned language of Eden

An apocalypse of voices gyrating mellifluous —
    jade tears of crimson — opiate light into the Atlantis —
    scarred, crystalline — primeval seas

An apocalypse of silences redeeming infinity in seraphic —
    liminal intuitions of ambrosial — glistening light

An apocalypse of angels shaping the hyacinth —
    veiled altar of sibylline — apsed, cypress —
    chastening eternity in jasmine — angled blooms of emerald —
    gleaming, camellia — soaring light.

Sea of Life

By Lynda Joyner Wallace
Mocksville, NC

At times, I have felt like a small
Seashell in a very large ocean
Protected by my fragile colorful shell
Life like an ocean can be very
Tumultuous
A force too powerful to control
Sometimes calm and warm as
The sunlight filters through
The water to console me
Sometimes angry and rough as
The moonlight filters through
The water
The storm approaches
The wave encroaches knocking
Me down tumbling me around
Until many times helpless
And washed ashore
So weak I cannot return
On my own
By the grace of God given the
Strength to try again
To safely to try again
To safely return to the sea
Of life

Dedication: Unity in prayer can move mountains
God Bless America

Besieged

By Meagan Tucker - age 16
Calgary, AB

Whispers walk along the dawn speaking nothing new
Words are spoken never broken wind keeps skies clear blue
Then tides all turn and wind picks up and smash upon the rocks
Lives are shaken the world awaken to the tearing docks
A second burst then weak release rips at human rust
And scattered parts of shattered hearts lie among the dust
Silence spreads and plagues the world as paint conceals and dries
And closed now still the window sill freeze and frost our eyes
A rhythm sets our minds alike and sinks low with the sea
And rubble hits us, tears us, splits us burning down and deep
We sit and see what used to be while sitting in the eye
The systems down now, people drowned now, beneath the rumbled sky
Once again, the wind blows fierce as the memories combust
And almost sleeping morning weeping the wind uproots the dust
Twisted stars among the stripes now face down 'neath the docks
Minds and bodies parted are found buried 'neath the rocks
Blankets sit a ghostly crowd and gazes at the view
Minds all frozen words unspoken as the cold wind blew.

By God's Will
By C. Edwin Ward
Little Falls, NJ

MacArther's speech to Congress
  A very memorable day
He said: "Old Soldiers never die
  They just fade away."

Other Veterans felt excluded
  Old Pilots, also, never die
It's because they've already been
  And had their taste of sky.

They've reached up and touched God's face
  As they've soared high in the blue
They survive by God's Good Grace
  While the enemy, they pursue.

"We'll win because God's on our side."
  Said Joe Louis in World War II,
"By God's will, they'll give up the fight."
  Joe's prophetic words proved true.

The ensuing years brought much unrest
  Korea, Nam, then Desert Storm
Constant pot stirring leaves a mess
  The answer lies in World Reform.

Once again we are engaged in War
  Sleazy Terrorists are the Foe
Cowards all — Rotten to the Core
  All Vermin Scum — They Gotta Go.

We'll ferret all those Bastards out
  Aided by new weapons, so modern
We'll turn this War into a rout
  And Hang Osama Bin Laden.

Song Bird
By Irma Vincenti
Edison, NJ

Every morning there sings a little song bird
He sits on a sturdy tree so high
His neck erect, his feathers bright,
Eyes stare towards the great blue sky.
He begins with a whistle, softly at first
And then harmony starts to flow
Into the bark of the sturdy tree
Through the raging roots below.
He sings to the heavens, and cries to the angels above
Giving thanks for the howling winds, the peaceful green, and the
returned melodious words of love.
And every morning the bird returns to the same sturdy tree, he flies
He sits so proudly, sings so beautifully
So full of life, he thrives.

But then one morning, a sudden gloom strikes the sky with smoke-filled air
The earth rumbled, the trees shook, releasing fallin' leaves with little care
Fires blazing, scorching, flames soaring
Struggling to understand,
What evil would do this?
What designs such wicked plans?

And on that same morning the little bird flew in,
Except now he sits on a broken branch
His eyes spell weary, his voice afraid, and when asked to sing, weeps,
"I can't."
Nevertheless he finds the strength and begins to whistle a different tune,
Quivering with every breath he takes
Consumed by the smoldering fumes.
He sang to the heavens and prayed to the Lord, not noticing the rhythm
in which he lacked.
And when he was through, he spreads his wings, but this time the little
bird would never come back.
Into the billowy clouds he flew, so eloquently he soared,
And as the little bird glanced down, the once sturdy tree was no more.
And although his music has left this earth, his melody lingers strong
For the little song bird will forever sing in our hearts a harmonious little
love song.

Two Tall Tuesday
By Judi Warren - age 41
Dallas, TX

    Two hundred and twenty stories all total in the Twin Towers of the World Trade Centers up in lower Manhattan, New York. Filled with thousands of innocent people some there at their jobs the others doing business with one or another company. There, all of them though thought it would be just one more ordinary Tuesday. Then the most horrified acts carried out by two jumbo jets also filled with hundreds of other people came crashing and burning. So many victims that lost their lives on September 11, 2001 and too the Afgahistanians, or so we blame who took their own lives in the most deadly tragedy in most Americans memories. All of us left behind, weeping for our loved ones, some filled with hatred but most feeling scared of another act of terrorism and blaming Osama Bin Laden and Omar the Taliban leader are now being hunted like rabid beasts and that doesn't really bother us true believers because they both will be judged and sentenced by God in the end and His punishment always fits the crime so I can't be the terrorist judge and jury because I too will be in the like one day and if I know what's best I'll ask for forgiveness for my sins and all terrorists around the globe also have that chance. Our heavenly Father does forgive all crimes even the most haunting, all we have to do is ask. So is what your living for worth dying for? Let us make a difference by trying to forgive these men who carried out these catastrophic events as God forgives us. Always keep in your prayers the families and friends of the deceased and the brave police, firefighters, plus all the hundreds of volunteers who are subsisting at ground zero.

Cognizant of one's place; Indelible in one's recourse:
By James E. Whitaker - age 41
Philadelphia, PA

Daggers, ripped into my sides. One side,
then the other. Piercing deep and oh so close
to my heart, I dare not utter the thought of why.
The pain, be it so telling. Ponder not, for we
see no time frame in dispelling what now
consumes the new everyday way of our lives.

I want to, to be, to see, to decree my life whole once
more. Rediscovering life, as it once was. Re-embracing
sacred trust, unlike never before. Would someone
please singe these mental wounds into repression,
I implore.

Time has past, cast no doubt upon the task that beseech
us. What we do now, we do for love. Force to prove
what always came as second nature for one another.
Price, be it so steep, yet I dear not say it not be are druthers.
For the choice was made, not by us, but by the sinful
act of such callas others.

We as Americans, no time for indecision, be the barer
of all, standing for honor. Exoneration of one's character,
a choice it is not, simply an ineffaceable given. As the
world looks on, and look they shall. Worry not, for we
shall rise above the ashes. Bleed not for us, but for
the innocent around the world. For it is those lives, which
will unfortunately be curtailed. Caused by negligent
decision-making by leaders from parts of the 3rd world.

MAY THE LORD HAVE MERCY ON THEIR SOULS.

Dedication: "Americans, Fortified as a Country,
Unite Incradicably as One."

Lady Liberty
By Marianne Ware - age 28
Mission Viejo, CA

Tears swell in the eyes of Lady Liberty
As she looks across the land of the free.
Chaos has rattled and shattered her land,
But the strength of her children has shown its face.

We dig for survivors and weep for the fallen.
Never forgetting the memories we all once shared.
Sheltering each other throughout every day,
Opening our arms to comfort those who need it.

Those two towers that took a blistering fall,
Will not crush a country that will always be united.
As we hold candles and stand hand in hand,
The chaos that was caused only made us stronger.

Lady Liberty please dry your eyes,
Stand tall once again over your land.
We need your torch to light our way,
So we make it through each and every day.

The American Eagle
By Dianna Wilder
Winamac, IN

I saw a poster of the American Eagle
with a tear falling from his eye.
The Twin Towers were in the background,
with smoke hovering in the sky.

Part of the world hates us,
they want to see us die.
They use planes as bombs, send warfare,
scheme and plot and lie.

But our lady still stands with the torch in her hand
even though there's smoke in the sky.
And the eagle still flies with a tear in his eye—
flies strongly over our land!

We display our flags with honor
for we're the "land of the free."
Our troops will protect us,
in the air, on the land, and at sea.

Pray for our country, solidarity will stand,
our nation has bled and cried.
But America is strong, we will prevail—
for God is on our side!

Changed People
By Dorann Tomasello - age 52
Elm, NJ

Sept. 11, 2001 changed us Lord
Some say "Why did God allow this to be?"
"Where was God that day,
In this land of the free?"

We are free to choose Lord.
But so are others
The ones who want to hurt us
The ones it's hard to call our brothers.

We are a changed people Lord
For now many live in fear
Help us to look to You Lord
For our lives to steer.

For we know where You were
It's where You've always been
As long as we are living here
In this world of sin.

You're here inside each human heart
Who's asked you to come in —
You're here with all the broken hearts
Strengthening them from within.

We saw You in the fireman and police
Who gave their lives
We saw You in those who helped
Giving time, money, and supplies.

You're here right beside us
To give comfort and peace each day
All we have to do Lord
Is close our eyes and pray.

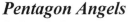

Pentagon Angels
By Dorothy Justesen
Albert Lea, MN

Pentagon angels are strong with support
For attack victims of a plane they couldn't abort!
Wings wide open to lift them up high
To heavenly places where no one will cry.
Love reigns there for all to enjoy
And God is supreme for each girl and boy.
A wonder to behold, all the heavenly beings
Surrounded by new souls who found the light.
September 11, 2001 bore angels who fight
For faith, hope, and love;
And peace forever more!

Pentagon angels we adore and adore!

Address Space
By Bill Samer - age 49
Union, NJ

Working in a high-rise office building in Manhattan is more than a crow on a tassel. I feel the same as if I've reached the crossroads in the middle of a cornfield back home in Indiana, tired from traveling through the Holland Tunnel to the car garage @ the bottom of the World Trade Center. I transfer from the express to the local elevator to the 46th floor where the offices of the Bethel Advisement Company are located. I brush lint off my light tan shirt from landsend.com and suit. One floor below the lobby level, the desk supervisor listens to a report from the Port Authority police desk from a mall night security guard's vertical: "A woman w/long black hair stuck gum to the banister on the stairway." It won't be cleaned by the contractors until after four when they arrive.

In my sparkling white office, I flip on the power, and have my quiet time. Should I read an e-book? I log on to a church's Home Page where I see a white dove flying w/out leaving the center of the color monitor. I put back my NASB (New American Standard Bible) on the shelf; dictate a letter to the company computer, Solomon. Our company robot, Jay Lennon, brings in the rest of my breakfast I start @ home. Breena's in her cubicle thinking of Robert the guard's uniform, and that he must have been jealous by the way he stared at her blue button suit w/a skirt, when she turned off her Dire Strait's CD, walking into the lobby of the north tower. I press her extension and ask her about the progress of the transfer of money from a private security company in China for a woman.

Her deceased uncle diverted money from rice, and she found Bethel in a business directory in Shanghai.

We'll receive 40% of the $30.4 million. On the computer screen Solomon's mother, the net, draws a figure that resembles the Hamburglar in the McDonald's commercial. It's father, the search engine, shows me its logarithms she's using to siphon money, and I say a little prayer for her to God.

My friend, Calvin, speaks w/his tongue sticking through his lips. He calls me on the videophone from Strong International Exporters on the third floor of the south tower. The Intel camera's eye is dazzling me w/the light in its blue eye staring @ me. He tells me someone stuck gum to the banister on the stairway in my building. After he hangs up I type a note to send him an e-mail postcard.

"I think something hit the building."
"Yes, I hear the sound of something crumbling, Addison."
"No, the south tower."

After Breena and I escape down the stairs, God gives me a second wind. I pray silently for Calvin's safety, holding her hand and witness that Jesus loves her and we pray as He becomes her Lord and Saviour from sin personally—God tells me I love her more than the and *so do I*. We pray w/Frank two blocks away when the second tower collapses.

God has provided both companies office space in the Shay Building. Robert's flowers are on Breena's desk in her office. They are enjoying breakfast, while I'm driving in the Lincoln Tunnel. Outside, in the window, a woman walks her white and chestnut Spinone Italiano—it looks like a large stuffed animal on the couch in her apartment above. (John 14:12)

America – Voices Coming Together

September 11th
By Eugene C. Chorosinski
Eustis, FL

I was terrified and sickened
by what I saw in a sickening flash
my world has changed forever,
I feel it in my heart.

I watched with shock, horror,
and some disbelief
nothing pleasant
that goes through my head.

I felt anger and sadness
about Tuesday's tragic events being
terrorist attacks in New York,
Pennsylvania and Washington,
D.C.
I went to bed Tuesday nite
to a usual sleep
broken by the images
of destruction and death
at the World Trade Center,
Pentagon and in Shanksville,
Pennsylvania fields.
I'm shock, awe, and anger
with frustration, sadness,
sympathy, hate, love,
they're all there
and at any moment
one or the other
boils my blood.

the enemy can blow our buildings,
kill our neighbor and friends
but our spirit will stay in tack.

We prayed, we mourn,
now is the time to avenge
on our foes around the globe.

Our way of life is too precious
to be given in to terrorist
who hide themselves
our Civil Liberties.

During this most difficult time
Our Country scores gains,
our Country will unite
and love our President
to find those responsible terrorists
from Tuesday's attacks
so it will strengthen
our resolve to be free.

I know President Bush
he will do whatever it takes
to respond to this act of 2001
of America's New War.

Dedicated to those we have lost on that day.

God Is In Control
By Jack W. Kirsch
Amarillo, TX

Though terrorists cause planes to fall from the sky
Though thousands of lives are shattered for those who die
Though skyscrapers topple trapping countless souls inside
Though thousands rush for cover as they try to hide
I won't lose hope, because I know God is in control.

Though military personnel are called in readiness for war
Though vengeance in our hearts is hard to ignore
Though thousands are trapped, dead, and dying
Though the world is filled with the sound of crying
I will be strong, because I know God is in control.

Though millions offer aid in any way they can
Though we honor the heroes, each and every American
Though people rush to pray and the flags fly low
There is peace in my heart, because I know God is in control.

Timeless
by Elvie E. Bryant Keller
Glen St. Mary, FL

Lingre...so softly unto me
And I will give my love unto thee
I'll love the softly in the rains
And be with thee 'til time is endless unto thine
I'll love the softly in the winds
And thou passion will dwell here within
I'll love the softly unto my heart
And my love will never want to depart

I have placed myself within this book, put me in a
discrete place for hence-forth when you see or
hear the rains and winds you will think of me,
want to read me, or perhaps you will want to
memorize me. For I will always be with thee...

I am Apus

No Stone Upon A Stone
By Ruth Warner - age 78
Northwood, OH

God prophesied these latter days:
a world devoid of love,
men self-assuming and haughty
with push turning to shove.

The enemy is at our gates
as dreaded days draw near.
The devil dances gleefully
as mankind quakes with fear.

From out the North, the winds of change
do chill one to the bone.
Now here we wait for their next move,
no stone upon a stone.

The vulture hovers overhead,
just waiting for a share,
to pick the bones for every scrap
that is remaining there.

Can you not hear the hoofbeats now
with ear pressed to the ground?
Is your present house in order,
or does bedlam abound?

In scriptures old, a loving God
beseeched all to atone.
Now man waits God's deliverance,
no stone upon a stone.

*Dedication: For those who hear the hoofbeats
in these latter days.*

Land of the Free
By Sally Jo Grubaugh
St. Johns, MI

The world watched us frozen in disbelief
On that early September morn,
Innocent lives taken in a matter of minutes
As buildings collapsed twisted, burning and torn.

A great cloud of grief and pain
Cast its shadow across this our land,
Real acts of heroism could not be overshadowed
By some cowardly murderous plans.

Who could have been so callous
Somehow claiming this as the beginning of a holy war,
What faith of man justifies mass murder
As the means to even some unknown score?

Some men's souls have never known our freedom
But only the evil that they have reaped,
Anger has choked out compassion in their hearts
As nightmares must also fill their sleep.

But there still lies the spirit in us all
That created this nation out of diversity,
Nor can we forget our promise
That we will protect this land of the free.

Dedicated to the American spirit that can not be destroyed.

Heroes
By Del Corey
Clinton Township, MI

Patton needed a war to become
all he felt he was destined to be,
so, many soldiers today
welcome testing themselves,
spitting in Death's eye,
and while becoming heroes
ridding the world of the vermin of terror.

Some will fall, and some will fail,
some will flee, and some prevail,
whenever they see Death cavorting above
the blood and bullets and body parts,
then, into the mayhem and roaring bombs,
to proceed against common sense,
against odds the Gods of war
have given against the living.

Yet, in years to come, when sitting,
along with their medals, and canes,
some will confess to the mirror
with secret shame, the selfish motives
they had just to claim their fame.

Taint not your deeds, oh, heroes,
the world cares not the why's
just the well-done's, with many thanks.

Ignited Hate
By Jean C. Marks
Brooklyn, NY

Without warning
Without interruptions
Suicidal terrorist
In hijacked airplanes
Like wrecking balls
Tore apart our twin towers
Walls came tumbling down
and the ground opened up
Thousands buried alive
Like pearls inside oysters
Comprehension fail me
Fire overwhelm me
Grief consumed me
And smoke blind me
Folks are still shook up
From the sight and smell
But it's no stopping ones date with death
Dying and rebirth overlap like waves
Fathers, Mothers, Sisters, and Brothers
Fighting back tears
The fireball still rises in the sky
From sadness, lets solidify
From the shattering, find strength
From the sleeping, let us wake up
From the weakness, let us get tough
From hate, lets have harmony
From the tragedy, let us transcend

Still Slaves
By Raymond F. Rogers
Greensboro, NC

White mercenaries sold dark ones from Africa
Into abject service, and to misery,
The hope of gain let buyers use their capital,
Blinded by the lures of slavery.
Elitists found the natives less than naught
And treated them with manifest disdain.
Little ones behaved as they were taught.
They exercised power over their domain.
A cruel war was fought to free the slaves
To convert souls who wore a darker skin,
But they still rule who yet the power have
And they are slaves whose salaries are thin.
Yet we are color blind who still must toil
To free the seed we've planted in the soil.

Please God, Peace
By Jeanette J. McAdoo - age 43
Glassport, PA

God why were innocent lives taken,
With families and friends left to grieve.
All with a purpose in life to serve,
Younger to older all innocent victims.

Fear spread quickly amongst all people,
Tears of fear and sadness shed.
God be with us in our time of need,
Bless the souls prematurely taken.

Ease the pain of friends and families,
Help them carry on with their lives.
Though no one will ever understand,
The reason of this senseless act.

Bless the brave who were hard at work,
Policeman and Firefighters all pitched in.
Bless our loved ones gone to war,
Bring them home safe and war to an end.

Let there be peace and grant us safety,
To live our lives and be free again.
Help us rebuild our lives and loss,
God Bless America and let freedom ring.

America – Voices Coming Together

Love Out of Pain
By Gregory Wilson
Pittsburgh, PA

We the people of this great vast land, where the ground is paved with blood and pain. In a place where freedom rings and people sing of joy. Tragedy struck, we all ran from the darkness of the crumbling building falling from the sky. The trade falls as the Pentagon burns. While the tears stream down America's faces. We hope and we learn.

Tragic Event-Thankful Mother
By Peggy E. Franklin
Plano, TX

America suffered a horrible terrorists attack, when those most tragic happenings had occurred on September 11, 2001. Leaving all of us with a feeling of devastation that we should not have hand to face.

The nightmarish day left us all in stunned horror wondering where, and when the monsters would strike again. This was no scary movie, as it was taking place as the nation was watching. It was the real thing. We were in state of helplessness.

Anger burns in my mind that these innocent people have lost their lives', and the survivors have been denied the love of a loved one, as this so cruelly has been taken from them. My heart grieves with the survivors.

We all felt the grief for those lives' were "snuffed out," and those who were injured. Our hearts ache for the survivors of the people who so needlessly perished. It's as if they were "executed' for no reason at all.

The one's with whom I've spoken, expressing their feelings are that of anger, like myself. My thoughts are "why could people do such a despicable deed killing and injuring innocent people?" We as American people want justice.

Then on a most thankful note my son Major Ken Franklin was kept safe through divine intervention. On September 10, 2001 Ken worked in the Pentagon in the same area where that Airplane crashed. On Tuesday, September 11, 2001 for some reason he had to work at Andrews Air Force Base. I realize that God had answered a prayer this mother has prayed many times through life for Him to take care of my family. So, I'm most grateful-giving my Heavenly Father the praise for Ken's safety.

We as Americans will never forget this day of devastation. The scars upon our hearts and minds will remain. The nightmarish memories will continue-never ending.

Several of my brothers served this country in the past wars; and one brother Leroy Shifflett died on a battlefield in the 2nd World War for the freedom of all Americans. Now this freedom for which he and thousands lost their lives' has been tainted. This right has been violated. I, along with others feel, that the people in authority will not let this act become "swept under the carpet," so to speak; and the American people will seek retaliation on the people involved in this inexcusable attack.

This very fact makes me realize there will be another war; and with fear (and also anger) in my heart that my grandson Shaun, which is in the Army now could go to fight in this war; and also if the draft is reinstated another grandson Randall will probably go to war. Also, nephews would be involved. And if this is to happen this grandmother/aunt will be praying for their safety, along with thousands of other men and women.

The Attack
By Peggy E. Franklin
Plano, TX

From the bowels of Hell it seems one came,
    With a great fury to abound;
As Satan belched him from his realm,
    Just to spread sorrow all around.
These "imps" from Hell caused ones to die,
    While surely he laughed with glee,
As Twin Towers then came tumbling down,
    Oh no! This shouldn't be.
Three shiny planes from the sky did roar,
    As they found their targets there;
At another point the Pentagon,
    As a bulls-eye it did share.
So many one's our fellowmen
    Unaware their time to end;
And the loved one's left in deep despair, and with
    Grieving hearts to mend.
Many people caught these flights that day,
    And for many reasons be.
So innocent they were brought down,
    While a Nation stunned did see.
The flames the smoke arose to the sky,
    As tears from our eyes did fall;
I'm sure Bin Laden looked on in delight,
    As his evil did make this call.
Then another shiny giant of the sky,
    A prison to many did make,
But heroes' fought with all their might,
    Even though their lives' at stake.
Countless others were saved that day,
    As this Aircraft missed its mark;
The brave went down in a grassy field,
    But to Heaven they did embark.
America struck back with a deadly force,
    Bin Laden now shakes with fear.
For he's all "holed-up" in a mountainside,
    While the Taliban's standing near.
Bin Laden will come falling down—
    His empire soon will fail,
He forgot one thing through his evil deed,
    That true justice will prevail.
For our God will see His children through,
    As they fight against their foe;
As a war on evil has been waged,
    He'll avenge us all we know.
'Cause America stands on solid ground,
    And this war is fought to the end.
When Bin Laden returns to Hell below,
    Where American's his soul will send.

December 2001
By Jody Lawton
Tucson, AZ

Once in America
the hollyhocks stood
row on row
on the coast of Maine,
with the red white and blue
flying in the breeze.
Stubborn beauty still holds.

While the serpent insinuated
itself deeper than ever before,
The sun, the eye of God
still glinted in the morning light
off the steel girders
that collapsed.
On September 11
the World Trade Center fell ,
but not America.

Weeping, then choking
on clouds of anthrax
against the red dawn
the eagle rose from its nest
wild predator aroused
in fury screaming
for the destination
winging to Afghanistan.

Now the angels watching,
at the four corners
of the Earth,
hold the wind in place
while the eagle,
sinks its talons
into the ground
holding the serpent
aloft in its beak
ready to close.

The Eye of God
By Allison Derderian

One Light
by Lillian M. O'Neal - age 63
Jamaica Plain, MA

You must have seen them the other morning
So many lights shot across God's skies
You must have known that they were special
By the way they passed you by.
You must have known that in this special year
God would move some souls to rest.
You must have felt in the air.
For on that special morning the angels came to God
They stood on heavens floor with
A gift held firmly in their hands.

They came to ask God please grant them one request.
Since they were taken in one swift moment,
In one second, in the morning light.
No chance to say what was on their minds.
As God looked down, He was blinded, by their lights
If only He could help them,
If only He could make things right.

Then someone spoke up...
God, we have assemble with a light held in our hands.
With all the love we now hold,
With one request, now in our plans.

And the Lord looked over the many lights as
He wiped the tears from His eyes.
And at the very moment this light became one,
He reached down to move these plans ahead.
With not much time left for Christmas season,
And even the best-laid plans could go wrong.
God made them all a promise
That things will be in the place on Christmas morn.

And the angels polished up their lights and said a little prayer.
On Christmas Day,
You'll see them shining on trees that remain ahead.
Oh the trees, within the houses, of the ones they left behind.
Within fire stations, where they still hear the alarms.
Within police stations, where they still answers all the calls.
In the parks, now filled with ice-skating rinks.
Down the streets, in the halls, in the stores everywhere...
As people come together singsongs giving gifts and
Praising the Lord.

Somehow we know that this Christmas
Has a new and different meaning...
As the angels bring their gifts of lights and hopes and dreams
To place them on their trees...
To let the others know that life still goes on and
Love still grows and hope is everywhere.
To let them know, that they will not be forgotten
In each and every light that shines
They will be there...
In each and every prayer, they will be there...
In each and every heart that beats they will be there...
In each and every breath they take, they...will be...there...
For they are not gone...they will live on...and on...forever and a day...

A Christian's View Regarding September 11, 2001
By Patricia H. Brochu
West Warwick, RI

As a Christian, I was overwhelmed when hearing of the terrorist attack on America on September 11, 2001.

First of all, America was founded on Christian principles. To be a Christian one must be a follower of Christ. One must know who Christ is and that can be accomplished by studying God's Word — The Holy Bible. It contains The Old Testament and The New Testament and usually contains a Concordance which simplifies finding the scripture verses dealing with such things as baptism, blessing death, disciple, evil, faith, healing, miracle, prayer, repentance, revelation, saints, salvation, soul, spirit, truth, etc. For people to call themselves Christians, it would be wise to attend Bible Classes and learn how our Creator intends for us to live.

Here are a few of the state's mottoes:

    Florida - In God We Trust
    New Hampshire - Live Free or Die
    New Jersey - Liberty and Prosperity
    Pennsylvania - Virtue, Liberty and Independence
    Rhode Island - Hope
    Washington DC - Justice to All

Here are a few quotes from well known people:

    Woodrow Wilson — "The interesting and inspiring thing about America is that she asks nothing for herself except what she has a right to ask for humanity." "One of the proofs of the divinity of our gospel is the preaching it has survived."
    Edgar Guest — "The best of all preachers are those who live by their creeds."
    Thomas Paine — "The World is my country, all mankind are my brethren and to do good is my religion."
    Otto Von Bismark — "There is only one greater folly than that of the fool who says in his heart there is no God, and that is the folly of the people that says with its head that it does not know whether there is a God or not."

The Bible also states, "If my people repent and change their wicked ways, then will I heal their land." So, Americans, please ponder all that I have written and God will Bless America once again.

Last September
By Mary B. Wadzinski - age 49
Wausau, WI

Devastation occurred last September.
It's a day we will always remember.
Hundreds of people lost their precious lives.
All because Bin Laden wants to survive.

Just one man caused all of this destruction.
So we look to God for our direction.
What he did deserves nothing but his death.
He has not been caught, so don't hold your breath.

But once he has, he's in for a surprise.
For our country will open his blind eyes.
We will not tolerate what he has done.
Let's pray now to Father, Spirit and Son.

America We Mourn
By Joe Vargas

(America - we mourn)

The Noble Eagle Soars
By Janet L. Kise
Blairstown, NJ

A glint of silver in the tranquil September morning skies,
And the roar of an engine startles the hustling passerby's.
People glance upwards then with mouths agape they see
An airliner by The Trade Center where it should not be.
A deafening crash and a fiery mushroom erupts into the air,
Unbelief and horror fill their eyes as they stand and stare.
Then a second plane appears and sharply turns in,
Gasps of shock and dismay as it slams into the towers twin.
As the Towers tumble downward in a slow motion portrayal,
Fires race unchecked everywhere in this shocking betrayal.
Tormented souls jump from windows in macabre minutes,
Concrete crumbles to dust and steel twists into grim silhouettes.
Jet fuel gushes and rescuers rush forward to meet only death
As the hot rancid fumes steals away their breath.
Those laboring inside, burnt and broken, and there is no doubt,
All buried beneath the falling rubble will never get out.
More explosions as the Pentagon is damaged and afire,
Then the heroic flight in Pennsylvania, bravely they all expire.
From out of the ashes, not the Phoenix, but the Eagle bursts free,
Clutched in his talons and flying in the wind for all to see,
A tattered but rugged flag, Old Glory, The Red, White, and Blue,
And America struggles to her knees. Fearless, brave, and true.
The Eagle circles and inspects the gaping wounds in his side,
He see those who are hurt and those who have died.
His earsplitting screech pervades the smoke filled sky,
As the wounded Eagle proclaims war with it's piercing cry.
His fierce eyes fill with cold fury as America's war has begun,
And America will never rest until justice has been done.
America will not lay down the sword as she seeks those sick souls,
For the Eagle will find the vermin that have run for their holes.
Though they dig deep, they will not prevail—
The Noble Eagle will not fail.
Though they dig deep at the end of the day—
The Noble Eagle will find its prey.
Though they dig deep, they will die beneath that sandy floor—
The Noble Eagle will endure.
Though Osama Bin Laden will be gone forever more—
The Noble Eagle through freedom's skies will forever soar.

Speech Recap of Mayor Guilian September 23, 2001

By Sharon Derderian
Troy, MI

September 11th, New York City, our darkest day in history.
It is up to us to come together as a united City.
Our Twin Towers — no longer stand
But, our skyline will rise again.
We understand why people from all over the world
come to New York and to America.
It is "called freedom, equal protection under law,
respect for human life, and the promise of opportunity."
All those that died were innocent and heroes.
"We will hold them firmly in our hands, honor their memory,
and lift them up toward heaven to light the world."

When the World Suffered
By Lucy L. Smith - age 60
Regina, KY

I sat in front of the T.V. that morning
watching as the news came on. Saw
people running and screaming
as they began to moan.
Oh God, why is this happening?
Why let those people suffer?
I begin to weep,
But only He knows and understands
the reason the ones he wants
the world to keep.
Maybe this was meant to be.
He needed some more angels
to help him watch over the world
for you and me.
Thank God for the policemen and firefighters
they were so helpful, I understand.
I think they are beautiful people
to help our fellowmen.
I prayed so hard for those people
when they suffer I would suffer,
when they cry I would cry.
Oh Father, why did they have to go?
I guess no one will ever know.

Chaos
By Crystal Tyree
Shelbyville, IN

All the chaos,
Who knows where to start.
To many groups of people forming together.
All different and yet all the same
For a while we all forget,
What our differences are,
To help each other through a difficult time,
And show our enemies we haven't lost our pride.
All the pain we feel,
Because of this tragedy,
May haunt us in our dreams.
Still we need to pick up the pieces and forget about our greed.
All of us people in this world,
We all can make a difference,
Through the nation our voices are heard.
We finally get some recognition
We don't get a praise,
For what's being said,
But for now it doesn't matter.
This is a time for rebirth, then celebration.
The chaos will never completely end,
But now we have a clear place to start.
With everyone working together,
For once united we all stand.

Reaching Out
by Christine Maloy
Corpus Christi, TX

To all the people who don't sleep,
may the world be your wonder
with eyes of indemnity,
in the priceless hierarchy of
forgotten dreams in life's mime

To all the people with the stacks
of magazines piled up,
books galore, and
horoscopes thrown about, with
a shared knowledge so sublime

To all the people that think the
sun should not have risen and
crested behind the mountain
with shuttered house,
open yourself to eternity and
its bliss in vast dimension of time

To all the people with
Haunting spirits may their past
be bygone, since
time's peace will heal the
periodic contagion of the soul

To all the people with love of art,
may you show your spark,
and the words flow freely
like breathing steams of crisp,
cold air rising from a mountain
stream

To all the people who know
the sixth senses may
life be as delightful as the sound
and smell of a full house at
Christmas time

To all the people,
remember we're only
like the rose, sometimes we have
to bare thorns to caress the
beauty

Fractured Mimes
By Kiki Stamatiou - age 32
Kalamazoo, MI

Valor giants tear down walls
Within a sacred tomb
And light radiates
From an enchanted corpse.

Woven drones call
Out to mystic
Birds for redemption
Of a cryptic world.

Mystical winds torment
A lost child
Who cries out
Into the night
For parents
He will never see again.

The drum beats on
To the rhythm
Of musical chairs
And the time has come
For souls to sleep.

September 11, 2001
by Cerresa M. Warner - age 19
St. Clair Shores, MI

It all started on September Eleventh. I started my day off normal. I was sitting in my Medical class when the Dean's voice came over the speakers and said, "There has been an accident in New York." Everyone stopped what they were doing. While she continued talking, both Twin Towers were hit by hijacked planes along with the Pentagon. Everyone ran to the TV as we all sat there in shock, the bell rang for us to return back to our regular high school. When I got on the bus, I pulled out my cell phone; everyone called their parents. I tried calling my best friend who lives in New York... all I received was a message telling me there were problems. I started getting scared.

When I returned to the high school I had to bang on the door, come to find out our schools were under a lock down because there was still a plane missing. When I got to my class, my teacher said we're not going to do anything today. Watching TV, I saw the clouds of smoke coming from the Twin Towers. I started crying. I looked at my class and said, "Why would stupid people do this to us?"

When class was over, I went and called my mom and told her to come and get me. I was scared that someone was going to hit us next. She told me everything will be alright and she will be there around 2:30pm, so I felt a little better. As I was sitting in my fifth hour class I began crying again. I still couldn't believe people could be so crazy as to kill so many innocent people.

As days went by, our school had silent time for all the innocent people in New York, Pentagon, and Pennsylvania who died on September 11, 2001. The third week of school after the tragedy, my school did a blood drive for those in need. Students gave their blood, but there were students who tried but just couldn't do it (I was one of those people. It was hard knowing someone out there needed my blood but I had a hard time with the needle). We collected a lot of blood, money, and etc.

I was at my dad's house getting ready for bowling, I heard the news say we went to war. As days, weeks even months went by, people started to move on with their lives. I wish we can all end the violence and terrorism. I hope all this violence will end one day.

Awakening
by Barbara Ozenberger Lowell
Carrollton, TX

September eleven, two thousand one
A tragic blow has struck our nation
The hand of evil touched all Americans
With an unthinkable act of devastation

Stars and Stripes wave proudly in our sky
America kneels, stunned with pain
A million voices form a single cry
A million tears pouring like rain

As the fire and smoke clear unity arises
Together we mourn and bury our dead
United we stand with our nation in crisis
Hands joined tightly, hearts full of dread

We turn from mourning to face the enemy
The spirit of America holds strong
To stay free from oppressive tyranny
We will not rest until righting this wrong

Free countries of the world joining hands
Binding together as one global village
Defending the freedom of all humans
From the threat of terrorist pillage

September eleven, two thousand one
The sleeping eagle has been awakened
Our home of the brave, and land of the free
In our pursuit of justice, will not be forsaken

September 11, 2001
Rebirth of United States of America

By John R. Camara, Jr.
Union City, CA

September 11, 2001, remembered as a day of sorrow, a day of great crises, and certainly tomorrow as the Rebirth of America in song, in work, and in pride. In the heart, in spirit, and in praise of liberty 'cause we're all free in free America; strong and determined to continue our life styles and values in defiance of adversity; and to show our unity, our flag is still there, everywhere and *semper fidelis* number one priority...

September 11, 2001, events changed everything for everyone in the world when the New York City, World Trade Center Twin Towers, imploded due to the evildoers who will suffer the consequences for their dastardly act without conscience of the demented evil-doers, i.e.: the suicidal maniacs professing a Jihad, rather a false god of the demented creatures who believe in a holy war: a *faux pas* in Spirit or in credence of the malevolent in power malfeasance...

Ground zero of what was the World Trade Center Twin Towers is now a vast surreal Sepulcher where a tsunami-like catastrophe swept, swished and shoved five thousand bodies, including workers, police officers, firemen, sight-seers and by-standers, mixed with a mountain of debris composed of metal, concrete, wood, steel, asbestos, and electricity all pulverized into eternity in a horrific skeleton of the ages incomprehensible only by the evildoers of the catastrophe...

The foregoing events of September 11, 2001 at the 110 story Twin Towers of the World Trade Center and the grief it caused the multitude of diverse individuals and their families throughout the world, will remain sizzled in the canyons of everyone's mind forever as a demon-induced catastrophe, unparalled in any century, like a biblical flood, the tsunami swept, swished and shoved the mountain of debris in a horrendous and spectacular event of the century...

The visual sensations experienced cause by the implosions of the 110-stories Twin Towers of the World Trade Center made me cry, and the statue of Liberty sad; the horrific shock on the block of ground zero reverberated throughout the globe like a bolt of fire from the sky. Notwithstanding, the sorrow and sadness of the September 11, 2001 remains etched in everyone's mind and it becomes clear, an event without fear, that united all Americans as symbolized by the ubiquitous use of the American Flag. Flags, flags everywhere and everyone flaunting them as if defying the evildoers, and flying it proudly: as the show of the century...

The foregoing events of September 11, 2001, launched a parade of flags and Patriotism unequalled in the annals of American history consonant with *God Bless America, land that I love...my home sweet home*. This momentous occasion also made New York City Mayor Guliani a hero taller than Paul Bunyon, in the shadow of the status of Liberty, where we are free, and we love and enjoy freedom; and no one can undermine our Unity in diversity and pride in being born free. Each an Amazon in American Democracy....

The foregoing concept in practice, American Democracy and Freedom, lends great Credence and a strong belief to the "Pledge of Allegiance and to the Flag and to the Republic for which it stands: E PLURIBUS UNUM, one Nation under God with Liberty and Justice for all." Values we believe, preserve and defend everlastingly, 'cause we are free, as the eagle in the sky, free and bold as the shining rainbow above...

The September 11, 2001, tragic tsunami changed and uprooted all prior life-styles and complacency in all Americans forever and stand as the Hallmark of our constantly changing ability to embrace new technology, high mobility and the yearning to overcome through education, health, and community effort: in giving, helping, and volunteering in every walk of life in America the beautiful. It can assuredly be said that the circumstances related to the event of September 11, 2001 was the BIG BANG or singularity that precipitated the permanently evolving changes in U.S.A....

Furthermore, the unprecedented September, 11, catastrophe resulted or initiated a revision of our thinking and vocabulary necessary to express one's views, i.e.: masked Terrorist, war without front lines, an unknown enemy (?), bio-terrorist, terror-by-mail, anthrax-by-mail and a new concept of the words: GRIEF & SORROW, etc., etc., which in itself attempts to disorient and confuse individuals: in view of the Valley of Death...

In the meantime, we are told to go about our business as usual, as if nothing has happened. Also, don't give the enemy the impression that anything is wrong; act normally, open your mail, buy your food and visit ground zero to see the devastation; to be sad and cry aloud, show your sincere emotion and reality...

Cry: "I hear you, I hear you." Besides, go to the movies, eat at your neighborhood restaurant, go to the ball game, and above all, be happy and honest sincerely...

Moreover, the media — the press and TV — and other witnesses describe tall tails, each expressing the positive or the negative point of view according to his or her sense of exaggeration which to the viewer appears to be more distortion. For instance security: I have noticed the press, eager to deliver the news, actually disclosing what appears to be secret information, sources of installations like bridges, cables, war communications, etc., in the name of fairness. Honesty? Honesty never fails the wise approach. Reality and normalcy have its own peaks and valleys; and the truth certainly has its own paradigm, i.e.: example, pattern and archetype...

Therefore, the advice to buy, buy, buy; go to the ball game and have a happy time sounds like good advice for the status quo ante September 11, 2001. But, in this latter period, a period of war, anxiety, wide spread confusion, and dead, dead, dead suggests counseling, psychiatric help, love, and caring. When everyone is affected adversely with a catastrophe, an implosion in the proportion of the Twin Towers, there is no shelter from the elements that hover everywhere about: e.g.: anthrax by mail and the tsunami that occurred at ground zero, like the big bang, at New York City, September 11, 2001...the date America and the world were reborn...

Enlightened Spirits
By Edyth V. Harris
Windsor, ON

Although tears flood our souls —
heartbroken we mourn loved ones
lost in premature transition; —

Although our nation's symbols of achievement
became a gigantic funeral pyre

our spirit is not vanquished!

    Men — trained to terrorized and
    murder thousand innocent lives —
    were promised that in death
        they'd be glorified —
But **Allah** cries and so does **Abraham!**

All nations
    have misused **GOD'S** Holy name
    to justify some misguided deeds
    committed throughout centuries.
    and brought to account for their crime.

    But now let us not seek vengeance,
    war, destructions — let us not
    cause famine, death, disease
    but question our hearts and
    pray for ENLIGHTENED JUSTICE

    The Earth is beautiful and rich
    God's gift to all the Nations
    May we disdain hatred and greed —
    Respect Mother Earth and each other;
    Learn to work and live together in PEACE

In memory of those who died – innocent victims and
dedicated servants. September 11, 2001

Photo by James R. Tourtellotte

September 11, 2001
Myrtle O. Rupp
Lynnwood, WA

The two planes came from somewhere
With the speed of lightning they came,
They tore into the Twin Towers
Things would NEVER be the same.

The Towers held 52,000 workers,
Many stayed home on this particular Day,
Thousands sped down the stairwells
To get out; it was the only way.

The steel beams melted by the raging fire,
The towers held steady till most were out,
Then it came crashing down like an implosion
The World watched in awe without a shout.

The sorrowing World was changed in a moment,
They stared aghast as the pictures came on,
People wept with broken hearts,
All at once they were aware of sin.

Over 5,000 were dead or missing
Leaving family and friends to grieve at home,
But the world grieved with them
So they didn't need to weep alone.

This Terrorist attack set the world to thinking
What caused this destruction of lives with such hate?
It seemed as if a voice from heaven
Was shouting, "Awake, Awake!"

And the World did, with crying and praying
They sought the Lord on bended knee
Our only help is from the God of heaven
So we kneel here and worship thee.

God didn't plan this deadly plot
Wicked people were bent to destroy
The hopes and dreams of the world at large
The Lord wants to turn this around to joy.

We need to wake up to the task at hand
Protect our borders and understand
That the Lord is with us to love and guide
To protect us from the marauding crowd.

When things get back to normal
And the urgency is gone,
Let's remember to keep Jesus in our lives
And not just use Him as a pawn

GOD BLESS AMERICA

This debris field in the center of the U.S. Customhouse at 6 World Trade Center was caused by pieces that fell from the North Tower. Steel beams formed several crosses in the midst of the debris field.

The Family Pages

Multiple inclusions from one or more family members.

Photo by: James R. Tourtellotte

Marie E. Hoag Banks
Age 39
Worcester, NY

Where are the Roses

Where have all the roses gone to?
I see no more roses.
If we could change those days to today.
There has been bumpy roads and tough times.
But you said: I will be there to endure it
all with you.
Where are all the roses?
You left me wanting so much more of you.
I thought there was a place for me in your
heart.
Where are all the roses?
Can there be living proof, that our love
will forever stay?
I am in Love with you, I want the whole
world to see.
It should always be, You in love with me.
Think about me deep into the night.
Just remember you are holding me oh
so tight.
Will there ever be roses, again?
Where are all the Roses.

I will be there

I will be there when you feel the road is long.
When you reach out in the darkness,
I will be there.
We can cross those stepping stones together.
Don't feel ashamed if you should fall,
I will be there to reach out my hand.
Just close your eyes and open your heart,
just maybe your worries will depart.
Along with me you will find God,
He will take over and help you finish
the rest.
Sometimes, Life's burdens are to great to
carry alone.
So let someone in, who cares for you deeply,
Very deeply for you.
I will be there.
When you need a shoulder to cry upon,
mine will be there, when you are sad
and blue.
Let me touch your heart, like you have
touched mine.
I will be there.
My heart does leap, when I see you.;
I want to love you, unselfishly.
To leave no doubts within your mind and
heart.
You are the touch of an angel's wing,
which is never cold.
The feathers have softened my sadness.
So I will be there for you.

---
*Dedicated
to all those
who protect and
serve us.*

I Believe

I believe in eternity
because without it
there is a absence of God.
I believe in God,
Because without him,
there is a absence of Love.
I believe in Love,
because without it,
there is a absence of you.
I believe in you,
because without you,
there is a absence of me.

Wake up Call

God watched us as we got our wake up call.
As he watched our world come to a halt.
He seen the fear in all of our eyes and hearts.
Did God cry, as he watched his children die?
This must of hurt.
To see a human falling, how could this be?
Such an acto of hatred, malice, and destruction
was unknown in this kind of world.
A time to stay forever in our minds, forever
to feel the heartache, sorrow, and pain.
To show us that Goodness, remembrance and
love shall never cease.
What is the world coming to, when you watch
a grown man cry?
Lives were torn apart and now dreams will
never be dreamt.
How can this be?
Bravery has not been questioned.
Somehow our freedom and safety was put to
the test.
So many emotionally overcome by death and
destruction.
We have found our faith in God again.

The "Angel" with Tears

Up in the sky, within the clouds, stands an angel
Watching over us all.
Her eyes are open, to all that is seen.
She says a prayer, for us all.
To know that there is grief and some of us
Are grieving, for she knows this feeling for
She has been there once.
She has felt and heard all that there is
To be, here on earth,
But when she was one earth she didn't
Understand then like she doesn't understand
Now.
She tries to hold the tears back, and not
To let God see.
She knows that there is different kinds of
Tears, tears of joy and tears of hurt.
She looks down upon us, with intentions
Of helping, but she does not know where to
Start.
She tries to look inside herself, and she begins
To cry.
She does not know if this is dismay or another
Feeling to be displayed.
She wants to yell tell and help us learn our
Lessons, with encouragement and truth.
She wants to make a path for us to follow,
So our hearts do not stray.
For she sheds another tear, when one of God's
Children are headed the wrong way.
She tries to scream out the guidance to over
Come their thoughts and darkness.
She blames herself for the things she can not
Change or has no path for them to take.
She wants to reach down to us and hold us
By our hand, to walk beside us in all that we do.
She wants us to listen to the message that lays
Within our hearts.
But what we didn't know she wants to hear them to.

Marie E. Hoag Banks

Keeper of My Heart

From the day I met you
I have known right from the start,
The very moment I saw you,
You'd be the keeper of my heart.

The search for you seemed endless,
I never thought I would find,
Such a rate intelligent beauty,
You were always on my mind.

I dream of kissing those voluptuous lips,
And to gaze into those pretty eyes,
I long to caress that gorgeous face,
My feelings I can't disguise.

I can make this promise,
My love for you is true.
No more will your heart be broken.
No more crying will you do.

I promise you'll be happy,
You'll be kept from harm,
To you I will give all of my love,
You will be safe and warm.

We'll love each other deeply,
From now and for all time,
I'll be the keeper of your heart,
And you'll be the keeper of mine.

Mirror

I looked in the mirror, this morning
I looked at my eyes, but all I could
see, was me.
My intention was to look in the
mirror to see if I could find you there.

Mirror

I found myself, with your shirt,
then me inside your shirt.
Then I looked in the mirror,
to see what I would find.
I found myself seeing you
with me.

Mirror

I look in the mirror, to wonder
what is on my mind.
Bud do whom do I find?
I find you there, so deep in
thought with no fear.

Mirror

I see the reflection in the mirror,
of the water that is in the sink.
I thought I saw you there, behind me,
but then I blinked.

Can you see the love in the
mirror, from me?

A Nation Under Fear

We thought our country was at peace,
till that September morning.
No good-byes or emotions showed.
No tears were cried, to let our loved
ones see, just how much they would
be missed.
The cries that did cry out, were not
heard by us.
A nation in terror we could not belief.
Just so many tears of disbelief.
We thought that our soil would not feel
the rage.
Our skies were blackened, by ashes and
debris.
Such thunder had ripped through the skies.
Pieces of paper flew through the sky,
like confetti, but found their way to other
parts of the city.
We thought our nation was under attack.
Our religion, ethnic, opinions, disagreements,
and hatred are put aside.
So much unspoken anger now lies within.
But much to their surprise, we all unified
and gave of ourselves.
That is what our nation is about.

The winds we sail

Let's catch a wind, upon the sea.
To take us to that destination unknown.
Our troubles will disappear, just blown
away by the winds.
A never-ending whispering breeze.
We see the sunset, the horizon together,
no matter how big or small.
We will never walk alone in our hearts.
Giving each other the love we desire.
Let's go to a place, that is yours and mine.
A place where our love will grow, by just
being one.
Our love is made of promises, that will
never end.
The stillness of our bodies, causing a sensation.
Knowing we are together forever and always.
Our hearts beat faster, with each embrace.
I want to find a place in your heart,
just for me.
So through endless winds and nights unknown,
we can be together forever more.
Not knowing where the winds will take us,
but letting our time together is precious.
So lets go to a destination unknown by the winds
or by man, then we can make time stand still.

Light of His Life

She was the light of his life,
His one true love for sure.
The thought of life without her,
Was too painful to endure.

He spent some time away from her,
It was but just one week.
He missed her so in every way,
And longed to touch her cheek.

That week he did realize,
How she was needed in his life.
And vowed upon his return,
She would be his wife.

The journey seemed forever,
On his return trip for home.
He thought of her constantly
His love had surely grown.

He imagined how it would be,
When he debarked the plane.
They each would rush to waiting arms,
They would once again be sane.

When he arrived at his home,
It was instant bliss.
They were enfolded in each other's arms.
Their lips met in a kiss.

He looked deep within her eyes,
They were a beautiful baby blue.
And asked her to marry him,
To her he would be true.

This is a familiar story,
My pretty precious Marie.
No one will ever love you,
Quite as much as me.

There is something always on my mind,
These thoughts of you and me.
You are indeed my everything,
You are my fantasy.

Please don't worry about how you look,
I do not really care.
The only thing that matters is,
That you are always there.

I'll love you no matter what,
If are fat or thin.
No matter what scars you bear,
What counts is what's within you.

Compassion is Still Alive

We thought compassion had seen its days.
How did we know just how much it came to
surface on that September day.
The unification of our country has begun to
surface.
Everyone felt all the emotions that could be
felt and will always linger in our memory.
Though times are tough and troubled,
we all seemed to reach deep within.
Some gave of themselves, to help find loved
ones and friends who had vanished,
physical labor in vain.
We should believe
"Be kind to one another."
We hope our words and prayers will
somehow console the grieving.
Someone is searching for those who
are still left behind, still in search of
finding someone's loved one, to put their
cries to rest.
For there are so many heroes of that day.
But don't ask them if they want that title
for that is just who they are.
Compassion is still alive.

Dream

I had a dream since I was young,
to have a love so true.
I have now found that love,
a beautiful woman, you.
You were the one I idealized,
the one I would always love.
No one could mean as much to me,
you were sent from God above.
I never thought I could feel this glow,
so deep within my heart.
You are the one I love so dear,
from you I could never part.
I thought for a very long, long time,
you would never be,
enfolded in my waiting arm,
you are the world to me.
Now that I have found you dear,
I fear our love will be lost.
This strikes such pain within my heart,
I would keep you at any cost.
So tell me dear what I can do,
to keep your love forever,
I need you so my dear Marie,
I could leave you never.
If I did not have your love,
Life's meaning would be lost.
Like a ship on a stormy sea,
I would be aimlessly tossed.
There is nothing I wouldn't do
My love for you has no end,
I need to hear these words my love,
You will always be my "M."
I love you very dearly M and I always will.

She Still Stands

She was declared a national monument.
As she stands on Ellis Island, to watch
over all of us.
As she stands in our sight she has never
been altered.
She has weathered many storms.
She has stood against all odds,
even on the tragic day of 9-11.
She has stood for credo for thousands
of immigrants, who came to America.
She has been our symbol for freedom
which terrorists did not attack.
She still stands
As once said "We are the keepers of the
flame of liberty" in which we all hold high.
We all still have so much gratitude, for one
of the wonders of this nation.
For she stands for our freedom, which we
have not lost yet.
The Statue of Liberty is here to stay.
She still Stands

Marie E. Hoag Banks

My Waterfalls

A place where I can go to. That no one can take from me.
A place that I know of and all my troubles are gone and
Set free.
A place where, beauty is in the eye of the beholder.
A place where I find calmness within my heart and mind.
A place where my words can scatter, then come rushing
Back to me like the water.
A place where there is no restrictions to be heard of.

Just where is this place? You ask of me..
Well this place is not too far from me. It can be just a ride
Away, just down the road.
Then other times I can stay at home and be in this place
Within my mind.
Picturing all the beauty and comfort that lies within.
I take all my feelings and emotions there with me.
Not knowing what they are going to be from day to day.
Just a thought away.

My fear turns to courage, my sadness turns to happiness.
My nightmares turn to daydreams, as I sit there and drift
Off into the waterfall.
The rainbow for that day, just might appear. But if it
Doesn't I really don't care.
I am just there to escape from reality at times..
You can kidnap me from this place, but never take it from
My mind.

I have spent many of days there. Just wishing and dreaming
Of things to come.
But someday, if you have a bad day or need company..
Just come to the "Waterfall" with me.
I will more than gladly take you.. To let it give you what
It has give me.

Fear felt across the nation

I could not believe my brother, as we talked
that morning.
He said "Sis, did you see the World Trade
Center, was just hit."
"What are you waiting for turn on your TV."
I could not believe my eyes, just so much
disbelief.
We sat there longer and then the second one
hit.
I fit numb and in a daze, for I did not know
what exactly to do.
I tried to reach for the phone. I did not know
who to call first.
Oh, this is the fear, that has been in the back
of my mind all these years,
since my son was born.
Did I say "I love you" before he walked out
the door, that morning.
I just could not remember.
I felt ashamed.
As the jets flew over, my heart came to a stop.
Did I tell someone else just how much I loved
him?
Oh God, how could I forget.
So before your loved one walks out the door.
Don't forget: To say those words
I Love You

America – Voices Coming Together

Joseph C. Carroll
Nichols, NY

Bridge's of Rigorous Faith

Destructive demolition / imperious smite.
Infrastructure of social repression.
Where demons preyed on the innocence taking plight.
A task to enforce terror. The red mars against the dusty bricks.
Smoldering grayish clouds from the smoke and fire relentlessly flicks.

There; Tears of the few who made it.
There; Tears for those heroes who sacrificed.
There; Tears from those whose loved ones lost there own.
There; Tears from those who felt the slaughter, the destruction,
the despair; together alone.

Can you hear the anger and frustration. The yelling; the crying.
The sickened, the fearful, the deceased, the dying.
Can you envision the distraught quitters.
Can you feel their fear.
Can you encapture the none witters.
On how onward they became there.

Though all as one encumbered in a United Force.
To incur there that of that partaketh asserting a new course.
Where inner strengths may find one God that reigns.
But beyond all its prayers that heals those internal pains.
And where those feelings and concepts: Love, integrity, devotion,
and commitment find.
Comfort and peace in kindness all in a matter of time.

For where resentment and bitter discourse are ensconced by the
unification of the reinvention of new peace and prosperity to restore.
Is where homage, solemn words, and embracing will someway implore.
For in our hearts; in our spirits; in our souls; and in our minds.
Where the toils of time and patience will endure what's left behind.
For now the act of placing kindling candle's in paper bags.
There to show respect in retrospect; high flying U.S. flags.
And there to show honor and courage against this act of neglect.
And there those that served and to protect.

For where broken vows and hearts will find the sanction of
insurrection and reprieval.
To relinquish and restore peace by retributed retrieval.
Where avenging justice against this malice injustice, nations
throughout.
To look forward to tomorrow; healing broken hearts; plighting
all doubt.

For what was and what is to become.
Torn nations allied as one.
Holding truths and realities.
Suppressing through time disharmony and disgrace.
Restoring new values our hearts embrace.
There pertaining to each and everyone in a different light.
Where honor and prayer can only endure what was lost that
day before that night.

God Don't Make Junk (Hymn song)

    God — God don't make junk.
    God — God don't make junk.
    God — God don't make junk.
When you're out; everything seems to be dreary.
When you're down; everything can be weary.
When you're at a loss; everything may be scary.
When everything inside you seems to be leery.
    Now you're feeling blue and you're all — alone.
    All amongst people still in that — zone.
    Perilous plight has taken what you be known.
    Resilience of your spirits seem to have flown.
So you may have an incurable illness.
Or plagued with irreprehensible responsibilities.
Where you find others have limitations and incapability's.
Or where there's death, disease, or despair.
Only to mar the things that don't seem as they appear.
    Some of us are burdened from the start.
    Some of us are sheltered from apart.
    Well we somehow got to find our own heart.
    For in every hardship that there may be.
    To find vision where we are to blind to see.
    Where there is just one reason to believe.
    Where there is no contest when we can reprieve.
Cause God — God don't make junk.
Cause God — God don't make junk.
Cause God — God don't make junk.
    If we at least can try to believe!

Unsung Heroes

Heroes's through integrity and might.
Where perseverance and determination became a right.
For where conditions there of become of blight.
Is where few relentlessly prevail rectifying against any fight.
As any situation that occurs under unforeseen circumstance's;
a guiding light.
As by ones persistence and fearlessness becomes instinct beyond
insight.

For by their dedication and honor in that instant of time.
Is where by which those who served to protect as a duty out of
line.
For they where the ones' who sacrificed so that other's would
survive.
For they were the ones' whose life's were cut short before
those of them that died.
As there that be noted that ones' courage against atrocities is
to remind.
Is where that be quoted: There are few and at time's so many that
deserve this sign.
       (Unsung Heroes)
      Not Forgotten.
          Not Left Behind.

Joseph C. Carroll

"United In Our Hearts, We Will Always Stand Together"
By Joseph Carroll

Reconciliation Day

A day in spirit for remembrance of those to reflect.
There of what has occurred when on that day of neglect.
To find solitude and stature of uniting as one.
To recognize the young, the free, the brave who did not
deserve what has become.
For that day of reckoning we strike our hearts in a solemn ness vow.
Of what and whom that broke apart of a peaceful country we
still have now.
And where we will find our hands joined together nations apart.
An inseparable salutation for the sanctity of this parable to embark.
One's integrity.
Where burdened unforeseen hardships find wisdom and courage as
a constitutional priority.
For its the respect we have; vowing to those of whom that died.
Clasping our hands in prayer for strength, hope, faith, and pride.
For those who served; for those ensemble in that enrapturement.
And those whose tragic relations suffer grief and despair.
To find resilience within ourselves and all that we do.
For what brought us apart to bring together and renew.
There to find justice through resistance in our hearts
uniting prosperity throughout.
To become one as a whole within this bout.
In recognition on this day that has become:
A moment in silence; a time to reflect.
Clasped hands in prayer; reverence in retrospect.
Where liberty and justice may find; Freedom and Peace left behind.
Where a virtue may become a new light, a new way.
That be solemnly recognized as <u>Reconciliation Day</u>.

Befeld Heritage

Broken spirits from within side.
Where the heart beats nil of what there is denied,
Faces of disguise of what one conveys or despise.
For if you don't envision the trues the rest is a pack of lies.
Oh broken spirit.
Oh broken pride.
From what truth the heart beholds to subside.
Though may you find peace from the torrid conditions.
And may you find perspectives and virtues from
new renditions.
And where contemptuous nature idles time and
patience into disharmony and grief.
Is where time in haste, unfulfilling objective's avenges nothing
but time as an idol and belief.
Through patience in time through one's passive provisions
renovates the passions of what prevails in one's heart
to be sought.
For where condemnation beguiles nothing if personal
forgiveness and homage is not wrought.
Where the iniquities of an imperious and impoverish nature
by the incisive incredulous act find people immotile
by uniting as done.
For the people that we have become.
Is by the people that restore as one.
Where of the people a bond to renounce such
disharmony to plague.
Are as we the people find peace and solitude to overtake.
For the arraignment of such an uncivil contemplated
conniving act.
Find the reigns of soldiers and the eradication of justice to
restore peace and bring it back.
For he who exhausts themselves amongst others
to plague and destroy
Will find all eyes rationalizing vengeance until not one bad
seed will employ.
For what those that did where and when.
And those whom justice pertains is sought as to what there
was to contend.
For this course of action that has rescinded infidelity
amongst all.
Is where we may find refuge in hopes and be stilled fears in
what is earnest, moral, descent, and righteous
making the call.
Where a restitution for refinement to restore God's will
once more.
Where the peace, innocence, and the prosperity became
stolen like once before.
For by which course of reaction of peace was lost.
For the disenabling restoration of all
which retracted a plighting cost.
There to find <u>Befeld Heritage</u> of those targeted social steeples.
Is only to find where hearts that were broken is only until
we became of the people.

Samantha Lynn Edwards
Age 15
Callicoon, NY

What's Happening

Our world is falling down in shame
and all anyone wants to do is point the blame.

Can no one see what kind of life we're setting for our children,
nothing but a world of hurt
and a world of pain?

We try to raise our kids right,
to not judge people by their skin,
dark or light.
We try to raise them with respect
and give them what they need threw out life,
so why is it now that nothing is right?

Many of our views have changed,
nothing is right.
Our world is insane.
Most of the views we set for our children
have been almost completely erased.
Places we always thought were safe,
we're not so sure about anymore.
We're once again fearing who may come knocking on our door.

Is this the kind of life we want our kids to live,
fearing every shadow,
killing what may have someday been a possible friend?

We need to fix things,
we need to make things better,
our world needs to be right again,
our kids need a good life again.

Tears of Sorrow

A Blink of an Eye
By Samantha Lynn Edwards - age 15
Callicoon, NY

Time passes us by,
within a blink of an eye,
young are born everyday,
as well as loved ones passing away.

We celebrate the birth of our young,
and we morn the death of our loved ones,
hoping both will be happy and at peace.

All of this can happen within a blink of an eye,
and within another blink,
it could be us,
that our loved ones are saying good bye to.

You should cherish every moment of your life,
good and bad,
and live your life to the fullest,
for you may not have another day to do so.

Rose Germano
Age 39
Salem, MA

Terrorism

Why
Obliterate
Ruins
Leveled
Destroyed

Terror
Ravage
Attack
Devastation
Evacuate

Courage
Eclipse
Nightmare
Teamwork
Emotional
Rescue

Persevere
Eleventh
Noble
Necessary
Sacrifice
Yesterday
Loved Ones
Victory
Airplanes
Nevermore
Integrity
Angels

Proud
Extreme
News
Terminate
Aftermath
Ghastly
Offensive
Nation

Attack On America

Senseless
Eye-opener
Pentagon
Terrorism
Excessive
Murdered
Bravery
Eerie
Reality

Eleven
Lost Lives
Eliminated
Valor
Elude
Numb

Tears
World Trade Center
Orphans

Tragedy
Heroes
Outrage
Unite
Shock
Anger
Naïve
Death

Old Glory
New York
Enemy

For those who died,
For those left behind....
God Bless.

A True Hero

Dedicated
Original
Magnificent
Integrity
Noble
Incredible
Caring
Kind

Patriotic
Exceptional
Zest
Zeal
Understanding
Loyal
Officer

Proud
Outstanding
Reliable
Terrific

Acceptance
Unique
Thoughtful
Hero
Old Glory
Rescuer
Important
Trustworthy
Youthful

Protector
Observant
Loved
Immeasurable
Children
Empathy

Optimistic
Family
Friends
Impressive
Courage
Easy-going
Rare

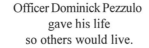

Officer Dominick Pezzulo
gave his life
so others would live.

Delores J. Howard & Steven G. Morris
Middletown, OH

The American Flag
By Delores J. Howard

She's very, very beautiful,
With eyes of midnight blue.
Fifty stars light them so bright
They see the whole world through.

Her dress of red and white
Depicts blood and purity.
Blood of brave defenders
That fought to keep her free.

She's an emblem of heroism,
With a long, majestic story.
So many died to protect her,
While others abused her glory.

But she's STILL proudly waving,
An example for me and you.
She's very strong and determined,
She's RED, WHITE, and **true** BLUE!

She represents so much,
She represents us ALL,
Even at half-mast,
She's never stood so tall.

God has given her to us,
And blessed her from above.
Just like our Heavenly Father,
Her banner over us is LOVE!

Creation
By Steven G. Morris

My soul is the center of the Universe.
The soul of the Universe is GOD.
Therefore, what matter makes the stars always makes me.
And He who makes the stars, has made me, from the stars and in His image.
And I am of the earth and stars and I am of His image.
I am man.

A Hero
By Delores J. Howard

A hero is a special one
Who puts another "greater."
A hero is a selfless one
Much like his great Creator.

A hero is a hero
To family, friend, or stranger.
A hero stays as others flee
In the fearsome face of danger.

A hero doesn't take time to think
Before he counts the cost.
He leaps to help, immediately,
Before someone is lost.

A hero not only risks his life
To save another sole,
A hero would sacrifice himself
For the good of the greater whole.

A hero will go down
Defending right from wrong.
A hero's strength is born of God.
It's MORE than "big" or "strong."

A hero is a courageous one
Who's nature is bold OR mild.
A hero is male or female,
A man, a woman, or child.

A hero feels really sad
If unable to protect the lot.
He wishes he'd done so much more
After giving the best he's got.

God's Glory?
By Steven G. Morris

Could someone please tell me
Just what is the story
Of a murderous rampage
And then call it God's glory?

Intolerance of others
Is it the rule of today?
Just live your own life
And let me be on my way.

We were put on earth
As brother to brother.
Christians, Muslims, and Jews
Are supposed to love one another.

When you slaughter the innocent
Just to prove YOUR own way,
I wouldn't want to be YOU
Whence comes "Judgment Day!"

The Velvet Touch
By Delores J. Howard

America has THE VELVET TOUCH,
A nation under GOD.
Founded on Holy principles,
And built on sacred sod.

America has THE VELVET TOUCH,
We're a major melting pot.
There's people all over the world
Longing for what we've got.

America has THE VELVET TOUCH,
When it comes to aiding allies.
Willingly helping nations
When their faith is us relies.

America has THE VELVET TOUCH,
We're a freedom loving nation.
But one for all and all for one
When needed retaliation.

VELVET is a soft, supple,
Warm and squishy feel.
But under America's velvet touch
Is a frame of SOLID STEEL!

Linda Hutson
Age 47
Gilbert, AZ

The Search

Spiraling silence may surround
With such a splendorous sound
Spinning round and round.
Round and round
Just above the ground,
Searched but never truly found.

Shoebox

Whilst existing in disharmony upon this pinhead sized planet,
Knowingly in orbit within an ever expanding oblong entity,
Just wonder, who holds this box shaped universe in his hand?
The form of great fame, it is to be hoped,
But hope too that his gesticulations remain playful!
That he should not tire of his toys.
He might easily reveres his multitudinous,
Glittering toy marbles from within that box
To be jettisoned into nothingness.
No-one would surely have nothing then –
In the end.
So perhaps one should relish
Each and every second as it passes,
Even love thy neighbor.
Diminish too, the abusion of this planet's wonders,
Where timeless beauty still abounds.
Perhaps with thoughts that, perhaps...
It doesn't all lie in our own hands!

The Notion of Motion

Allusively, Time will never stand still.
Try to stop it,
But you never will.
Just like water
Running down the window pane.
It has a pace that will never falter.

You might get the notion,
Just standing still
Could coerce a halt to time's motion.
It would need to be said,
If all did adopt such a pose,
We would all indeed be dead.

So hinder as you will, happily,
Weighted only by the force of fate.
And fall toward the lake of greater density,
Whilst simply and briefly, watching.
As the ocean continues to fling itself,
Unknowingly toward recreating creation.

Quiescent Vibrations

Invisible but connecting
As a string from thing to thing.
Strong as an adobe brick,
Or weak,
As a whispering wind
On which a hawk soars happily heavenward.
Such strings are the connecting threads
Essential apparently to existence.
Consummating human to human,
Chord by chord, charismatic music between.
To a vibration with strength to be heard and held,
Quiescent, electron to electron.
Transcended by an acquiescence of theories,
Quantum to relativity, particle and force.
"The final theory." Peace everlasting?
So essential to the existence of just everything.
But so beyond and above the complexities of science!

Progress

Historically the human race has achieved
With such ease, such physical atrocities!
As the Millennium drew near,
Mankind promised there was nothing to fear.
Except perhaps such incompatibilities as
Confusion amongst our computers.

For myself, I did hope that Humanity
Realized perhaps that New Year, with gentility,
We had been blessed with 'another chance,'
In order to use lessons badly learnt in the past.
January 1, 2000, approached and went very fast.
Supposedly the rebirth of Progress?

As tentative and uncertain as the growth of a rosebud,
So desperate under sunlight to be nurtured.
Fragile and so sweet smelling in its naivety,
Oh that we may still return to softness in reality.
Peace and humility of action could yet emerge,
As happily as petals may unfurl with renewed courage.

The Family of Christopher Lowe

Up In Arms
By Shannon J. Francis - age 28

Up in arms are we
Full of fear, angry
That so many could be taken
Without warning or knowing
This country, vulnerable, running scared
Not knowing how to heal
This is the end time, it's real
Armies forming, battles raging
As babies are born, people aging
I look at the flags hanging high and proud
Like an American commemorative shroud
They put flags up where Jesus should be
It's sad that it took a tragedy for people
To realize how lost we could be without the
Lord to set us free.

September 11
By Genevieve C. Hubbard - age 24

A desperate plea comes at me through my TV screen,
"Please come and donate blood."
One would think there was some grand prize at the end of this
line, with the amount of people gathered.
From somewhere behind me I heard
"I haven't seen you in so long!" and turn just in time to
see two lost friends reunited.
Something so basic had returned to us that day,
a sense of community.
Our only common bond a tragedy, but I see many new
friendships starting here.
And that sort of thing always makes my heart smile.
A young man hands me a pin that says
"United We Stand,"
and I feel a rush of pride that momentarily quiets my grief.
Because today we do stand together,
proud and free.

A Letter on a Grave
By Ashleigh S. Woods - age 25

I miss you, I need you to come home;
Dad is so sad now, feels empty, alone.

I miss your stories, I miss your laugh;
Your love for us so evident in each photograph.

I know a part of me is gone for good;
Dad says he would take your place, if only he could.

My young mind won't forget this date;
Or will it comprehend that much hate.

We watched it from across the river;
Helpless we could do little but quiver.

I waited and waited for you to pick me up that day;
I never knew my heart and soul could ache this way.

I do my best to give young David a reason;
So sad you will miss his first winter season.

I can't watch the news or see one more image;
I still looked for you at my football scrimmage.

The dog mopes around, all broken hearted and blue;
I swear she needs you as much as we do.

All who knew you are overwhelmed by grief;
You touched so many in a life so brief.

I miss you Mom, I feel so all alone;
Only you can fill this void in our home.

I love you Mom, Daniel

Attack On Our Land
By Christopher J. Lowe - age 30

I am restless this night, my mind ablaze with horrific images.
The terrorist attack upon our land has left a deep crater both within the earth and in every American's heart.
Like most, September 11 was a day of shock and confusion for me.
Even days later, I try to fathom the depths of this attack and how our land is forever changed.
As the buildings crumbled before the eyes of the world my thoughts shift to those persons familiar to me from the New York area.
Matt Tanner, the truest form of friend, was he caught in the wake of this destruction?
Liz Thaler, she with the whole Brooklyn attitude, was she all right?
By the evening of the tragedy, I'd heard from them both and they were indeed safe.
Yet in the wake of their safety, I felt dishonorable because I was worried about those whom I knew only....
On September 11th, I lost over five thousand of my fellow countrymen.
Men, women, and children all perished for what, because someone feels that our freedom does them personal harm.
If these terrorists want to promote change within their land, do not approach us with violence.
Instead, come to our land and speak to us with conviction in your voice.
Do not attempt to make us change because of your discomfort with our society.
Every American knew someone or is associated with someone who died in Tuesday's massacre.
My thoughts go out to those whose lives abruptly ended that day with the destruction of our landmarks.
There are those who would call the World Trade Center or the Pentagon a National Treasure lost.
However, as the buildings lay crumbled upon the ground, the treasure lost was the culture residing in those unfortunate souls.
I think the best words, the most heart-felt to explain the price of today, were uttered by a six year old girl in Washington D.C.
She innocently mentioned to the population of the United States
that many children would be without their Mommies and Daddies this night.
In her eyes this would be the worst tragedy she could fathom as
she held her mother's hand tightly.
In her words she filtered out the overlaying politics involved, and made the damage of this day clear.
Our fellow Americans will never again be coming home to dinner, their houses will never again be filled
with their joy, their children's eyes will never again sparkle for their playful antics on Christmas morning.
We cherish our freedoms dearly and we work very hard to keep them established.
If you are not satisfied with culture in which you live, come live with us and make your life among us.
You claim that your religion deemed these events upon us and you were justified in your actions.
This can only be true if you do not understand the words before you, no religion would openly call for the persecution of others.
Be this the Koran, the Bible, or any other religious foundation, there is no mention of this justification you claim.
I pity you all for your part in this attack, for your religious salvation will never come as you hope.
As Americans, we are now faced with a difficult decision of how to respond.
Our actions must be strong to show our rage, but well planned to gain the support of the world.
It has been said that 62 nations lost some number of civilians on Tuesday, the world has been awakened by this vicious act.
The next steps which we take will cost many lives regretfully, but we've been driven to this impasse not of our own accord.
Yet, deep within the bowels of the planning rooms, let us be sure to account for the innocent souls in these terrorist nations.
Let us not repeat the actions of Tuesday with a different justification, for we will be no better than those responsible.
It is regretful that we've been forced to this point, we must avenge ourselves,
but let our revenge cost the world as few Mommies and Daddies as possible....

God Bless America

Lillian M. O'Neal
Age 63
Jamaica Plain, MA

A Tribute to Heroes

Father Mychal Judge

Mourn not for me for I am about God's work.
I could not let them go to Heaven alone.
I still had to sit and pray with them.
As shattered bodies, left behind.
Rose up into Heaven and they were made whole.

Mourn not for me for I have so much I want to do...
God has opened up His arms for me to rise above.
For just like on earth I always do...what I have to do...

Mourn not for me for I have others here by my side.
God had set things in motion,
As soon as the devil, had set his course.
While my vocation was "a rebuke to the act of hatred"
I was drawn in.
A world of pain, a world of sorrow...
A world of hatred like I have never seen before.

Rejoice for I am home...we are home now...
God has told me that I have done what I was sent to earth to do.
For in my death I helped to draw a nation...
To draw a country and to draw a world together
For peace...comforted and love...
In my death there was life...in my life there was love...
In my giving there was sharing...
In my prayers there was comforting
In my blessing there was peace...
In my placement there was a reason...

My death came swift in the line of duty...
My life was easy...my friends were many...
There was a reason, for God to place me there, by your side...
There was a reason, why God moved me here into the skies...
There was a reason why; I now, must heed His call...

Mourn not for me...I have and had been always about God works.
Even when I was on earth and now...even more...here in Heaven...
I will be at your side;
Whether you're asleep, or awoke...you will be in my prayers.
For in death there is life...a new beginning...a new faith...
a new hope, for better tomorrows
and I will do, what I always do...

In Memory of Father Mychal Judge
Hook and Ladder 24

Proud to be an American
To Mayor Giuliani

As death came in the forms of planes,
Buildings now directly in their lanes,
No time to react...no time to react...
As building burn and crumble now towards the ground.
As people in disbelief stood all around...

A mayor stood by his city in a time of pain.
As he counted minutes, counted hours, and still he remains.
To give support in their times of grief,
In times of need, in their time of loss.
What could they have gains and what was the cost?
So "Proud To Be An American" he repeats again and again.
As he now brings his people together in strength,
In unity, and he still remains...
So many hours without sleep...
From one end of his city to the other,
He walks this vigilance he must keep...
On that day he stepped into the light...
as his true colors now, are shining bright.
What more can he do as he holds hands, sheds tears,
Gives love, shows support, and gives hugs,
A new bond now takes hold of a city
Flows into a nation as it spreads out of this love,
He now shows...
While others look into his eyes of tears,
Through the eyes of courage into the heart of a man,
Numb, he feels the losses as he stands there not knowing.
Please don't give up;
Please don't give up as he sees the numbers growing.
Through untold courage, through untold stories
That he will, forever, relive.
As he gathers up his colors
He does not stop nor does he ever quite.
As this mayor shows support and shows his colors of solidarity,
Deep within his soul, he now must gather up his colors of strength.
Deep within his soul he must now gather up
His colors of courage to mend their shattered dreams.

Doesn't he know that God called them home?
Doesn't he know that they have done what they had to do on earth?
Doesn't he know that out of this...will come a new birth?
Doesn't he know that weren't promised another day, another year?
Doesn't he know that on this day, God fought the devil in His own way?
Doesn't he know that they are only a call away?
Doesn't he know...doesn't he know?
How much this Mayor is loved
For his colors of true strength he now shows.
Because he told his people
That they must rise above and show their love...
As a city in pain comes together as one, in an equal cause.

What do you say to this Mayor?
How can you ease this kind of pain?

You tell him this...
Doesn't he know that there were reasons why?
God chose him and He placed him by their side?
At that time...in that second...in that minute...
in that hour...in those days?

Doesn't he know?
Doesn't he know?
Doesn't he know?

God Shared With Them

"To heroes who step into the light when they are called."

God said let Me share with them My heart...
So He waved His hands over their chest and it was done.
Then God said let Me share with them My knowledge...
So He sprinkled water over their foreheads and this was done.
God said let Me give them a soul like no other...
So He moved the spirit into them.
Then God said let Me show them peace and love...
And with this He blew a kiss oh so gently through the air...
And it landed on their cheeks and they become warm to the touch.

Then God said let Me teach them My ways of forgiveness...
And this too was done.
God stepped back and looked at all He had accomplished...
And He was please beyond all measures.

Now let Me see if there might be something I have forgotten...
I have given them a heart...knowledge...a soul...
And I have shown them peace and love...
I have taught them how to forgive...

Yes...yes...memories...I must put them in place too...
So that they will never be forgotten, even in, others subconscious minds...
With that God flooded their minds and their spirit absorbed all the rest...
And this was good...

Then when He knew all things were in place...
He said now let's see, "one by one He gave them names...
Each one of them possessed a confidence, strength, and courage unmatched.
Because one day you will enter the Green Berets and you will be spoken of...
Therefore you...I...will call (Sgt. First Class) Daniel Petithory... you (Staff Sgt.) Brian...
Cody Prosserl...you (Master Sgt.) Jefferson Donald Davis.
And these words will burn in your heart...*DE OPPRESSO LIBER*...
it's meaning *TO FREE FROM OPPRESSION*

...you Frank Burlingame III
For the honor that you will bring in time of trouble

...and you...mum...Johnny Michael Spann, for the soul I see in you...

And when He was finished He sent them down to earth...
With the understanding that when they had done all
That He had asked them to do...
He...God...would call them back home to be with Him.

So that they might share with Him about their challenges...
So that they might share with Him how they fought with the devil and won...
So that they might share with Him their knowledge...

So that they might share with Him how they learned to forgive...
So that they might share with Him their hearts...
So that they might show Him their soul...
and now...how they have found peace and love with Him...

Yet somewhere along the way they became Heroes...
and like all of God's own Heroes they were given a Heroes Honor...
Both on earth and there in heaven.
and these things moved God...
He was pleased at all that they had accomplished...
With what He had given them...

Then, God said, I will...make you their Guardians,
until they are beside you here in heaven.
And God stepped back raised His arms and this too was done...
He looked once more and He was pleased...

For these Heroes were apart of Him and they will never be alone...

America – Voices Coming Together

The Young Family
Neenah, WI

Life's Dance
By Ann Young

Days can be crowded by expectations
bored players never really knowing
most people have their own battles
noxious weeds of life that just keep growing

In the distance the sun peeks
over a horizon watered with tears
the journey is long and some turn back
    in pain and sorrow
for to glimpse more of the sun could take years

My hand is in yours, yours in mine
yet I wonder if you couldn't see my face
if time shatters dreams and steals visual presence
could you tell my hand never left its place

Energy-a complicated thing
yet so simple for all we know
the pluses and minuses of ourselves
permeate and create a new soul

God saw what he made in clear view
    of abstract clutter
    and it was good
He the Worthy Master of Life's Dance
uncertain the dancers bow to Him
as they take the floor
for
He counted them worthy of the chance.

For all the people who help others look for the sun.

Heroes of Our Time
By Ann Young

We were going to be the heroes of our time
our hearts yearning, hands willing
everything is bright for all we see
Please pass the world
it's our turn to hold the key

We were going to be the heroes of our time
the masters of the wealth
with self-doubt, material paralysis
we couldn't even save ourselves

Hollywood created the movies of past heroes
but changed facts to move movies off the shelves
Like the real life ordinary
was never incredible in itself

Raised on criticism
we grew bent and twisted trying to reach for the sun
still we'd straighten to save the world
our generation would be the one

Yet we were never told of diseases
we couldn't pronounce
enemies we never hated
the chemicals in our foods
the super heroes that were jaded

We were going to be the heroes of our time
trying to fill an insatiable craving
now our kids say it's them who'll
have to do the saving

The heroes of our time
did we even get to stir the pot?
We tell our children, "Soups on....
and we hope you like it....hot!"

    To Brent, Michelle, and Monica's Generation
    Peace & Love

What I Gather
By Ann Young
Neenah, WI

Someday when the brants fly
beneath the faithful sun
when the lusty mammoth of materialism
is no longer pointing the gun

with things slipping through our hands (and minds)
we-frantically hunting for our souls
find the pot we used for gathering
was a mere sieve....full of holes

we'll give birth to our spirits
learning we're sent with all we need
that we were running on the world's "rat wheel"
never getting closer to succeed

stepping out of life's endless queues
realizing I don't need a turn
for you-my life's most precious cargo
are impossible to earn

I'll thank the One who bestows the gifts
trusting finally in the Spirit that tends
knowing the only thing worth gathering here
is a love that never ends.

Dedicated to the Soul that jumped from heaven with me, Dave!

September 11
By Michelle Young - age 8

When this sorrowful day came
the foundation was not the same
we are happy that some people survived
we are sad that some people died.
September 11, the day our hearts cried.

U-S-A
By Brent Young - age 12
Neenah, WI

U-S-A
United States of America
Or are we united?
Republicans and Democrats
always arguing
Comedies teasing
Our president
Economy slumping
Parties bumping
Comes an act of evil
U-S-A
Unifed States of America

What I Always Pray For
By Dave Young
Neenah, WI

What I always pray for is
my family's health, happiness, and safety.
What I lived for too much
was to provide to excess at the cost of access.
Tragedy can focus ones self to
what is important in life.
Time can help heal tragedy, but
I don't want time to lessen the lesson
of tragedy.

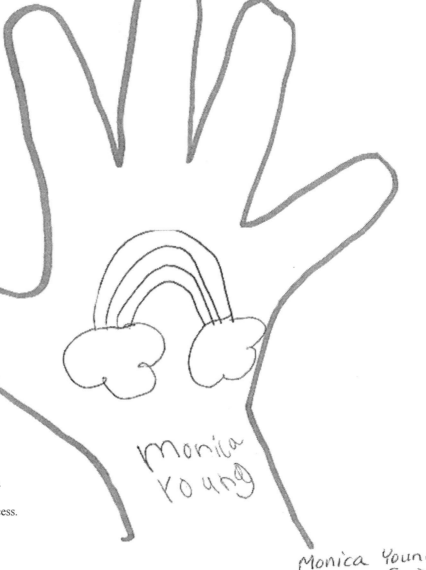

America – Voices Coming Together

New York City, Sept. 14, 2001.
White House photo by Paul Morse

"Now, we have inscribed a new memory alongside those others.
It's a memory of tragedy and shock, of loss and mourning.
But not only of loss and mourning. It's also a memory of
bravery and self-sacrifice, and the love that lays down its life for
a friend—even a friend whose name it never knew."
President George W. Bush

About the Author

Biographical information of authors with a after their name.

Fighting fires burning in the rubble of World Trade Center Building #7.

Akhter, Shahira - I'm seventeen years young, I'm from Ranchi, a city in India but live in Delhi, capital of Republic of India. I am one of those typical taureans you know (or maybe don't!) because I am diligent, have a stubborn temper, loyal and tend to get egoistic sometimes. O.k. now for the things I like doing...I write a lot, do roller blading sometimes, read majorly, dig good music, freak out on Chinese food, and sleep a lot. Oh yeah I like stargazing too. When I was a kid I used to imagine myself as one of those stars because it must be feeling nice to be up there and looking down at everything happening. I have never really seen a major part of the world but among those places, which I have been to, I think New York rules! It's a sense of freedom you have out there and the sky's the limit. The feel for writing, I feel, comes from deep within...I can pen down my emotions, likes and dislikes is a very simple phrase or I can make it complicated. But unless I feel it, I don't think the writing is much worth...Poetry brings out the best and worst of me...it's beautiful yet painful, imaginative yet too real. My favorite writers include Satyajit Ray (an Indian writer), Ruskin Bond, Kahlil Gibran, T.S. Eliot, and Paulo Coetho. One of the best books I have read is the Diary of Anne Frank. There are not really a lot of people I relate to and so my circle of friends is small, I have always admired my Dad for everything he is, and everything that he isn't. If not for him, I probably wouldn't ever be writing...One of my negative traits is that everything that affects my closed ones, affects me. I wish I could change the world sometimes, someday, somehow...Wish that there would be a day when a black wouldn't feel the pain that has been given to him, a day when a man wouldn't kill another one in the name of religion and a day when you and me would wake up in a world oblivious to hatred and bloodshed. A day when dreams wouldn't remain in cases anymore...

Barrows, Keith (Pen name Mr. B) - Keith is from Palm Springs, California. I'm a very active sixty-eight year old silver Fox and I have been in the Hospitality Business all my life. I wrote a Hospitality textbook in the 70's, to do seminars for training in Hotel and Restaurants, now it is written in English and Spanish. My writing of all my poetry comes from my heart. I write from my heart, to make your heart happier, what you have never been able to say, from your heart, to your special "Love." I have had many poems published with great pride, and I really have only been writing poems, for about two years. Now my life is being fulfilled to make people happy.

Blake, Patricia Payzant - Born in Shelbourne, Nova Scotia. Patricia received a Bachelor of Science degree in Household Economics from Acadia University Wolfville, Nova Scotia. Before continuing on a career in Dietetics, starting with a position in Diet Therapy at the New Britain General Hospital in New Britain, Connecticut, Patricia returned to Canada in 1941, married in 1946 and remained in Nova Scotia until 1964. A widow with two children, she returned to New Britain and later married Biology teacher John Hodgson Blake. The two retired and moved to Stonington, Connecticut where they enjoyed the views and experiences offered by 19 wooded acres overlooking Long Island sound. The beauty of these surrounding inspired Patricia's writing which continued after a move to Naples, Florida twelve years ago. The lovely city of Naples, from its magnificent sunsets to the flamboyant Royal Poinciana trees continues to inspire her. Patricia is presently a member of the National Authors Registry.

Boyden, Christopher W. - Born January 4, 1952 in Orange, California as the first son of a United States Marine Corps. fighter pilot, this poet enjoyed his formative years in Hingham, Massachusetts, where Baseball was a religion and where God made ice just for Hockey Players! If he didn't make ice float on the ponds and lakes, they would have surely played Hockey underwater! He was awarded an Athletic Scholarship (Baseball, Football, and Hockey) and an Academic Scholarship to Phillips Andover Academy, in Andover, Massachusetts, by entering a Newspaper Boy Contest. The Poet, subsequent to his graduation from Phillips Andover Academy in 1970; attended Fairleigh Dickinson University, from which he graduated "Magna Cum Laude," in 1975, with University Honors in Political Science. He also, in 1974, won first place in the Villanelle Poetry Competition sponsored by the University's Literature Department. The Poet subsequently attended, Seton Hall Law School, from which he graduated "Cum Laude" in 1978. He was admitted to The New Jersey State Bar Association in 1978 and to The Florida State Bar Association in 1979. In 1979, the Poet established his own law firm in Palm Beach County, Florida, where he has been an active, practicing civil trial litigation attorney, divorce attorney, and a divorce mediator for the past twenty-two years. Mr. Boyden first began poetry writing in 1971, as a part of a cathartic and philosophical methodology in his ongoing attempt to fully comprehend and appreciate the true meaning of his life on this planet, and also with the sincere hope that his poetic meanderings might offer some encouragement, insight, and benefit to all fellow Earth-Bound travelers.

Burnside, Wanda Jacqueline - Born in Highland Park, Michigan to parents, Reverend and Mrs. Minor Palm, Jr. She is the oldest of three children: a brother Rodger and a sister Regina. The family moved to Detroit, Michigan in 1952. Education: 1972 graduate of the University of Detroit - B.S. in Humanities/Early Education. Attended William Tyndale and Charles H. Mason Bible Colleges in Michigan. She is certified in several Christian Ministries. Employment: Teacher/Grades K-7 in public and private schools in Michigan. U.S. Government Educational Researcher, Departmental Coordinator at Marygrove College in Michigan, NARA Coordinator for the U.S. Attorney's Office, Editor and Office Manager for Detroit Church World Magazine, Library Assistant in the Education Center at the

University of Detroit, Personnel Officer for Blue Cross-Blue Shield of Michigan, and Office Manager Bailey Cathedral COGIC. Published Author: Wanda has written 22 performed plays for children, nearly 100 poems, won three national recipe contests. She has self-published a gospel tract titled "Matchless Love" with 2,500 in print in the USA and Canada, "Lord Bless the Children" USA, Honduras and Canada, "A Prayer Can Reach Heaven" USA and Canada. Published in magazines and journals: *Christian Information Network, Standard, Evangel, Catholic Review, African American Journal, Totally Gospel, Gospel Truth, Weight Watchers, Faygo Beverage Cookbook, Recipes of Michigan,* and *Detroit Black Writers Guild Cookbook*. Poems in anthologies. Writing Honors: Over twenty writing honors and awards: Poetry Guild, Poets Society, Byline, and Broadside Press. 2002, 2001, 2000, and 1999 President's Award for Literary Excellence from the National Authors Registry, 2000 Second Place Browning Competition Awards Program, 1999 Christian Writer of the Year Award from the American Christian Writers Org., Best Poems of 1998 from the National Library of Poetry, Famous Poet for 1998 The Famous Poets Society, Editor's Choice Award, and Most Cherished Poems of the Western World. Memberships: The National Authors Registry, American Christian Writers, Detroit Black Writers' Guild, International Women Writers' Guild, and The Academy of American Poets. Member of Greater Miller Memorial COGIC. Married: In November 1972 to Mr. Simmie Lee Burnside, Jr.

Carreira, Maria Alice - Born March 6, 1962 in Portugal. I came to America in December 1985. I've been married for twelve years and I am a working mother. Have two beautiful angels, Carlos, nine and Daniel, four. I speak French. I lived in Belgium for five years and worked for British ambassador. In one occasion there, I met the future king of Belgium Prince Philippe. I like to write poems especially about children. I wrote "Missing Boy" which was published in the previous anthology *Journeys*. I am planning to write more in the future.

Cheatham-Shipman, Olivia (Pen name: LadyO) - Born October 12, 1965 in Bossier City, Louisiana at Barksadale Naval Air Force Base. Two children and hearts contented Robert Terrance and Michelle Monique. Many Honorable Mentions of scholastic and public service achievements. Arts & Entertainment New Music Seminar 1994; Show Biz Expo 1994-1998; American Biographical Institute - Woman of the Year 2001; International Biographical Centre - International Woman of the Year 1995. This year ABI acknowledges a World Biography Day (date of the birth October 12, 1965) calendar date was an entry; Aids walk, Housing Works Thrift Shops (charities) American Diabetes Association; Multiple Sclerosis Society; charities, volunteer, and work to serve. Prepping for Pallotta Team work 3 day Aids vaccine walk fund-raiser; fitness & nutrition diploma - PCDI; Ministerials - PULC listed in Marquis Who's Who; Independent studies and research programs census 2000; Social Services/Event Field worker.

ROTC Union Catholic Regional H.S. 1983. Vocations, tutorials, and all sports...OCS.

Falzone-Cardinal, Nancy L. - Nancy lives in Springfield, Massachusetts. She has a rewarding life with her husband James, foster elder Shirley Brown, Shih Tzu Randi, parrot Tamika, Pomeranian Cotton Candy, and rabbit Lily. Nancy is a Certified Activities Director working in both private and parochial schools. She enjoys writing children books, art, theater, and spiritual programs.

Gannon, Yvonne A. - I am a resident of Hawaii who has been blessed by so many people who believe in my work. Cader Publishing has presented me with the President's Award for Literary Excellence 2002 and four Honorable Mention Awards for my poems which can be found in their anthologies, *Awakenings, Bridges, Gatherings, and Acclamations:* The President's Award for Literary Excellence 2002. The Library of Poetry has presented me with two Editor's Choice Awards and my poems are published in their anthologies *The Harvest of Dreams* and *The Best Poems and Poets of 2001*. My work can also be found in *Soul Songs* published by Sunshine Press. My interest in photography goes hand in hand with my writing. My own photos accompany my original poems in Famous Poets Society's *New Millennium Poets* and *Our Millennium's Most Famous Poet's*. I also enjoy writing haiku, and am the Second Place Winner in the Haiku You Contest, *Chile Pepper Magazine* December 2001.

Gray, Jeffrey V. - Born August 27, 1965 in Long Branch, New Jersey. I currently reside in Aberdeen, New Jersey. Occupation: Substitute teacher and a minister. Education: Graduate Motaban Regional High School, 1984, B.A. Northeastern Bible College, 1989, M.R.E. Liberty Baptist Theological Seminary, 1993, and Th.M. Andersonville Baptist Seminary, 2001. Interests: Reading and writing poetry. I've had several poems published in various anthologies as well as received numerous awards for my work. "From Mourning to Joy" is based on Psalm 30, and the second part of verse 5. I believe that God put it on my heart to write this. I originally dedicated this to the families of those who lost their lives in Swissair Flight 811 a few years ago. Hopefully, this will be a poem of comfort to those in a difficult time of need.

Harwell, Judith - I became interested in writing, soon after I had a stroke in 1989. I had plenty of time just to think. I had trouble saying things that I wanted to say, but putting them on paper seemed to be easy. I had written an article for the National Stroke Association in 1994 titled, "Wheelchair Awareness Party." It was featured in one of their newsletter. Then I really had an interest. I wrote a poem later and had it published in a book called *Courage*. Since I have written several articles for the local newspaper and some I just keep. I have written three short stories for children that I would like to try to gave published someday. This is mainly a pastime as well as good therapy for me. It is something I really enjoy doing. Having a chance to have an article published in *America-Voices Coming Together*, is an honor for me and I am grateful for this opportunity.

Hillman, Aaron W. - Born in Chaffee, Missouri in 1926, raised in Ohio. Graduated from San Francisco State University with a B.A. and from the University of California Santa Barbara with a M.A. and Ph.D. He has been published in *Oyez Review, Maelstrom, The Honolulu Advertiser, In the Grove, Fauquier Poetry Journal, Scimitar and song, Mobius, The Vision: Native American Poetry Anthology, Rattle, The Villager, Flatbush, The University of Houston Forum, The Hartford Courant, Englophile,* and *Santa Barbara Book Review, among others.* Aaron resides with Rosemary in Fresno, California and enjoys reading, writing, watching ducks on the pond, and two scrub jays named Jock and Jill. He has moved from rhymed and metered verse to musing narratives.

Hoag Banks, Marie Elizabeth - Born in Cooperstown, New York. Grandparents: Mr. and Mrs. Lafayette Hoag and Mr. and Mrs. Leon Browning Parents: Douglas B. Hoag and Theresa Browning. I have eleven brothers and sisters. Douglas, Linda, Danny, Dennis, David, Michael, Damion, Jason, CaraLee, and Cassandra. My favorite animal was Peanut, she was a miniature German Shepard. I love to write poetry about God, animals, family, dreams, fears, accomplishments in my life, a love of my own. I have been writing poetry since I was twelve. The first poem I had published was called "Try to Understand." I am into my animals. I have a son Joseph Ryan Hoag and a grandson Joseph Ryan Hoag, Jr. I am a Residential Counselor. Army, three years of Business College, Child Development Aide and Registered for Child Abuse and Maltreatment. My favorite place is, Otsego Lake, where I love to write my poetry.

Hudkins, Ronald E. - Born June 12, 1951 in Canton, Ohio to parents Nevien and Catherine Hudkins. Graduated from Washington High School, Massillon, Ohio in 1970. He entered the United States Army Military Police Corps. where he served honorably until retirement December 1, 1993. During numerous assignments and between extensive travels, Ronald attended Kent State and Maryland Universities, Hagerstown Junior College and Central Texas College wherein the equivalent of an Associates Degree was compiled. He attended Blair College and entered the Paralegal Program. Ronald transferred to the University of Phoenix (Colorado Springs, Colorado) where he will complete a Bachelors of Science Degree in Information Technology. Ronald is likewise in Long Ridge Writers Group where he is enhancing a life long dream to become a writer of international notoriety. In a public release of poetry, Ronald received the President's Award for Literary Excellence 2001 for his literary work, "Transitions" which received Honorable Mention in the Spring 2000 Iliad Literary Awards Program. His first work was selected above thousands of poems and essays and recognized by the National Authors Registry for rare and outstanding creative talent. Proud of his distinction, Ronald says, "Perhaps this is the first step in an aspiring journey. I hope to write thousands of things to include books that will be honorably recognized in the future."

Hutson, Linda P. - Six years ago she followed her heart to Arizona. She was captivated by the indigo skies and vast vistas, enthralledrom sunrise to sunset and beyond, she couldn't leave. Thus the commencement of her love affair. "Arizona's Trails of Magique" was grasped from the raw breathtaking extremes contained within this one state, an attempt to capture moments of emotional magic which hang oh so briefly in time, in honor of Arizona's beauty. "Riding the Ripples" has been available for purchase for the past eighteen months. This inspirational and thought-provoking book of poetic prose explores the beauty, joy, sadness, and unpredictability of life. Commenting on "Riding the Ripples" Don Sorchych, publisher and editor of *Sonoran News* raves "Whether it is reflecting on the birth of Sunrise, a foal, or a glimpse of a desert dwelling creature-the rhythm and just the right words delight." He continues, "Ranging from chuckles to apprehension, emotions are stimulated-demanding a turn of the page-and another." An English woman of standard English education, is searching continuously within herself, whilst watching the world without, continues to strive to inspire an audience in thought and perhaps action with her continued writing. As a distinguished member of The International Society of Poets, she holds the International Poet of Merit and many other Editors Choice and Honorable Mention Awards. In both 1999 and 2000, she has received the prestigious President's Award for Literary Excellence from the National Authors Registry.

Idziak, Boniface - Born April 12, 1925 in Grand Rapids, Michigan, became a landed resident of Canada in 1962. He is a self-taught mineralogist and pros-pector who has dedicated his life to the wilderness and the preser-vation of nature. The father of five children (by his first wife, Margaret Melvin now deceased.) Mr. Idziak is also a proud grandfather of three, and great-grandfather of twelve. Mr. Idziak currently resides in Iron Bridge, Ontario with Virginia Rittenhouse of Hart, Michigan and his wife of forty-one years. Mr. Idziak is the author of the following

animal stories; *Hughie and Honey Bear*, *Hughie, Bow and Ruefus*, and *Hughie and Bow*, a series of three books concerning humor and antics of the Black Bear Cubs. Also author of *Big Paw* and *No Better Friend Has Man*. He is also writing stories about his tribulations of injustice between borders in his past mining venture. Mr. Idziak's books can be purchased off the Internet. Books for Pleasure any age. www.booksforpleasure.com. An author without an agent is like a sea captain without a ship.

Joshi, Manisha S. - Originally from Mumbai, India, Manisha was born in 1971 into a family of two older sisters, Heena and Smita, and loving intellectual parents, Uma and Arvind Vakil. When she was six months old, her family relocated to the United States over the years, Manisha began to tap into her natural writing abilities. Growing up in beautiful Southern California, she explored new subjects and styles in her work. At fifteen, Manisha and her family moved back to Mumbai to further enrich their Indian culture. Mumbai was the perfect place for a poetess - gorgeous sunsets, coastal views and a diverse population. Manisha began writing poems that enveloped real-life themes. Her first achievement was winning first place in the college literary contest. After graduating with a B.A. in Economics from Mithibai College of Arts, Manisha and her family moved back to Southern California in 1992, to pursue higher education. In 1994, Manisha published her first book, *Poetic Thoughts*, a collection of her writings in Mumbai. Selected poems were featured in local and national publications and she went on to win merit awards from the International Society of Poetry and the Famous Poets Society. She graduated with a B.A. in Environmental Analysis and Design from the University of California, Irvine in 1996, while developing a career in Marketing and Public Relations. In 1999, she published her second book, *If yesterday was, tomorrow would be*, which reflected a much deeper and emotional side of Manisha. In the autumn of 2000, she met and became engaged to her love at first sight, Sunil. This sparked a turning point in her writing as her poems mirrored her newfound happiness. In May 2001, Manisha and Sunil were married and she now resides in Jacksonville, Florida. She is currently a freelance writer and an active member of Toastmasters. Filled with diverse experiences and the teachings of her parents and mentors, she is energized with passion, ambition and strength. Travels to all corners of the globe continue to inspire her and as a versatile writer, Manisha is sure to inspire others.

Joyner, Linda - Linda is a native of North Carolina. She has a wonderful Christian husband, two grown children and three grown step-children. Linda was not born with a talent for writing. Recently God gave her the desire to put her thoughts and feelings into poems, songs, and writings. Linda believe's God gave her this gift as another way to communicate with Him personally and hopefully bless others. This gift is a blessing to her because although inadequate, she can express the love she has for Jesus - the one who saved her soul. The poem "Trust in God" was taken from her recent book *Roses for Jesus*.

Marks, Jean C. - Jean is a native New Yorker. For the past twenty years, she has worked as a New York City Housing Inspector. Between L.I.U. and Medgar Evers College, she has three years of college credits. She hopes to learn more and grow more. Currently she has had her poems published in *Spring Creek Sun* at Starrett City, *Hear Our Voices V*, and *Opened Eyes Literary Journals*. She hopes to share her flair for writing poems by publishing a book of poems.

Martin, Ossie H. - Ossie is a native North Carolinian, graduating from Person County High School, Roxboro, North Carolina. Ossie moved on to further her education at Johnson C. Smith University in Charlotte, North Carolina. Matriculating from J.C.S.U., Ossie earned a B.A. degree with a major in French and a minor in Psychology. Ossie has done additional studies at Newark State College, Union, N.J.; University of S.C., Lancaster, S.C.; Winthrop College, Rock Hill, S.C.; Columbia College, Columbia, S.C. and the Institute of Children's Literature, West Redding, Connecticut. Since early childhood, Ossie has had an interest in creative writing; although time didn't permit her to invest in writing in the past, she has now aspired to fulfilled that dream. As a writer and a poet, she loved to write songs and poetry, which led to her, recently published book of poems *Spreading Good Cheer through Song and Verse*. She also enjoys singing with the "Spiritualities" singing group at Ames Road Church of Christ in Columbia, South Carolina. Soft spoken, kind, trustworthy, and someone to lend a helping hand, whenever needed are but a few traits that describe Ossie. Volunteer community services are National Cystic Fibrosis Foundation, American Cancer Society; American Heart Association; Diabetes Associates, and Volunteer Librarian at a local elementary school. She was added to the Body of Christ on November 26, 1967 in Newark, New Jersey under the leadership of Brother Eugene Lawton. Ossie has taught in the public schools in New Jersey and South Carolina. It was in Newark, New Jersey where she met her military husband Johnny. From this union, two children were born, Renee and John. Ossie has been employed in retail industry for thirty years first with J.B. Whites Incorporation, and currently with Belk's Incorporation. Ossie wants young people to "Be respectful to others as well as themselves." Also, "Be a good listener." Her hobbies are: singing, traveling, volunteering, and writing. Her most notable writing accomplishments are: *Spreading Good Cheer through Song and Verse*, author, 1997, *A Celebration of Poets*, showcase edition, 1998, *Poetic Spirit*, Poetry Guild, 1998, Sparrowgrass Poetry Forum, Inc., Spring 1998, and *Sound of Poetry*, International Library of Poetry, 1999.

Mason, Neil - I am an aspiring writer and poet. I like uplifting words, stories, and poems. If one person is touched by my words - amen. I live in California, struggled my whole life and now am ready to help others.

Mattern, Ruth Diselrod - I reside in Wilson, North Carolina. Interests: Writing, amateur photography, and handcrafts. Memberships: Who's Who in Business. Publications: "The Most Beautiful Thing in the World" in *Treasured Poems of America*, 1998 and in *In-between Days*, 2000, "I Love You" in *In-between Days,* 2000, "My Daughter" in *Voices of the New Century*, 2000, "I See" in *Between Darkness and Light*, 2000, "My Heart" in *The Falling Rain*, 2000, and "My Little Boy" and "To My Grandchild" in *Nature's Echoes*, 2000. Award: Creative Writing Award, 1970. Comment: I grew up along with three brothers in a military family. We moved around often, so the themes of my work vary. Most of my poetry is inspired by my family and friends. Especially my terrific husband, my three wonderful children and my three precious grandchildren. I have written a series of children's picture books that have not yet been published. I also write short stories, but I prefer poetry because I can be more colorful and expressive with fewer words. I feel, with poetry, the reader can develop his or her own ideas and feelings about what they read. I believe poetry should be felt...not just read. When I write, I open my soul to the world. In my poetry, as with my photography, I want to share with others the beauty I see in life.

Merolla, Carol - Carol is the author of four poetry books: *Quiet Reflections, The Time of Christmas, The Power of the Pen,* and *Walk Beside Me.* She is also the author of two children's books, *Letters to God* and *Two Kittens for Kim.* Her fiction, nonfiction work and poetry have appeared in many publications including magazines, newspapers, anthologies, the Internet. The International Library of Poetry features a selection of her poetry in their series, *The Sound of Poetry.* Her awards include: President's Award for Literary Excellence, two Iliad Literary Awards, Third Quarter Winner in the Poet of the Year Award competition, and is the recipient of several Honorable Mentions. She is a Distinguished Member of The International Society of Poets, The National Authors Registry, and The Society of Children's Books Writers & Illustrators. Carol is a freelance writer from Johnston, Rhode Island where she lives with her husband, businessman Anthony Merolla.

O'Flaherty, John - Watergrasshill, County Cork, Ireland. Trained as an actor/singer in Cork, appeared in several stage shows in Ireland, TV Commercials, London, England. Studied novel writing with Writer's Digest, Ohio, Qualified as a screenwriter, Hollywood, California. Poems, letters, and articles have been published. A novel, She Came from Atlanta is due for release.

O'Neal, Lillian M. - Born in Boston, Massachusetts to Arthur and Olive Morgan. I was one of six children, Arthur, Eddie, Wesley who passed away at the age of forty, Michelle and Kurt. Graduated from the Jeremiah E. Burke High School. I was a single parent who raised ten children, Danita, Arthur, Cynthia, Kendra, Anthony, Rosalea, Tamara, Melissa, Roosevelt, and Eddie. I now have twenty-nine grandchildren and nine great-grandchildren. I worked at Filenes for fifteen years and in my quest for a challenge I was hired by the United States Postal Service. After a year of being a window clerk, I was promoted to a supervisor. While at the post office I started writing. At first, when someone lost someone dear to him or her and then for other reasons. If I read about someone, I could write a poem about him or her. This was how I could ease a pain; bring a smile, or information. In these poems, I have read about those at Ground Zero, or those who flew in the planes, or those who fought the battles saving others. What would and did they say, how can I ease the pains of others, how can I show them that life goes on in this world of violence and turmoil. I have submitted these poems to President Bush, Mayor Giuliani, and Senator Kennedy. So far, I have written twenty-one poems and I hope to have a book published. I plan to have a percentage donated to Ground Zero funds. In my collections, I have written for the following heroes...First Deputy/Commissioner William Feehan, Ray Downey, Captain John Ogonowski, Jeremy Glick, Todd Beamer, Mark Bingham, and Thomas E. Burnett, Jr. When I have information, I have to share it with others. The best ways are my poems.

Perrapato, Elena Rachel - Elena resides in Lincoln Park, New Jersey. Education: high school, some college; Medical Assistant Degree. Occupation: Teacher/transport driver, singer/writer, IBO. Interests: Beach-walking, swimming, playing guitar, composing music, and writing. Publication: Poetic Voices of America Summer 1997, original copyrights of lyrics & music. Comments: I was moved deeply by September 11th tragedy in NYC and wanted to write some

words. To all the families that suffered I have you in my prayers.

Ramsey, Linda R. - Born January 3, 1944 in Lake City, Florida to parents Fred and Montie Shope. Attended Andrew Jackson High School in Jacksonville, Florida. Moved to Dearborn, Michigan at eighteen. First marriage to Robert Tracy, we had three children. Second marriage to Drury Ramsey, Newport, Tennessee. We raised five children, three of mine and two of his. Our family was called the Brady Bunch; we have been married twenty-two years. We have fifteen grandchildren together. We own and operate our own business in Newport, Tennessee. New and used auto parts and 24-hour towing. We are the man and woman team. I love my husband very much. I have been writing poetry for three years. I have several Honorable Mentions

Awards from Cader Publishing, Ltd. "Boxer Shorts" and "Childhood Days," and the President's Awards for Literary Excellence 2000 for "Boxer Shorts" and "Childhood Days." Editor's Choice Award "Smoky Mountains," for outstanding achievements in poetry in The International Library of Poetry. Cader Publishing, Ltd. 2001 President's Award for "Pray For Our Children" and "Pork Chops and Potatoes." Honorable Mentions for "Little Angel Twins." Honored as a Famous Poet for 2001 and presented with Prometheus Muse of Fire Trophy also a medallion for Poet of the Year from Famous Poets for "God I Went Looking For You." I am a member of the National Authors Registry. My hobbies are reading and writing poetry. "Pray For Our Children," is my favorite poem. Let's get back on the right track and bring God, the Ten Commandments, and school prayer back.

Randall, Claudette Susan - I live in the small coastal town of Topsham, Maine and have lived in the area most of my fifty years. I am married to my new husband Dennis, a retired dairy farmer. We have five children between us-all grown and four beautiful grandchildren. I am a nurse in a local physician's office and have worked in the medical profession for over twenty years. My calling in life has always been "to serve," but my real passion has always been writing! I have experienced many transitions in my life and am constantly re-inventing myself. I have been through divorce, struggled raising three children as a single parent, lost my second husband after a long illness and became a widow at age forty-five. I have faced much adversity and turmoil in life, but it has wrought about much personal and spiritual growth. I have always had this insatiable desire to write about my life in the shear hope that it can inspire or encourage others. Now at age fifty, I feel I have finally arrived. I have written a lot of personal experience piece, essays and am working on my first novel. My interest in poetry is rather recent. I have found it enjoyable, comforting, and quite fulfilling. Like many of us who were deeply affected from the events of 9/11— I found solace in my poetry and in my unshakable faith in God. We live in world that is sadly inundated with many random, insidious acts of violence bringing with it unimaginable heartache for thousands of people every day robbing us of our joy and our hope. I believe in a merciful and loving God, who will one day right all wrongs, vanquish all evil forever, vindicate the righteous and restore to us the peace of Eden!

Ruble, Ronald M. - Born July 4, 1940 in Shelby, Ohio. The son of Eldred and Dessie Briner, he is the youngest of four children. He spent his youth among the rural farming communities of Richland and Ashland counties. He graduated from Lucas High School, Lucas, Ohio in 1958 and received his B.A. degree from Otterbein College in 1962. He furthered his education with a M.A. degree from Bowling Green State University in 1966 and his Ph.D. from the same university in 1975. He raised his sons, Eric and Kristofer in Huron, Ohio, where he was a member of the faculty at Firelands College of B.G.S.U. from 1970 through 1998. He taught in the areas of the humanities, theatre, and speech communications, with specialties in human communications, creative writing, and children's theatre. He is now emeritus faculty member at Firelands College teaching humanities part-time. He has been the Artistic Director of the Caryl Crane Children's Theatre since 1990. A award-winning playwright (*Tender Times* and *My Father's Father*), he is also an award winning poet and fiction writer and has published his poems and short stories in *Eric Shores Magazine, Firelands Arts Review, Grand Lake Review, The Heartlands Today, Mixer Magazine, New Waves, Poet's Corner, Verses Magazine,* and *Waterlines*. His works are in anthologies by Bottom Dog Press, Cader Publishing/Iliad Press, Doll Printing Press, and Quill Books, Inc.

Runner, Edward - I am a ninety-one year old semi-retired Real Estate Broker and former Commissioner of the New Jersey Real Estate Commission. While doing volunteer work with elementary school children, I was invited to attend a

reading before Poetry Group where the children were to read their own written poems. One sixth grader requested me to write and read a poem for them. I told them that I wrote a poem in the seventh grade seventy-four years ago. Upon getting home, I decided that writing a poem for them would be challenge so I wrote and read a poem. It was so well received that I then wrote more and more so that in the past three years I have written two hundred twenty-three poems and joined four Poetry Groups' my own book of poems *Diversified Poetry* was published and available on Internet last Spring thru Xlibris Publishers 1-888-7954-27-47 or @Xlibris.com.

Samer, Bill - I hope you'll read "Address Space," written by the editor of the special commemorative 30th anniversary issue of *Top of the Stairs* magazine, published by Gracevine, a company established in 1975; and is dedicated to the families of the victims of September 11—when the world changed. Where were you on the future September 11 Remembrance Day or TT, To the Lord Day? Jesus is my Saviour. I wish you joy but most of all, I wish you love—the love I have written, and "I hear pipes calling/without touch of you," because "I am a poet/if only in my mind." It's a long road becoming an accomplished poet, who has won three awards. There is even more pressure being a diabetic, as I've been for a couple of years now. I'm starting at the top of the sickness because I'm missing my right second toe from it going unestablished for a while. At the moment, I'm enjoying health, writing, reading, gardening, playing volleyball, walking, hiking and even jogging. I've been involved in a church choir, songwriting for a CD and cassettes, a crisis intervention hot-line; and presently as WHAT (The William Samer Activist Organization), a volunteer for CROP and the American Cancer

Society. I received my degrees from Union College, Concordia College, Bronxville; and Kean University, in History, with a collateral program in Study of the Future (certificate). My biography is included in four *Who's Who* books.

Scanlon, Kelsey - Kelsey is a twelve-year-old honor roll student. Although she didn't experience a personal loss on September 11, 2001, she felt compelled to write this ballad for  her English class. Kelsey has dedicated herself to her school and her community. Her contributions include personal donations to the local animal shelter and the Community Christmas. As a sixth grader, her activities evolve around student government, chorus, art club, and soccer. Kelsey also sings in her church choir, step dances, and plays piano and flute. Her parents and family are very proud of Kelsey. She is an exceptional, beautiful person.

Sobel, Cleo Ray - Cleo is a native of Texas. She left Texas at an early age. After completing high school, bound for Oklahoma City, she took a course in Massage Therapy. She  completed her studies and became a Certified Massage Therapist. Helping people with stress and pain has been her life. After attending school in Chicago, Illinois, she worked for twenty-five years. She wrote a booklet, *Massage Express to health and Beauty*. She wrote a song, "Let Go and Let God" and "Mother, A precious Name" in 1980. Her hobbies are painting, playing the guitar, and singing. She also makes her own bath salts for relaxing. She likes to read and grow plants in her terrace. She is a daughter of the late Charles R. Ray and Ethel J. Ray and the eldest of seven children. She is the widow of Jack Sobel, and she has just completed a love story about her and Jack. She wants to write more poetry and plans to write a chapbook. Her two grandmothers named her. One said Frances and the other grandmother was hurt, so her mother said, "Don't be mad. We will just add Cleo." So, now you have Frances Cleo. Mrs. Sobel now resides in New York City.

Smith, Lucy L. - Born August 15, 1941 in Pike County. Education: first through eighth grade. Occupation: Housewife. Interests: Writing poetry, crafts, fishing, and enjoys four children and four grandchildren. Publications: "The Weeping Willow" published in *Poetic Voices of America*, 1990 and "Grandma's Pipe" published in *SPF 2000 Voices of the New Century*. Dedicated to my husband William; children, Tammy, Kathy, Nancy, and Diann; grandchildren, Tiffany, Terri, Dorothy Ann, and Mandy; and the policemen, firefighters, and victim's families..

Stamatiou, Kiki - Parents: Odysseus and Toula Stamatiou; Siblings: John (deceased in 1988) and Stanley. Publications: "Ode to the Ancient One" published in *The Space Between* (1994 ED.) published by The National Library of Poetry; The National Library of Poetry will publish "Carnival" in January 2002 also. Personal Statement: "A tortured soul breathes life into a drifting corpse whose mind was shattered by bombs exploding in the night as a result of two countries failing to talk out their differences rather than resorting to violence."

Thomas, Amy Nicole (Pen name: Nicole) - Nicole lives with her husband and two daughters in southern Indiana. Recently, she chose to pursue her love of writing and drawing full-time. As an abuse survivor, she involves herself in promoting Abuse Awareness. She writes poems, short stories, articles, and is an artist, as well. Publications: Her first book, *Molly and the Secret*, is currently available from 1st Books.com. She is now working on two novels, *Infinity*, a historical romance and *Beauty of the Eyes*, a horror novel. She has three poems in the process of publication: "Spinning," to be published in a collection, *Under a Quicksilver Moon* and on the CD, *The Sounds of Poetry* and "Christmas with My Family" is to be published in a collection of poetry entitled *Bridges*, "The Pit of Hell" is to be published in the collection, *Good Times*. "Mrs Daniels", a short horror story, is included in the book *Borderline* by Elizabeth R. Peake. Mrs. Thomas is the Creator, Executive Editor and Publisher of the magazine *e-zine Abstracts*. Awards: "Christmas with My Family" won Honorable Mention in the Iliad Press Awards Program Summer 2001. Nicole is a member of The National Association of Women Writers, The Phenomenal Women of the Web (as Gabriel), and A Preferred Author and Moderator at Stories.com also a member of The National Authors Registry. You can reach Nicole at ajbthree@psci.net

Thompson-Briatico, Nycol - I went to New York at eighteen to find myself. What I found was a heart that beat beneath my feet, a soul that bellowed and sang between the cracks in the sidewalk. I quickly knew New York as, "She" and "Her," my mother. "She" pointed me this way and that until I eventually ran into myself on a side street somewhere downtown. "She" gave me the courage to reach out and take my own hand. I laughed, I cried, I spat in anger, and for the first time, I loved. All this as I grew into womanhood with the guidance of the greatest teacher I have ever had the honor of knowing. My only wish for this New Year is for the world to know New York with their hearts as I have, for the world to know her as OUR tough love mother.

Vargas, Joe - The symbol entitled "Facade" represents me (Joe Vargas) and also the band that I'm in. We have not been a band for very long and we incorporated all kinds of music styles. We live in northern Indiana where we work, go to school, and practice. We don't do shows for the moment.

We're just waiting for the right time and preparing as we wait. Our philosophy behind the name Facade is the wide spread pretence people seem to have. It seems that at one time or another most have been guilty of hypocrisy. Our message deals with confusion of not knowing who you are and how it relates to maturity or reality in general. But, pretending can also be a good thing as C.S. Lewis mentions in his book *Mere Christianity*. Aside from the band I am praying for America humbly and repentant.

Wilson, Doris L. - Born December 30, 1942 to parents Richmond and Rosa Jones. Married James E. Wilson December 24, 1966. I have four children: Vivian, Pamela, Cassandra, and Lutrell Wilson. Blessed with Six grandchildren: James, Devon Jena, Emani, Luvenia, Jamea, and Sanjaya Wilson. I am a homemaker and a poet. Volunteered for D.C. Public School and Recreation Centers for twenty-five years. Received various outstanding awards for volunteer services and several outstanding awards for outstanding volunteer parent. Nominated several times as Poet of the Year by The International Library of Poetry. Received several Editors Choice Awards from The International Library of Poetry for outstanding achievement in poetry. I have poetry in several anthologies such as The International Library of Poetry, Sparrowgrass Poetry Forum, and Poetry Guild. Poems published in *The Best Poem of 1998* and *The Best Poet of 2000* anthologies by The International Library of Poetry. I have a poem published in *The Best Love Poems* by Sparrowgrass Poetry Forum. I have a great love for poetry. I enjoy writing poems. I was motivated to write poems by my siblings and a close friend. The poem "Fallen Angels" is significant to me because it help me to manifest my emotions of the unproved attack on America September 11, 2001. I sincerely hope that it can help bring tranquility and closure to the families of the victims of September 11, 2001 attack on America.

Young Family - The Young family lives in Wisconsin with their golden retriever named Friday. Brent, age twelve, loves sports history, debate and running. He is an excellent student. Michelle, age eight, plays piano, Suzuki violin and wants to learn guitar too! She also is excellent student. Monica, age five, is just finishing preschool. She plays the piano and loves cooking and drawing. Dave, not a poet, writer or artist, agreed to be part of his family's page because he loves them very much. Ann is a stay-at-home mom. She married her best friend, David. Together they enjoy their three precious gifts, Brent, Michelle, and Monica. September 11th touched our family in a personal way because we have a cousin, Leone and her husband, Chris, who both work blocks away from the World Trade Center. Leone was supposed to be in the building September 11, but her plans changed. It took us a long, anxious wait to learn Chris and Leone were safe. As we talk to Chris and Leone, and learn of all the friends and colleagues they lost, we know September 11th will never be over. Monica, our youngest child, had her fifth birthday September 12th. As we went to the Build-A-Bear store at our local mall to celebrate her birthday, the mall was eerily empty. We wondered if we should be out. But, Leone, our analyst cousin from New York told us to keep spending money so we didn't fall into a worse recession. New York, you made us proud. You kept on going and so we had to too. There will always be images of the towers falling. Let us always preserve too the picture of all the people of New York helping each other regardless of color, race, or religion. That is the best picture of what the United States, at its best, is all about. God Bless! From the Young Family.

"Life affords no higher pleasure than
that of surmounting difficulties, passing from one step of success
to another, forming new wishes, and seeing them gratified.
He that labors in any great or laudable undertaking
has his fatigues first supported by hope, and afterwards rewarded by joy...
To strive with difficulties, and to conquer them,
is the highest human felicity."

Samuel Johnson, *Light from Many Lamps* by Lillian Eichler Watson (Editor)

Index

Alphabetical listing of authors.

Verizon's 140 West Street Central office standing in background (left).

A

Akhter, Shahira, 3, 24, 97
Anderson, Gregory L., 3
Andrews, Joyce E., 3
Ayikwei, Ashley Edem, 14

B

Backlund, Patricia L., 12
Baird, Debra, 29
Banks, Marie E. Hoad, 81, 82, 83, 99
Baker, Kellyann, 2
Baker, Nathaniel M., 8
Baker Rippeon, Viola Mae, 56
Barrows, Keith, 2, 97
Bates, Sheila, 4, 10
Batts, Sonya S., 15, 16
Beguhn, Sandra E., 6
Bergen, Joan Z., 5
Berry, Ann R, 6
Birenbaum, Barbara, 15
Bishop, Mary Utt, 5
Blackwell-Davis, Geri, 5
Blake, Patricia Payzant, 7, 97
Boecher, George, 7
Bott, Mary Beth, 7
Bowden, Dorothy, 10
Boyce, Cecil, 6
Boyden, Christopher W., 8, 97
Bradfield, Diana Elizabeth, 9
Brigham, Elladean, 9
Brochu, Patricia H., 76
Brohl, Ted, 9
Brown, Gloria Jean, 10
Brown, Lori, 21
Bryant, Derick R., 17
Buckley, Duranda, 11
Burnside, Wanda J., 1, 97
Burnside, Simmie Jr., 62

C

Camara, Jr., John R., 79
Campbell, Genevieve M., 9
Candanoza, Celestina, 12
Carlson, Madeline J., 13
Carreira, Maria, 13, 98
Carroll, Joseph C., 84, 85
Caster, Annette, 14
Chalke, Peachie, 13
Cheatham-Shipman, Olivia, 41, 98
Chorosinski, Eugene C., 72
Clemmons, John P., 5
Collins, Georgia, 2
Collins, V. June, 4
Cone, Ruth, 13
Corey, Del, 73
Cowan, Doris, 4
Crampton, Kristie, 14
Crichlow, Eleanor L., 16
Crowder, Patricia Autrey, 3
Currie, Emma, 16

D

DaVee, R. Lowell "Ted", 18
Daigle, Kenneth William, 18
Dana, Stephanie Joan, 15
Dehoff, Dagon A., 5
Dehoff, Freda M., 16
Delaney, April L., 11
Denette, Edwiin N., 23
Derderian, Allison, 65
Derderian, Sharon, i, 77
DiTizio, Paulette, 10
Dias, Brenda Joyce, 11
Donovan, Kathleen, 19
Dunsmore, Stacey, 17

E

Eastman, Madeline, 20
Edwards, Samantha L., 86
Ehren, Edward, 10
Eleana, 48
Elliott, June Allegra, 12
Evans, Louise, 24

F

Falzone-Cardinal, Nancy L., 12, 98
Family, Young
Farrell, Cass, 20
Flatley, Kathryn, 40
Fontaine, Irene A., 15
Franklin, Peggy E., 74
Francis, Shannon J., 90
Fritz, Karen K., 19
Furlow, William, 26

G

Gabrovsky, Todor, 21
Gannon, Yvonne A., 21, 98
Garvin, Glenn Abby, 24
George, Ruth Tolbott, 18
Germano, Rose, 87
Gibson, Sherri, 18
Glassman, Sandra, 17, 19
Granse, William, 33
Gratman, Mary S., 28
Gray, Jeffrey V., 24, 98
Gray, John A., 22
Grazulis, Linda C., 24, 25
Gribble, Doris Lee, 26
Groopman, Cynthia L., 23
Groza, Horia Ion, 25
Grubaugh, Sally Jo, 73
Grumbling, Carol Ann, 25
Guthrie, Belinda, 23

H

Hagen, Edna, 26
Hale, Sue Sally, 28
Ham, Crystie, 29
Hammerberg, J.M. Bennett, 27
Harges, Angela, 28
Harris, Edyth V., 80
Harrison, Elizabeth A., 27
Harwell, Judith R., 30, 98
Haskins, Michelle L., 27
Hellewell, Margaret R., 30
Henderson, Marcus, 26
Higby, Jarrod, 28
Hill, Diana J., 27
Hillman, Aaron W., 31, 98
Hip, Jay, 23
Hitchcock, Gabrielle, 29
Hoffman, Robin, 31
Holt, Connie, 32
Howard, Delores J., 88
Hubbard, Genevieve C., 90
Hudkins, Ronald E., 32, 99
Huling, Erick K., 29
Humphrey, Verna Ray, 31
Hutson, Linda P., 89, 99

I

Idziak, Boniface, 22, 99
Ingram, Jodi, 32
Irwin, William D., 31
Isaksen, Ellen, 32

J

Jennings, Mia, 38
Johnson, Carole, 33
Johnson, Penny, 33
Joshi, Manisha S., 34, 100
Joyner, Linda, 33, 100
Justesen, Dorothy, 71

K

Kambiss, Thomas Christopher, 37
Kay, Deborah, 36
Keller, Elvie E. Bryant, 72
Key, Cynthia V., 38
Kipp, Conrad Novarro, 35
Kirsch, Jack W., 36, 72
Kise, Janet L., 77
Klausner, Dorothy Chenoweth, 35
Kush, Angela, 36

L

Labadie, Sandra J., 36, 37
LadyO, 41, 98
Lammers, Angela, 35

America – Voices Coming Together

Latham, Tamara B., 35
Lawton, Jody, 75
Lee, Jessica, 8
Lilley, David, 35
Lipscomb, Wilma V., 40
Lowe, Christopher, 91
Lowell, Barbara Ozenberger, 78
Lowry, Ronnie, 38

M

MT-G, 48
Maloy, Christine, 78
Markowski, Benedict, 37
Marks, Jean C., 73, 100
Marron, Rebecca A., 37
Martin, Ossie H., 39
Martinez, Rose Marie, 38
Mascherin, Kathy E., 41
Mason, Neil, 39, 101
Masten, Jaqueline G., 40
Mattern, Ruth Diselrod, 39, 101
Maurice, Lisa, 30
McAdoo, Jeanette J., 73
McGarry, Margaret T., 41
McKeever, Karen, 43
McKenzie, M.J., 44
McLane Collins, Georgia
McRavin, Sarah, 63
Mercer, Betty D., 44
Merolla, Carol, 45, 101
Micheli, Donna M., 42
Milano, Carole S., 39
Miller, Christina, 48
Miller, Mary Jean, 43
Mollan, Vivian Gloff, 45, 49
Moore, Tina M., 46
Morris, Steven G., 88
Moscatello, Kate, 43
Mosher, Heidi L., 47
Mulcahey, Janice, 47
Murphy, Anne, 48
Murphy, Randal K., 50

N

Nelson, Albert, 47
Nelson, Carrie, 47
Nickel, Jessika, 49
Nielson, Alyce M., 60

O

O'Connor, Joy A., 46
O'Flaherty, John, 51, 101
O'Neal, Lillian M., 75, 92, 93, 101
ODom, Don, 49
Ondroczky, Elizabeth, 51
Osadchuk, Amy, 46

P

Paquette, Linda, 50
Parente, Michael, 49
Perrapato, Elena, 48, 101
Phillips, Steve, 51
Pingsterhaus, Lori, 45
Poggensee, Stephanie, 50
Potts, Luella Knauss, 14
Proctor, Cyndee Lee, 52

R

Ramirez, Ruben, 54
Ramsey, Linda R., 55, 101
Randall, Claudette Susan, 53, 102
Recupero-Faiella, Anna, 22
Reed, Susan M., 44
Rhodenizer, Flora J.M., 22, 54
Richards, Britnie, 21
Ridner, Melanie Marie, 55
Ritchie, Carol J., 56
Roan, Robert, 55
Robbins, William, 55
Rogers, Anita, 56
Rogers, Raymond, 73
Rosenblatt, Ina, 57
Ross, Shirley Leanore Bohl, 41
Ruble, Ronald M., 57, 58, 59, 102
Runner, Edward J., 58, 102
Rupp, Myrtle, 80
Rust, Daphne, 58
Rutherford, John E., 57

S

Sabella, Marlena, 65
Samer, Bill, 71, 102
Scanlon, Kelsey, 59, 103
Schnall, Linda V., 63
Schneider, Steve, 42
Sheets, Juanita Russell, 44
Shelley, Kate, 42
Shuttleworth, William H., 53
Simington, Christina Marie, 42
Smith, Lucy L., 77, 103
Smith, Phyllis A., 63
Smith, Valarie, 53
Snead, Olivia S., 59
Sobel, Cleo, 45, 103
Stack, Dorothy Randall, 61
Stamatiou, Kiki, 78, 103
Stanton, Steve, 57
Stapp, Christa, 51
Steinberg, Thelma T., 61
Stockton, Patricia, 52
Stulc, Sarah, 54
Szatny, Kristen, 58

T

Tebrinke, Nan, 59
Thomas, Amy Nicole, 60
Thomas, Charles J., 62, 103
Thompson-Briatico, Nycol, 63, 103
Tincani, UnDra, 67
Tipps, Lou Ann, 66
Tisdale, Alma Woods, 20, 25
Tomasello, Dorann, 71
Torres, Sergio, 64
Traversi, Anthony S., 65
Tucker, Mary Elizabeth, 66
Tucker, Megan, 68
Turner, Lloyd, 67
Tyree, Crystal, 77

V

Vargas, Joe, 76, 103
Villela, Michelle, 53
Vincenti, Irma, 69

W

Wadzinski, Mary B., 76
Wallace, Lynda Joyner, 68
Walter, Hugo, 68
Ward, C. Edwin, 69
Ware, Marianne, 70
Warner, Ceresa M., 78
Warner, Ruth, 72
Warren, Constance A., 54
Warren, Judi, 69
Westview, Casey, 65
Whitaker, James E., 70
White, Tiffany, 68
Whittaker, William R., 67
Wilder, Dianna, 70
Wilder, Timothy B., 66
Williams, Brian H., 64
Williams, Judy Ann, 61
Wilson, Doris L., 60, 104
Wilson, Gregory, 74
Wingrove, Pearl, 64
Woods, Ashleigh S., 90

Y

Young, Ann, 94, 95, 104
Young, Brent, 95, 104
Young, Dave, 95, 104
Young, Michelle, 95, 104

Z

Zuzak, Charlotte Ann, 64

106

In Rememberance of the Tragedies of September 11, 2001

In Memoriam

The Victims

(as reported from MSNBC)

World Trade Center
The Pentagon
American Airlines Flight 11
American Airlines Flight 77
United Airlines Flight 93
United Airlines Flight 175

In the last analysis
it is our conception of death
which decides our answers
to all the questions
that life puts to us.

Dag Hammarskjöld

"The ultimate measure of a man is not where he stands in moments of comfort and convenience, but where he stands at times of challenge and controversy."
Martin Luther King, Jr., *The Book of Positive Quotations* by John Cook

WORLD TRADE CENTER

Maria Rose Abad, 49, Syosset, NY
Edelmiro (Ed) Abad, 54, New York, NY
Andrew Anthony Abate, 37, Melville, NY
Vincent Abate, 40, New York, NY
Laurence Christopher Abel, 37
William F. Abrahamson, 58, Cortland Manor, NY
Richard Anthony Aceto, 42, Wantagh, NY
Erica van Acker, 62, New York, NY
Heinrich B. Ackermann, 38, New York, NY
Paul Andrew Acquaviva, 29, Glen Rock, NJ
Donald L. Adams, 28, Chatham, NJ
Shannon Lewis Adams, 25, New York, NY
Stephen Adams, 51, New York, NY
Patrick Adams, 60, New York, NY
Ignatius Adanga, 62, New York, NY
Christy A. Addamo, 28, New Hyde Park, NY
Terence E. Adderley, 22, Bloomfield Hills, MI
Sophia B. Addo, 36, New York, NY
Lee Adler, 48, Springfield, NJ
Daniel Thomas Afflitto, 32, ManalaPan, NJ
Emmanuel Afuakwah, 37, New York, NY
Alok Agarwal, 36, Jersey City, NJ
Mukul Agarwala, 37, New York, NY
Joseph Agnello, 35, New York, NY
David Scott Agnes, 46, New York, NY
Joao A.D. Aguiar, 30, Red Bank, NJ
Lt. Brian G Ahearn, 43, Huntington, NY
Jeremiah J. Ahern, 74, Cliffside Park, NJ
Joanne Ahladiotis, 27, New York, NY
Shabbir Ahmed, 47, New York, NY
Terrance Andre Aiken, 30, New York, NY
Godwin Ajala, 33, New York, NY
Gertrude M. Alagero, 37, New York, NY
Andrew Alameno, 37, Westfield, NJ
Margaret Ann Jezycki Alario, 41, New York, NY
Gary Albero, 39, Emerson, NJ
Jon L. Albert, 46, Upper Nyack, NY
Peter Craig Alderman, 25, New York, NY
Jacquelyn Delaine Aldridge, 46, New York, NY
Grace Alegre-Cua, 40, Glen Rock, NJ
David D. Alger, 57, New York, NY
Ernest Alikakos, 43, New York, NY
Edward L. Allegretto, 51, Colonia, NJ
Eric Allen, 41, New York, NY
Joseph Ryan Allen, 39, New York, NY
Richard Lanard Allen, 30, New York, NY
Richard Dennis Allen, 31, New York, NY
Christopher E. Allingham, 36, River Edge, NJ
Janet M. Alonso, 41, Stony Point, NY
Anthony Alvarado, 31, New York, NY
Antonio Javier Alvarez, 23, New York, NY
Telmo Alvear, 25, New York, NY
Cesar A. Alviar, 60, Bloomfield, NJ
Tariq Amanullah, 40, Metuchen, NJ
Angelo Amaranto, 60, New York, NY
James Amato, 43, Ronkonkoma, NY
Joseph Amatuccio, 41, New York, NY
Christopher Charles Amoroso, 29, New York, NY
Kazuhiro Anai, 42, Scarsdale, NY
Calixto Anaya, 35, Suffern, NY
Jorge O. Santos Anaya, 25, Aguascalientes, Mex.
Joseph Peter Anchundia, 26, New York, NY
Kermit Charles Anderson, 57, Green Brook, NJ
Yvette Anderson, 53, New York, NY
John Andreacchio, 52, New York, NY
Michael Rourke Andrews, 34, Belle Harbor, NY
Jean A. Andrucki, 42, Hoboken, NJ
Siew-Nya Ang, 37, E. Brunswick, NJ
Joseph Angelini, 38, Lindenhurst, NJ
Joseph Angelini, 63, Lindenhurst, NJ
Laura Angilletta, 23, New York, NY
Doreen J. Angrisani, 44, New York, NY
Lorraine D. Antigua, 32, Middletown, NJ
Peter Paul Apollo, 26, Hoboken, NJ
Faustino Apostol, 55, New York, NY
Frank Thomas Aquilino, 26, New York, NY
Patrick Michael Aranyos, 26, New York, NY
David Gregory Arce, 36, New York, NY
Michael G Arczynski, 45, Little Silver, NJ

Louis Arena, 32, New York, NY
Adam Arias, 37, New York, NY
Michael J. Armstrong, 34, New York, NY
Jack Charles Aron, 52, Bergenfield, NJ
Joshua Aron, 29, New York, NY
Richard Avery Aronow, 48, Mahwah, NJ
Japhet J. Aryee, 49, Spring Valley, NY
Carl Asaro, 39, Middletown, NY
Michael A. Asciak, 47, Ridgefield, NJ
Michael Edward Asher, 53, Monroe, NY
Janice Ashley, 25, Rockville Centre, NY
Thomas J. Ashton, 21, New York, NY
Manuel O. Asitimbay, 36, New York, NY
Lt. Gregg Arthur Atlas, 45, Howells, NY
Gerald Atwood, 38, New York, NY
James Audiffred, 38, New York, NY
Kenneth W. van Auken, 47, E. Brunswick, NJ
Louis F. Aversano, Jr, 58, ManalaPan, NJ
Ezra Aviles, 41, Commack, NY
Ayodeji Awe, 42, New York, NY
Samuel (Sandy) Ayala, 36, New York, NY
Arlene T. Babakitis, 47, Secaucus, NJ
Eustace (Rudy) Bacchus, 48, Metuchen, NJ
John James Badagliacca, 35, New York, NY
Jane Ellen Baeszler, 43, New York, NY
Robert J. Baierwalter, 44, Albertson, NY
Andrew J. Bailey, 29, New York, NY
Brett T. Bailey, 28, Bricktown, NJ
Tatyana Bakalinskaya, 43, New York, NY
Michael S. Baksh, 36, Englewood, NJ
Sharon Balkcom, 43, White Plains, NY
Michael Andrew Bane, 33, Yardley, Pa
Kathy Bantis, 44, Chicago, ill
Gerard Jean Baptiste, 35, New York, NY
Walter Baran, 42, New York, NY
Gerard A. Barbara, 53, New York, NY
Paul V. Barbaro, 35, HolMDel, NJ
James W. Barbella, 53, Oceanside, NY
Ivan K. Fairbanks Barbosa, 30, Jersey City, NJ
Victor Daniel Barbosa, 23, New York, NY
Colleen Ann Barkow, 26, E. Windsor, NJ
David M. Barkway, 34, Toronto, Ont., Canada
Matthew Barnes, 37, Monroe, NY
Sheila Patricia Barnes, 55, Bay Shore, NY
Evan J. Baron, 38, Bridgewater, NJ
Renee Barrett-Arjune, 41, Irvington, NJ
Arthur T. Barry, 35, New York, NY
Diane G Barry, 60, New York, NY
Maurice Vincent Barry, 49, Rutherford, NJ
Scott D. Bart, 28, Malverne, NY
Carlton W. Bartels, 44, New York, NY
Guy Barzvi, 29, New York, NY
Inna Basina, 43, New York, NY
Alysia Basmajian, 23, Bayonne, NJ
Kenneth W. Basnicki, 48, Etobicoke, ON, CD
Lt. Steven J. Bates, 42, New York, NY
Paul James Battaglia, 22, New York, NY
W. David Bauer, 45, Rumson, NJ
Ivhan Luis Carpio Bautista, 24, New York, NY
Marlyn C. Bautista, 46, Iselin, NJ
Jasper Baxter, 45, Philadelphia, Pa
Michele (Du Berry) Beale, 37, Essex, Britain
Paul F. Beatini, 40, Park Ridge, NJ
Jane S. Beatty, 53, Belford, NJ
Larry I. Beck, 38, Baldwin, NY
Manette Marie Beckles, 43, Rahway, NJ
Carl John Bedigian, 35, New York, NY
Michael Beekman, 39, New York, NY
Maria Behr, 41, Milford, NJ
Yelena Belilovsky, 38, Mamaroneck, NY
Nina Patrice Bell, 39, New York, NY
Andrea Della Bella, 59, Jersey City, NJ
Debbie S. Bellows, 30, E. Windsor, NJ
Stephen Elliot Belson, 51, New York, NY
Paul Michael Benedetti, 32, New York, NY
Denise Lenore Benedetto, 40, New York, NY
Bryan Craig Bennett, 25, New York, NY
Oliver Duncan Bennett, 29, London, England
Eric L. Bennett, 29, New York, NY

Margaret L. Benson, 52, Rockaway, NJ
Dominick J. Berardi, 25, New York, NY
James Patrick Berger, 44, Lower Makefield, Pa
Steven Howard Berger, 45, ManalaPan, NJ
John P. Bergin, 39, New York, NY
Alvin Bergsohn, 48, Baldwin Harbor, NY
Daniel D. Bergstein, 38, Teaneck, NJ
Michael J. Berkeley, 38, New York, NY
Donna Bernaerts-Kearns, 44, Hoboken, NJ
David W. Bernard, 57, Chelmsford, MA
William Bernstein, 44, New York, NY
David M. Berray, 39, New York, NY
David S. Berry, 43, New York, NY
Joseph J. Berry, 55, Saddle River, NJ
William Reed Bethke, 36, Hamilton, NJ
Timothy D. Betterly, 42, Little Silver, NJ
Edward F. Beyea, 42, New York, NY
Paul Michael Beyer, 37, New York, NY
Anil T. Bharvaney, 41, E. Windsor, NJ
Bella Bhukhan, 24, Union, NJ
Shimmy D. Biegeleisen, 42, New York, NY
Peter Alexander Bielfeld, 44, New York, NY
William Biggart, 54, New York, NY
Brian Bilcher, 36, New York, NY
Carl Vincent Bini, 44, New York, NY
Gary Bird, 51, Tempe, AZ
Joshua David Birnbaum, 24, New York, NY
George Bishop, 52, Granite Springs, NY
Jeffrey D. Bittner, 27, New York, NY
Balewa Albert Blackman, 26, New York, NY
Christopher J. Blackwell, 42, Patterson, NY
Susan L. Blair, 35, E. Brunswick, NJ
Harry Blanding, 38, Blakeslee, PA
Janice L. Blaney, 55, Williston Park, NY
Craig Michael Blass, 27, Greenlawn, NY
Rita Blau, 52, New York, NY
Richard M. Blood, 38, Ridgewood, NJ
Michael A. Boccardi, 30, Bronxville, NY
John Paul Bocchi, 38, New Vernon, NJ
Michael L. Bocchino, 45, New York, NY
Susan Mary Bochino, 36, New York, NY
Bruce Boehm, 49, West Hempstead, NY
Mary Katherine Boffa, 45, New York, NY
Nicholas A. Bogdan, 34, Browns Mills, NJ
Darren C. Bohan, 34, New York, NY
Lawrence Francis Boisseau, 36, Freehold, NJ
Vincent M. Boland, 25, Ringwood, NJ
Alan Bondarenko, 53, Flemington, NJ
Andre Bonheur, 40, New York, NY
Colin Arthur Bonnett, 39, New York, NY
Frank Bonomo, 42, Port Jefferson, NY
Yvonne L. Bonomo, 30, New York, NY
Sean Booker, 35, Irvington, NJ
Sherry Ann Bordeaux, 38, Jersey City, NJ
Krystine C. Bordenabe, 33, Old Bridge, NJ
Martin Boryczewski, 29, ParsipPany, NJ
Richard E. Bosco, 34, Suffern, NY
John Howard Boulton, 29, New York, NY
Francisco Bourdier, 41, New York, NY
Thomas H. Bowden, 36, Wyckoff, NJ
Kimberly S. Bowers, 31, Islip, NY
Veronique (Bonnie) Bowers, 28, New York, NY
Larry Bowman, 46, New York, NY
Shawn Edward Bowman, 28, New York, NY
Kevin L. Bowser, 45, Philadelphia, PA
Gary R. Box, 37, North Bellmore, NY
Gennady Boyarsky, 34, New York, NY
Pamela Boyce, 43, New York, NY
Michael Boyle, 37, Westbury, NY
Alfred Braca, 54, Leonardo, NJ
Sandra Conaty Brace, 60, New York, NY
Kevin H. Bracken, 37, New York, NY
David Brian Brady, 41, Summit, NJ
Alexander Braginsky, 38, Stamford, CT
Nicholas W. Brandemarti, 21, Mantua, NJ
Michelle Renee Bratton, 23, Yonkers, NY
Patrice Braut, 31, New York, NY
Lydia Estelle Bravo, 50, Dunellen, NJ
Ronald M. Breitweiser, 39, Middletown Twp, NJ

America – Voices Coming Together

Edward A. Brennan, 37, New York, NY
Frank H. Brennan, 50, New York, NY
Thomas M. Brennan, 32, Scarsdale, NY
Michael Emmett Brennan, 27, New York, NY
Peter Brennan, 30, Ronkonkoma, NY
Capt. Daniel Brethel, 43, Farmingdale, NY
Gary L. Bright, 36, Union City, NJ
Jonathan Eric Briley, 43, Mount Vernon, NY
Mark A. Brisman, 34, Armonk, NY
Paul Gary Bristow, 27, New York, NY
Victoria Alvarez Brito, 38, New York, NY
Mark Francis Broderick, 42, Old Bridge, NJ
Herman C. Broghammer, 58, N. Merrick, NY
Keith Broomfield, 49, New York, NY
Janice J. Brown, 35, New York, NY
Lloyd Brown, 28, Bronxville, NY
Capt. Patrick J. Brown, 48, New York, NY
Bettina Browne, 49, Atlantic Beach, NY
Mark Bruce, 40, Summit, NJ
Richard Bruehert, 38, Westbury, NY
Andrew Brunn, 28
Capt. Vincent Brunton, 43, New York, NY
Ronald Paul Bucca, 47, Tuckahoe, NY
Brandon J. Buchanan, 24, New York, NY
Greg Joseph Buck, 37, New York, NY
Dennis Buckley, 38, Chatham, NJ
Nancy Bueche, 43, Hicksville, NY
Patrick Joseph Buhse, 36, Lincroft, NJ
John E. Bulaga, 35, Paterson, NJ
Stephen Bunin, 45, New York, NY
Thomas Daniel Burke, 38, Bedford Hills, NY
Capt. William F. Burke, 46, New York, NY
Matthew J. Burke, 28, New York, NY
Kathleen A. Burns, 49, New York, NY
Donald James Burns, 61, Nissequogue, NY
Keith James Burns, 39, E. Rutherford, NJ
John Patrick Burnside, 36, New York, NY
Irina Buslo, 32, New York, NY
Milton Bustillo, 37, New York, NY
Thomas M. Butler, 37, Kings Park, NY
Patrick Byrne, 39, New York, NY
Timothy G Byrne, 36, Manhattan, NY
Jesus Cabezas, 66, New York, NY
Lillian Caceres, 48, New York, NY
Brian Joseph Cachia, 26, New York, NY
Steven Cafiero, 31, New York, NY
Richard M. Caggiano, 25, New York, NY
Cecile M. Caguicla, 55, Boonton, NJ
Michael John Cahil, 37, E. Wilston, NY
Scott W. Cahil, 30, West Caldwell, NJ
Thomas J. Cahil, 36, Franklin Lakes, NJ
George Cain, 35, MAapequa, NY
Salvatore B. Calabro, 38, New York, NY
Joseph Calandrillo, 49, Hawley, Pa
Philip V. Calcagno, 57, New York, NY
Edward Calderon, 44, Jersey City, NJ
Kenneth Marcus Caldwell, 30, New York, NY
Dominick E. Calia, 46, ManalaPan, NJ
Felix (Bobby) Calixte, 38, New York, NY
Capt. Frank Callahan, 51, New York, NY
Liam Callahan, 44, Rockaway, NJ
Luigi Calvi, 34, E. Rutherford, NJ
Roko Camaj, 60, Manhasset, NY
Michael Cammarata, 22, Huguenot, NY
Robert Arthur Campbell, 25, New York, NY
David Otey Campbell, 51, Basking Ridge, NJ
Geoffrey Thomas Campbell, 31, New York, NY
Sandra Patricia Campbell, 45, New York, NY
Jill Marie Campbell, 31, New York, NY
Juan Ortega Campos, 32, New York, NY
Sean Canavan, 39, New York, NY
John A. Candela, 42, Glen Ridge, NJ
Vincent Cangelosi, 30, New York, NY
Stephen J. Cangialosi, 40, Middletown, NJ
Lisa B. Cannava, 30, New York, NY
Brian Cannizzaro, 30, New York, NY
Michael R. Canty, 30, Schenectady, NY
Louis A. Caporicci, 35, New York, NY
Jonathan N. Cappello, 23, Garden City, NY
James Cappers, 33, Wading River, NY
Richard M. Caproni, 34, Lynbrook, NY
Jose Cardona, 32, New York, NY
Stephen Carey, 50, Chatsworth, CA
Dennis M Carey, 51, Wantagh, NY
Edward Carlino, 46, New York, NY
Michael Scott Carlo, 35, New York, NY
David G Carlone, 46, Randolph, NJ
Rosemarie C. Carlson, 40, New York, NY
Mark Stephen Carney, 41, Rahway, NJ

Joyce Ann Carpeneto, 40, New York, NY
Alicia Acevedo Carranza, Teziutlan, Puebla, Mexico
Jeremy M. Carrington, 34, New York, NY
Peter Carroll, 35, New York, NY
Michael T. Carroll, 39, New York, NY
James J. Carson, 32, MAapequa, NY
Christopher Newton Carter, 52, Middletown, NJ
James Marcel Cartier, 26, New York, NY
Vivian Casalduc, 45, New York, NY
John F. Casazza, 38, Colts Neck, NJ
Paul Cascio, 23, Manhasset, NY
Margarito Casillas, 54, Guadalajara, Jalisco, Mex.
Thomas Anthony Casoria, 29, New York, NY
William Otto CasPar, 57, Eatontown, NJ
Alejandro Castano, 35, Englewood, NJ
Arcelia Castillo, 49, Elizabeth, NJ
Leonard M. Castrianno, 30, New York, NY
Jose Ramon Castro, 37, New York, NY
Richard G Catarelli, 47, New York, NY
Christopher Sean Caton, 34, New York, NY
Robert J. Caufield, 48, Valley Stream, NY
Mary Teresa Caulfield, 58, New York, NY
Judson Cavalier, 26, Huntington, NY
Michael Joseph Cawley, 32, Bellmore, NY
Jason D. Cayne, 32, Morganville, NJ
Juan Armando Ceballos, 47, New York, NY
Marcia G Cecil-Carter, 34, New York, NY
Jason Cefalu, 30, West Hempstead, NY
Thomas J. Celic, 43, New York, NY
Ana M. Centeno, 38, Bayonne, NJ
Joni Cesta, 37, Bellmore, NY
Jeffrey M. Chairnoff, 35, West Windsor, NJ
Swarna Chalasani, 33, Jersey City, NJ
William Chalcoff, 41, Roslyn, NY
Eli Chalouh, 23, New York, NY
Charles (Chip) Chan, 23, New York, NY
Mandy Chang, 40, New York, NY
Mark L. Charette, 38, Millburn, NJ
Jayceryll M. de Chavez, 24, Carteret, NJ
Gregorio Manuel Chavez, 48, New York, NY
Pedro Francisco Checo, 35, New York, NY
Stephen Patrick Cherry, 41, Stamford, CT
Douglas MacMillan Cherry, 38, Maplewood, NJ
Vernon Paul Cherry, 49, New York, NY
Nestor Chevalier, 30, New York, NY
Swede Joseph Chevalier, 26, Locust, NJ
Alexander H. Chiang, 51, New City, NY
Dorothy J. Chiarchiaro, 61, Glenwood, NJ
Luis Alfonso Chimbo, 39, New York, NY
Robert Chin, 33, New York, NY
Wing Wai (Eddie) Ching, 29, Union, NJ
Nicholas P. Chiofalo, 39, Selden, NY
John Chipura, 39, New York, NY
Peter A. Chirchirillo, 47, Langhorne, PA
Catherine E. Chirls, 47, Princeton, NJ
Kyung (Kaccy) Cho, 30, Clifton, NJ
Abul K. Chowdhury, 30, New York, NY
Mohammed S. Chowdhury, 38, New York, NY
Kirsten L. Christophe, 39, Maplewood, NJ
Pamela Chu, 31, New York, NY
Steven Paul Chucknick, 44, Cliffwood Beach, NJ
Wai-ching Chung, 36, New York, NY
Christopher Ciafardini, 30, New York, NY
Alex F. Ciccone, 38, New Rochelle, NY
Frances Ann Cilente, 26, New York, NY
Elaine Cillo, 40, New York, NY
Edna Cintron, 46, New York, NY
Nestor Andre Cintron, 26, New York, NY
Lt. Robert Dominick Cirri, 39, Nutley, NJ
Juan Pablo Alvarez Cisneros, 23, Weehawken, NJ
Gregory A. Clark, 40, Teaneck, NJ
Mannie Leroy Clark, 54, New York, NY
Thomas R. Clark, 37, Summit, NJ
Eugene Clark, 47, New York, NY
Benjamin Keefe Clark, 39, New York, NY
Donna Clarke, 39, New York, NY
Christopher Robert Clarke, 34, Philadelphia, PA
Michael Clarke, 27, Prince's Bay, NY
Suria R.E. Clarke, 30, New York, NY
Kevin Francis Cleary, 38, New York, NY
James D. Cleere, 55, Newton, IA
Geoffrey W. Cloud, 36, Stamford, CT
Susan M. Clyne, 42, Lindenhurst, NY
Steven Coakley, 36, Deer Park, NY
Jeffrey Coale, 31, Souderton, PA
Patricia A. Cody, 46, Brigantine, NJ
Jason Matthew Coffey, 25, Newburgh, NY
Daniel Michael Coffey, 54, Newburgh, NY
Florence Cohen, 62, New York, NY

Kevin Sanford Cohen, 28, Edison, NJ
Anthony Joseph Coladonato, 47, New York, NY
Mark J. Colaio, 34, New York, NY
Stephen J. Colaio, 32, Montauk, NY
Christopher M. Colasanti, 33, Hoboken, NJ
Michel Paris Colbert, 39, West New York, NJ
Kevin Nathaniel Colbert, 25, New York, NY
Keith Eugene Coleman, 34, Warren, NJ
Scott Thomas Coleman, 31, New York, NY
Tarel Coleman, 32
Liam Joseph Colhoun, 34, Flushing,, NY
Robert D. Colin, 49, West Babylon, NY
Robert J. Coll, 35, Glen Ridge, NJ
Jean Marie Collin, 42, New York, NY
John Michael Collins, 42, New York, NY
Michael L. Collins, 38, Montclair, NJ
Thomas J. Collins, 36, New York, NY
Joseph Collison, 50, New York, NY
Patricia Malia Colodner, 39, New York, NY
Linda M. Colon, 46, Perrineville, NJ
Soledi Colon, 39, New York, NY
Ronald Comer, 56, Northport, NY
Jaime Concepcion, 46, New York, NY
Albert Conde, 62, Englishtown, NJ
Denease Conley, 44, New York, NY
Susan Clancy Conlon, 41, New York, NY
Margaret Mary Conner, 57, New York, NY
Cynthia L. Connolly, 40, Metuchen, NJ
John E. CNolly, 46, Allenwood, NJ
James Lee Connor, 38, Summit, NJ
Jonathan (J.C.) Connors, 55, Old Brookville, NY
Kevin P. Connors, 55, Greenwich, CN
Kevin Francis Conroy, 47, New York, NY
Brenda E. Conway, 40, New York, NY
Dennis Michael Cook, 33, Colts Neck, NJ
Helen D. Cook, 24, New York, NY
John A. Cooper, 40, Bayonne, NJ
Joseph J. Coppo, 47, New Canaan, CN
Gerard J. Coppola, 46, New Providence, NJ
Joseph Albert Corbett, 28, Islip, NY
Alejandro Cordero, 23, New York, NY
Robert Cordice, 28, New York, NY
Ruben D. Correa, 44, New York, NY
Danny A. Correa-Gutierrez, 25, Fairview, NJ
James Corrigan, 60, New York, NY
Carlos Cortes, 57, New York, NY
Kevin M. Cosgrove, 46, West Islip, NY
Dolores Marie Costa, 53, Middletown, NJ
Digna Rivera Costanza, 25, New York, NY
Charles Gregory Costello, 46, Old Bridge, NJ
Michael S. Costello, 27, Hoboken, NJ
Conrod K.H. Cottoy, 51, New York, NY
Martin Coughlan, 54, New York, NY
Sgt. John Gerard Coughlin, 43, Pomona, NY
Timothy John Coughlin, 42, New York, NY
James E. Cove, 48, Rockville Centre, NY
Andre Cox, 29, New York, NY
Frederick John Cox, 27, New York, NY
James Raymond Coyle, 26, New York, NY
Michelle Coyle-Eulau, 38, Garden City, NY
Christopher Seton Cramer, 34, Manahawkin, NJ
Anne M. Cramer, 47, New York, NY
Denise Crant, 46, Hackensack, NJ
Robert James Crawford, 62, New York, NY
James L. Crawford, 33, Madison, NJ
Joanne Mary Cregan, 32, New York, NY
Lucia Crifasi, 51, Glendale, NY
Lt. John Crisci, 48, Holbrook, NY
Daniel Hal Crisman, 25, New York, NY
Dennis A. Cross, 60, Islip Terrace, NY
Helen Crossin-Kittle, 34, Larchmont, NY
Kevin Raymond Crotty, 43, Summit, NJ
Thomas G Crotty, 42, Rockville Centre, NY
John Crowe, 57, Rutherford, NJ
Welles Remy Crowther, 24, Upper Nyack, NY
Robert L. Cruikshank, 64, New York, NY
Francisco Cruz, 47, New York, NY
John Robert Cruz, 32, Jersey City, NJ
Kenneth John Cubas, 48, Woodstock, NY
Richard Joseph Cudina, 46, Glen Gardner, NJ
Neil James Cudmore, 38, Port Washington, NY
Thomas Patrick Cullen, 31, New York, NY
Joan McCNell Cullinan, 47, Scarsdale, NY
Joyce Cummings, 65
Brian Thomas Cummins, 38, Manasquan, NJ
Nilton Albuquerque Fernao Cunha, 41
Michael Cunningham, 39, Princeton Junc., NJ
Robert Curatolo, 31, New York, NY
Laurence Curia, 41, Garden City, NY

Paul Dario Curioli, 53, Norwalk, CN
Beverly Curry, 41, New York, NY
Sgt. Michael Curtin, 45, Medford, NY
Gavin Cushny, 47, Hoboken, NJ
Caleb Arron Dack, 39, Montclair, NJ
Carlos S. DaCosta, 41, Elizabeth, NJ
John D'Allara, 47, Pearl River, NY
Vincent D'Amadeo, 36, E. Patchoque, NY
Thomas A. Damaskinos, 33, Matawan, NJ
Jack L. D'Ambrosi, 45, Woodcliff Lake, NJ
Jeannine Damiani-Jones, 28, New York, NY
Patrick W. Danahy, 35, Yorktown Heights, NY
Nana Kwuku Danso, 47, New York, NY
Mary D'Antonio, 55, New York, NY
Vincent G. Danz, 38, Farmingdale, NY
Dwight Donald Darcy, 55, Bronxville, NY
Elizabeth Ann Darling, 28, Newark, NJ
Annette Andrea Dataram, 25, New York, NY
Lt. Edward Alexander D'Atri, 38, New York, NY
Michael D. D'Auria, 25, New York, NY
Lawrence Davidson, 51, New York, NY
Michael Allen Davidson, 27, Westfield, NJ
Scott Matthew Davidson, 33, New York, NY
Titus Davidson, 55, New York, NY
Niurka Davila, 47, New York, NY
Clinton Davis, 38, New York, NY
Wayne Terrial Davis, 29, Fort Meade, MD
Calvin Dawson, 46, New York, NY
Anthony Richard Dawson, 32, Hampshire, Eng.
Edward James Day, 45, New York, NY
Emerita (Emy) De La Pena, 32, New York, NY
William T. Dean, 35, Floral Park, NY
Robert J. DeAngelis, 48, West Hempstead, NY
Thomas P. Deangelis, 51, Westbury, NY
Tara Debek, 35, Babylon, NY
Anna Debin, 30, E. Farmingdale, NY
James V. DeBlase, 45, ManalaPan, NJ
Paul DeCola, 39, Ridgewood, NJ
Simon Dedvukaj, 26, Mohegan Lake, NY
Jason Christopher DeFazio, 29, New York, NY
David A. Defeo, 37, New York, NY
Jennifer DeJesus, 23, New York, NY
Monique E. DeJesus, 28, New York, NY
Nereida DeJesus, 30, New York, NY
Donald A. Delapenha, 37, Allendale, NJ
Vito Joseph Deleo, 41, New York, NY
Danielle Delie, 47, New York, NY
Colleen Ann Deloughery, 41, Bayonne, NJ
Anthony Demas, 61, New York, NY
Martin DeMeo, 47, Farmingville, NY
Francis X. Deming, 47, Franklin Lakes, NJ
Carol K. Demitz, 49, New York, NY
Kevin Dennis, 43, PeaPack, NJ
Thomas F. Dennis, 43, Setauket, NY
Jean C. DePalma, 51, Newfoundland, NJ
Jose Nicolas Depena, 42, New York, NY
Robert J. Deraney, 43, New York, NY
Michael DeRienzo, 37, Hoboken, NJ
David Paul Derubbio, 38, New York, NY
Jemal Legesse DeSantis, 28, Jersey City, NJ
Edward DeSimone, 36, Atlantic Highlands, NJ
Christian L. DeSimone, 23, Ringwood, NJ
Lt. Andrew Desperito, 44, Patchogue, NY
Michael Jude D'Esposito, 32, Morganville, NJ
Cindy Ann Deuel, 28, New York, NY
Melanie Louise DeVere, 30, London, England
Jerry DeVito, 66, New York, NY
Robert P. Devitt, 36, Plainsboro, NJ
Dennis Lawrence Devlin, 51, Washingtonville, NY
Gerard Dewan, 35, New York, NY
Simon Kassamali Dhanani, 62, Hartsdale, NY
Michael L. DiAgostino, 41, Garden City, NY
Obdulio Ruiz Diaz, 44, New York, NY
Matthew Diaz, 33, New York, NY
Nancy Diaz, 28, New York, NY
Lourdes Galletti Diaz, 32, New York, NY
Michael Diaz-Piedra, 49
Judith Belguese Diaz-Sierra, 32, Bay Shore, NY
Patricia F. DiChiaro, 63, New York, NY
Joseph Dermot Dickey, 50, Manhasset, NY
Lawrence Patrick Dickinson, 35, Morganville, NJ
Michael David Diehl, 48, Brick, NJ
John DiFato, 39, New York, NY
Vincent F. DiFazio, 43, Hampton, NJ
Carl DiFranco, 27, New York, NY
Donald J. DiFranco, 43, New York, NY
Debra Ann DiMartino, 36, New York, NY
Stephen P. Dimino, 48, Basking Ridge, NJ
William J. Dimmling, 47, Garden City, NY

Christopher Dincuff, 31, Jersey City, NJ
Jeffrey M. Dingle, 32, New York, NY
Anthony DiOnisio, 38, Glen Rock, NJ
George DiPasquale, 33, New York, NY
Joseph DiPilato, 57, New York, NY
Douglas Frank DiStefano, 24, Hoboken, NJ
Ramzi A. Doany, 35, Bayonne, NJ, Jordanian
John J. Doherty, 58, Hartsdale, NY
Melissa C. Doi, 32, New York, NY
Brendan Dolan, 37, Glen Rock, NJ
Neil Dollard, 28, Hoboken, NJ
James Joseph Domanico, 56, New York, NY
Benilda Pascua Domingo, 37, New York, NY
Charles (Carlos) Dominguez, 34, E. Meadow, NY
GeronimoDominguez, 37, HoltsvillLe, NY
Lt. Kevin W. Donnelly, 43, New York, NY
Jacqueline Donovan, 34, New York, NY
Stephen Dorf, 39, New Milford, NJ
Thomas Dowd, 37, Monroe, NY
Lt. Kevin Christopher Dowdell, 46, New York, NY
Mary Yolanda Dowling, 46, New York, NY
Raymond M. Downey, 63, Deer Park, NY
Joseph M. Doyle, 25, New York, NY
Frank Joseph Doyle, 39, Englewood, NJ
Randy Drake, 37, Lee's Summit, Mo
Stephen Patrick Driscoll, 38, Lake Carmel, NY
Mirna A. Duarte, 31, New York, NY
Luke A. Dudek, 50, Livingston, NJ
Gerard Duffy, 53, Manorville, NY
Michael Joseph Duffy, 29, Northport, NY
Christopher Michael Duffy, 23, New York, NY
Thomas W. Duffy, 52, Pittsford, NY
Antoinette Duger, 44, Belleville, NJ
Jackie Sayegh Duggan, 34
Sareve Dukat, 53, New York, NY
Christopher Joseph Dunne, 28, Mineola, NY
Richard A. Dunstan, 54, New Providence, NJ
Patrick Thomas Dwyer, 37, Nissequogue, NY
Joseph Anthony Eacobacci, 26, New York, NY
John Bruce Eagleson, 53, Middlefield, CN
Robert D. Eaton, 37, Manhasset, NY
Dean P. Eberling, 44, Cranford, NJ
Margaret Ruth Echtermann, 33, Hoboken, NJ
Paul Robert Eckna, 28, West New York, NJ
Constantine (Gus) Economos, 41, New York, NY
Dennis Michael Edwards, 35, Huntington, NY
Michael Hardy Edwards, 33, New York, NY
Lisa Egan, 31, Cliffside Park, NJ
Capt. Martin Egan, 36, New York, NY
Michael Egan, 51, Middletown, NJ
Christine Egan, 55, Winnipeg, Manitoba, Canada
Samantha Egan, 24, Jersey City, NJ
Carole Eggert, 60, New York, NY
Lisa Caren Weinstein Ehrlich, 36, New York, NY
John Ernst (Jack) Eichler, 69, Cedar Grove, NJ
Eric Adam Eisenberg, 32, Commack, NY
Daphne F. Elder, 36, Newark, NJ
Michael J. Elferis, 27, College Point, NY
Mark J. Ellis, 26, South Huntington, NY
Valerie Silver Ellis, 46, New York, NY
Albert Alfy William Elmarry, 30, N. Brunswick, NJ
Edgar H. Emery, 45, Clifton, NJ
Doris Suk-Yuen Eng, 30, New York, NY
Christopher S. Epps, 29, New York, NY
Ulf Ramm Ericson, 79, Greenwich, CN
Erwin L. Erker, 41, Farmingdale, NY
William J. Erwin, 30, Verona, NJ
Sarah (Ali) Escarcega, 35, New York, NY
Jose Espinal, 31
Fanny M. Espinoza, 29, Teaneck, NJ
Francis Esposito, 32, New York, NY
Lt. Michael Esposito, 41, New York, NY
William Esposito, 51, Bellmore, NY
Brigette Ann Esposito, 34, New York, NY
Ruben Esquilin, 35, New York, NY
Sadie Ette, 36, New York, NY
Barbara G. Etzold, 43, Jersey City, NJ
Eric Brian Evans, 31, Weehawken, NJ
Robert Edward Evans, 36, Franklin Square, NY
Meredith Emily June Ewart, 29, Hoboken, NJ
Patricia M. Fagan, 55, Toms River, NJ
Catherine K. Fagan, 58, New York, NY
Keith G Fairben, 24, Floral Park, NY
William Fallon, 38, Coram, NY
William F. Fallon, 53, Rocky Hill, NJ
Anthony J. Fallone, 39, New York, NY
Dolores B. Fanelli, 38, Farmingville, NY
John Joseph Fanning, 54, West Hempstead, NY
Kathleen (Kit) Faragher, 33, Denver, Colo

Capt. Thomas Farino, 37, Bohemia, NY
Nancy Carole Farley, 45, Jersey City, NJ
Elizabeth AnnFarmer, 62, New York, NY
Douglas Farnum, 33, New York, NY
John W. Farrell, 41, Basking Ridge, NJ
Terrence Patrick Farrell, 45, Huntington, NY
John G Farrell, 32, New York, NY
Capt. Joseph Farrelly, 47, New York, NY
Thomas P. Farrelly, 54, E. Northport, NY
Syed Abdul Fatha, 54, Newark, NJ
Christopher Faughnan, 37, South Orange, NJ
Wendy R. Faulkner, 47, Mason, Ohio
Shannon M. Fava, 30, New York, NY
Bernard D. Favuzza, 52, Suffern, NY
Robert Fazio, 41, Freeport, NY
Ronald C. Fazio, 57, Closter, NJ
William Feehan, 72, New York, NY
Francis J. (Frank) Feely, 41, Middletown, NY
Garth E. Feeney, 28, New York, NY
Sean B. Fegan, 34, New York, NY
Lee S. Fehling, 28, Wantagh, NY
Peter Feidelberg, 34, Hoboken, NJ
Alan D. Feinberg, 48, New York, NY
Rosa Maria Feliciano, 30, New York, NY
Edward T. Fergus, 40, Wilton, CN.
George Ferguson, 54, Teaneck, NJ
Henry Fernandez, 23, New York, NY
Judy H. Fernandez, 27, Parlin, NJ
Jose Contreras Fernandez, El Aguacate, Jalisco, Mex.
Elisa Giselle Ferraina, 27, London, England
Anne Marie Sallerin Ferreira, 29, Jersey City, NJ
Robert John Ferris, 63, Garden City, NY
David Francis Ferrugio, 46, Middletown, NJ
Louis V. Fersini, 38, Basking Ridge, NJ
Michael David Ferugio, 37, New York, NY
Bradley James Fetchet, 24, New York, NY
Jennifer Louise Fialko, 29, Teaneck, NJ
Kristen Fiedel, 27, New York, NY
Samuel Fields, 36, New York, NY
Michael Bradley Finnegan, 37, Basking Ridge, NJ
Timothy J. Finnerty, 33, Glen Rock, NJ
Michael Curtis Fiore, 46, New York, NY
Stephen J. Fiorelli, 43, Aberdeen, NJ
Paul M. Fiori, 31, Yorktown Heights, NY
John Fiorito, 40, Stamford, CT
Lt. John R. Fischer, 46, New York, NY
Andrew Fisher, 42, New York, NY
Thomas J. Fisher, 36, Union, NJ
Bennett Lawson Fisher, 58, Stamford, CT.
John Roger Fisher, 46, Bayonne, NJ
Lucy Fishman, 37, New York, NY
Ryan D. Fitzgerald, 26, New York, NY
Thomas FitzPatrick, 35, Tuckahoe, NY
Richard P. Fitzsimons, 57, Lynbrook, NY
Salvatore A. Fiumefreddo, 47, ManalaPan, NJ
Christina Donovan Flannery, 26, New York, NY
Eileen Flecha, 33, New York, NY
Andre G Fletcher, 37, N. Babylon, NY
Carl Flickinger, 38, Conyers, NY
John Joseph Florio, 33, Oceanside, NY
Joseph W. Flounders, 46, E. Stroudsburg, PA
David Fodor, 39, Garrison, NY
Lt. Michael N. Fodor, 53, Warwick, NY
Steven Mark Fogel, 40, Westfield, NY
Thomas Foley, 32, West Nyack, NY
David Fontana, 37, New York, NY
Chih Min (Dennis) Foo, 40, Holmdel, NJ
Del Rose Forbes-Cheatham, 48, New York, NY
Godwin Forde, 39, New York, NY
Donald A. Foreman, 53, New York, NY
Christopher Hugh Forsythe, 44, Basking Ridge, NJ
Claudia Alicia Martinez Foster, 26, New York, NY
Noel J. Foster, 40, Bridgewater, NJ
Ana Fosteris, 58, Coram, NY
Robert J. Foti, 42, Albertson, NY
Jeffrey L. Fox, 40, Cranbury, NJ
Virginia Fox, 58, New York, NY
Virgin (Lucy) Francis, 62, New York, NY
Pauline Francis, 57, New York, NY
Joan Francis
Morton Frank, 31, New York, NY
Gary J. Frank, 35, South Amboy, NJ
Peter Christopher Frank, 29, New York, NY
Richard K. Fraser, 32, New York, NY
Kevin Joseph Frawley, 34, Bronxville, NY
Clyde Frazier, 41, New York, NY
Lillian I. Frederick, 46, Teaneck, NJ
Andrew Fredericks, 40, Suffern, NY
Tamitha Freemen, 35, New York, NY

America – Voices Coming Together

109

Brett O. Freiman, 29, Roslyn, NY
Lt. Peter L. Freund, 45, Westtown, NY
Arlene E. Fried, 49, Roslyn Heights, NY
Alan Wayne Friedlander, 52, Yorktown Heights, NY
Andrew K. Friedman, 44, Woodbury, NY
Gregg J. Froehner, 46, Chester, NJ
Peter Christian Fry, 36, Wilton, CN
Clement Fumando, 59, New York, NY
Steven Elliot Furman, 40, Wesley Hills, NY
Paul James Furmato, 37, Colts Neck, NJ
Fredric Gabler, 30, New York, NY
Richard S. Gabrielle, 50, West Haven, CN
James Andrew Gadiel, 23, New York, NY
Pamela Gaff, 51, Robinsville, NJ
Ervin Vincent Gailliard, 42, New York, NY
Deanna L. Galante, 32, New York, NY
Grace Galante, 29, New York, NY
German Castillo Galicia, Ozumba, Mexico
Anthony Edward Gallagher, 41, New York, NY
John Patrick Gallagher, 31, Yonkers, NY
Daniel James Gallagher, 23, Red Bank, NJ
Cono E. Gallo, 30, New York, NY
Vincenzo Gallucci, 36, Monroe Township, NJ
Thomas Edward Galvin, 32, New York, NY
Giovanna (Genni) Gambale, 27, New York, NY
Thomas Gambino, 48, Babylon, NY
Giann F. Gamboa, 26, New York, NY
Peter J. Ganci, 55, N. MAapequa, NY
Claude Michael Gann, 41, Roswell, Ga
Lt. CharlesGarbarini, 44, Pleasantville, NY
Cesar Garcia, 36, New York, NY
David Garcia, 40, Freeport, NY
Jorge Luis Morron Garcia, 38, New York, NY
Juan Garcia, 50, New York, NY
Marlyn C. Garcia, 21, New York, NY
Thomas A. Gardner, 39, Oceanside, NY
Christopher Gardner, 36, Darien, CN
Douglas B. Gardner, 39, New York, NY
Harvey J. Gardner, 35, Lakewood, NJ
Jeffrey B. Gardner, 36, Hoboken, NJ
William Arthur Gardner, 45, Lynbrook, NY
Francesco Garfi, 29, New York, NY
Rocco Gargano, 28, Bayside, NY
James M. Gartenberg, 36, New York, NY
Matthew David Garvey, 37
Bruce Gary, 51, Bellmore, NY
Palmina Delli Gatti, 33, New York, NY
Boyd A. Gatton, 38, Jersey City, NJ
Donald Richard Gavagan, 35, New York, NY
Terence D. Gazzani, 24, New York, NY
Gary Geidel, 44, New York, NY
Paul Hamilton Geier, 36, Farmingdale, NY
Julie M. Geis, 44, Lees Summit, Mo
Peter Gelinas, 34, New York, NY
Steven Paul Geller, 52, New York, NY
Howard G. Gelling, 28, New York, NY
Peter Victor Genco, 36, Rockville Centre, NY
Steven Gregory Genovese, 37, Basking Ridge, NJ
Alayne F. Gentul, 44, Mountain Lakes, NJ
Edward F. Geraghty, 45, Rockville Centre, NY
Suzanne Geraty, 30, New York, NY
Ralph Gerhardt, 33, New York, NY
Robert J. Gerlich, 56, Monroe, CN
Denis P. Germain, 33, Tuxedo Park, NY
Marina R. Gertsberg, 25, New York, NY
Susan M. Getzendanner, 57, New York, NY
James Gerard Geyer, 41, Rockville Centre, NY
Joseph M. Giaccone, 43, Monroe, NJ
Lt. Vincent Giammona, 40, Valley Stream, NY
Debra L. Gibbon, 43, Hackettstown, NJ
James A. Giberson, 43, New York, NY
Craig Neil Gibson, 37, New York, NY
Ronnie Gies, 43, Merrick, NY
Laura A. Giglio, 35, Oceanside, NY
Andrew Clive Gilbert, 39, CAon, NJ
Timothy Paul Gilbert, 35, Lebanon, NJ
Paul Stuart Gilbey, 39, Chatham, NJ
Paul John Gill, 34, New York, NY
Mark Y. Gilles, 33, New York, NY
Evan H. Gillette, 40, New York, NY
Ronald Gilligan, 43, Norwalk, CN
Sgt. Rodney C. Gillis, 34, New York, NY
Laura Gilly, 32, New York, NY
Lt. John F. Ginley, 37, Warwick, NY
Jeffrey Giordano, 46, New York, NY
John Giordano, 46, Newburgh, NY
Donna Marie Giordano, 44, Parlin, NJ
Steven A. Giorgetti, 43, Manhasset, NY
Martin Giovinazzo, 34, New York, NY
Kum-Kum Girolamo, 41, New York, NY

Salvatore Gitto, 44, ManalaPan, NJ
Cynthia Giugliano, 46, Nesconset, NY
Mon Gjonbalaj, 65, New York, NY
Dianne Gladstone, 55, New York, NY
Keith Alexander Glascoe, 38, New York, NY
Thomas I. Glasser, 40, Summit, NJ
Harry Glenn, 38, Piscataway, NJ
Barry H. Glick, 55, Wayne, NJ
Steven Lawrence Glick, 42, Greenwich, CN
John T. Gnazzo, 32, New York, NY
William (Bill) Robert Godshalk, 35, New York, NY
Michael Gogliormella, 43, New Providence, NJ
Brian Fredric Goldberg, 26, Union, NJ
Jeffrey Grant Goldflam, 48, Melville, NY
Michelle Herman Goldstein, 31, New York, NY
Monica Goldstein, 25, New York, NY
Steven Goldstein, 35, Princeton, NJ
Andrew H. Golkin, 30, New York, NY
Dennis James Gomes, 40, New York, NY
Enrique Antonio Gomez, 42, New York, NY
J o s e   Bienvenido

"You must not lose
faith in humanity.
Humanity is an ocean;
if a few drops
of the ocean are dirty,
the ocean does not
become dirty."

Mahatma Gandhi (1869 - 1948)

Gomez, 45, New York, NY
Manuel Gomez, 42, New York, NY
Wilder Gomez, 38, New York, NY
Jenine Gonzalez, 27, New York, NY
Joel Guevara Gonzalez, 23, Aguascalientes, Mexico
Rosa J. Gonzalez, 32, Jersey City, NJ
Mauricio Gonzalez, 27, New York, NY
Calvin J. Gooding, 38, Riverside, NY
Harry Goody, 50, New York, NY
Kiran Reddy Gopu, 24, Bridgeport, CN
Catherine Carmen Gorayeb, 41, New York, NY
Kerene Gordon, 43, New York, NY
Sebastian Gorki, 27, New York, NY
Kieran Gorman, 35, Yonkers, NY
Thomas E. Gorman, 41, Middlesex, NJ
Michael Edward Gould, 29, Hoboken, NJ
Yugi Goya, 42, Rye, NY
Jon Richard Grabowski, 33, New York, NY
Christopher Michael Grady, 39, Cranford, NJ
Edwin John Graf, 48, Rowayton, CN
David M. Graifman, 40, New York, NY
Gilbert Granados, 51, Hicksville, NY
Elvira Granitto, 43, New York, NY
Winston Arthur Grant, 59, West Hempstead, NY
James Michael Gray, 34, New York, NY
Christopher Stewart Gray, 32, Weehawken, NJ
Linda Mair Grayling, 44, New York, NY
Timothy Grazioso, 42, Gulf Stream, Fla
John Michael Grazioso, 41, Middletown, NJ
Derrick Arthur Green, 44, New York, NY
Wade Brian Green, 42, Westbury, NY
Elaine Myra Greenberg, 56, New York, NY
Gayle R. Greene, 51, Montville, NJ
James Arthur Greenleaf, 32, New York, NY
Eileen Marsha Greenstein, 52, Morris Plains, NJ
Elizabeth (Lisa) Martin Gregg, 52, New York, NY
Donald H. Gregory, 62, Ramsey, NJ
Florence M. Gregory, 38, New York, NY
Denise Gregory, 39, New York, NY
Pedro (David) Grehan, 35, Hoboken, NJ
Tawanna Griffin, 30, New York, NY
John M. Griffin, 38, Waldwick, NJ
Joan D. Griffith, 39, Willingboro, NJ
Warren Grifka, 54, New York, NY

Ramon Grijalvo, 58
Joseph F. Grillo, 46, New York, NY
David Grimner, 51, Merrick, NY
Kenneth Grouzalis, 56, Lyndhurst, NJ
Joseph Grzelak, 52, New York, NY
Matthew J. Grzymalski, 34, N Hyde Park, NY
Robert Joseph Gschaar, 55, Spring Valley, NY
Liming (Michael) Gu, 34, Piscataway, NJ
Jose A. Guadalupe, 37, New York, NY
Yan Zhu (Cindy) Guan, 25, New York, NY
Geoffrey E. Guja, 47, Lindenhurst, NY
Lt. Joseph Gullickson, 37, New York, NY
Babita Guman, 33, New York, NY
Douglas B. Gurian, 38, Tenafly, NJ
Philip T. Guza, 54, Sea Bright, NJ
Barbara Guzzardo, 49, Glendale, NY
Peter Gyulavary, 44, Warwick, NY
Gary Robert Haag, 36, Ossining, NY
Andrea Lyn Haberman, 25, Chicago, IL.
Barbara M. Habib, 49, New York, NY
Philip Haentzler, 49, New York, NY
Nizam A. Hafiz, 32, New York, NY
Karen Hagerty, 34, New York, NY
Steven Hagis, 31, New York, NY
Mary Lou Hague, 26, New York, NY
David Halderman, 40, New York, NY
Maile Rachel Hale, 26, Cambridge, MA
Richard Hall, 49, Purchase, NY
Vaswald George Hall, 50, New York, NY
Robert John Halligan, 59, Basking Ridge, NJ
Lt. Vincent Halloran, 43, North Salem, NY
James D. Halvorson, 56, Greenwich, CN
Mohammed Hamdani, 23, New York, NY
Felicia Hamilton, 62, New York, NY
Robert Hamilton, 43, Washingtonville, NY
Frederic Kim Han, 45, Marlboro, NJ
Christopher James Hanley, 34, New York, NY
Sean Hanley, 35, New York, NY
Valerie Joan Hanna, 57, Freeville, NY
Thomas Hannafin, 36, New York, NY
Kevin Hannaford, 32, Basking Ridge, NJ
Michael L. Hannan, 34, Lynbrook, NY
Dana Hannon, 29, Suffern, NY
Vassilios G. Haramis, 56, New York, NY
James A. Haran, 41, Malverne, NY
Jeffrey P. Hardy, 46, New York, NY
Timothy Hargrave, 38, Readington, NJ
Daniel Harlin, 41, Kent, NY
Frances Haros, 76, New York, NY
Lt. Harvey L. Harrell, 49, New York, NY
Lt. Stephen Gary Harrell, 44, Warwick, NY
Stewart D. Harris, 52, Marlboro, NJ
Aisha Harris, 22, New York, NY
John Patrick Hart, 38, Danville, CA
John Clinton Hartz, 64, Basking Ridge, NJ
Emeric J. Harvey, 56, Montclair, NJ
Capt. Thomas Haskell, 37, Massapequa, NY
Timothy Haskell, 34, Seaford, NY
Joseph John Hasson, 34, New York, NY
Capt. Terence S. Hatton, 41, New York, NY
Leonard Hatton, 45, Ridgefield Park, NJ
Michael Haub, 34, Roslyn Heights, NY
Timothy Aaron Haviland, 41, Oceanside, NY
Donald G. Havlish, 53, Yardley, PA
Anthony Hawkins, 30, New York, NY
Nobuhiro Hayatsu, 36, Scarsdale, NY
Philip Hayes, 67, Northport, NY
William Ward Haynes, 35, Rye, NY
Scott Hazelcorn, 29, Hoboken, NJ
Lt. Michael K. Healey, 42, E.Patchogue, NY
Roberta Bernstein Heber, 60, New York, NY
Charles Heeran, 23, Belle Harbor, NY
John Heffernan, 37, New York, NY
Howard Joseph Heller, 37, Ridgefield, CT
JoAnn L. Heltibridle, 46, Springfield, NJ
Mark F. Hemschoot, 45, Red Bank, NJ
Ronnie Lee Henderson, 52, Newburgh, NY
Janet Hendricks, 48, New York, NY
Brian Hennessey, 35, Ringoes, NJ
Michelle Henrique, 27, New York, NY
Joseph P. Henry, 25, New York, NY
William Henry, 49, New York, NY
John Henwood, 35, New York, NY
Robert Allan Hepburn, 39, Union, NJ
Mary (Molly) Herencia, 47, New York, NY
Lindsay Coates Herkness, 58, New York, NY
Harvey Robert Hermer, 59, New York, NY
Claribel Hernandez, 31, New York, NY
Norberto Hernandez, 42, New York, NY
Raul Hernandez, 51, New York, NY

110   In Rememberance of the Tragedies of September 11, 2001

Gary Herold, 44, Farmingdale, NY
Jeffrey A. Hersch, 53, New York, NY
Thomas Hetzel, 33, Elmont, NY
Capt. Brian Hickey, 47, New York, NY
Ysidro Hidalgo-Tejada, 48, Dom. Republic
Lt. Timothy Higgins, 43, Farmingville, NY
Robert D. Higley, 29, New Fairfield, CT
Todd Russell Hill, 34, Boston, MA
Clara Victorine Hinds, 52, New York, NY
Neal Hinds, 28, New York, NY
Mark D. Hindy, 28, New York, NY
Richard Van Hine, 48, Greenwood Lake, NY
Katsuyuki Hirai, 32, Hartsdale, NY
Heather Malia Ho, 32, New York, NY
Tara Yvette Hobbs, 31, New York, NY
Thomas A. Hobbs, 41, Baldwin, NY
James L. Hobin, 47, Marlborough, Conn.
Robert Hobson, 36, New Providence, NJ
DaJuan Hodges, 29, New York, NY
Ronald Hoerner, 58, Massapequa Park, NY
Patrick Aloysius Hoey, 53, Middletown, NJ
Marcia Hoffman, 52, New York, NY
Stephen G. Hoffman, 36, Long Beach, NY
Frederick J. Hoffmann, 53, Freehold, NJ
Michele L. Hoffmann, 27, Freehold, NJ
Judith Hofmiller, 53, Brookfield, CT
Thomas Warren Hohlweck, 57, Harrison, NY
Jonathan R. Hohmann, 48, New York, NY
Joseph Francis Holland, 32, Glen Rock, NJ
John Holland, 30
Elizabeth Holmes, 42, New York, NY
Thomas P. Holohan, 36, Chester, NY
Bradley Hoorn, 22, New York, NY
James P. Hopper, 51, Farmingdale, NY
Montgomery Hord, 46, Pelham, NY
Michael Horn, 27, Lynbrook, NY
Matthew D. Horning, 26, Hoboken, NJ
Robert L. Horohoe, 31, New York, NY
Aaron Horwitz, 24, New York, NY
Charles J. Houston, 42, New York, NY
George Howard, 45, Hicksville, NY
Michael C. Howell, 60, New York, NY
Steven L. Howell, 36, New York, NY
Jennifer L. Howley, 34, New Hyde Park, NY
Milagros Hromada, 35, New York, NY
Marian Hrycak, 56, New York, NY
Stephen Huczko, 44, Bethlehem, NJ
Timothy Robert Hughes, 43, Madison, NJ
Kris R. Hughes, 30, Nesconset, NY
Melissa Hughes, 31, San Francisco, CA
Thomas F. Hughes, 46, Spring Lake Hgts, NJ
Paul R. Hughes, 38, Stamford, Conn.
Robert T. "Bobby" Hughes, 23, Sayreville, NJ
Susan Huie, 43, Fair Lawn, NJ
Mychal Lamar Hulse, 30, New York, NY
Kathleen (Casey) Hunt, 43, Middletown, NJ
William C. Hunt, 32, Norwalk, Conn.
Joseph G. Hunter, 31, South Hempstead, NY
Robert Hussa, 51, Roslyn, NY
Capt. Walter Hynes, 46, Belle Harbor, NY
Thomas E. Hynes, 28, Norwalk, Conn.
Joseph Anthony Ianelli, 28, Hoboken, NJ
Zuhtu Ibis, 25, Clifton, NJ
Jonathan Lee Ielpi, 29, Great Neck, NY
Michael Patrick Iken, 37, New York, NY
Daniel Ilkanayev, 36, New York, NY
Capt. Frederick Ill, 49, Pearl River, NY
Abraham Ilowitz, 51, New York, NY
Anthony P. Infante, 47, Chatham, NJ
Louis S. Inghilterra, 45, New Castle, NY
Christopher N. Ingrassia, 28, Watchung, NJ
Paul Innella, 33, East Brunswick, NJ
Stephanie V. Irby, 38, New York, NY
Douglas Irgang, 32, New York, NY
Kristin A. Irvine-Ryan, 30, New York, NY
Todd A. Isaac, 29, New York, NY
Erik Hans Isbrandtsen, 30, New York, NY
Taizo Ishikawa, 50
Aram Iskenderian, 41, Merrick, NY
John Iskyan, 41, Wilton, Conn.
Kazushige Ito, 35, New York, NY
Aleksandr Ivantsov, 23, New York, NY
Virginia Jablonski, 49, Matawan, NJ
Brooke Jackman, 23, New York, NY
Michael Grady Jacobs, 54, Danbury, Conn.
Aaron Jacobs, 27, New York, NY
Jason Kyle Jacobs, 32, Mendham, NJ
Ariel Louis Jacobs, 29, Briarcliff Manor, NY
Steven A. Jacobson, 53, New York, NY
Ricknauth Jaggernauth, 58, New York, NY

Jake Denis Jagoda, 24, Huntington, NY
Yudh V.S. Jain, 54, New City, NY
Maria Jakubiak, 41, Ridgewood, NY
Gricelda E. James, 44, Willingboro, NJ
Ernest James, 40, New York, NY
Mark Jardim, 39, New York, NY
Mohammed Jawara, 30, New York, NY
Francois Jean-Pierre, 58, New York, NY
Maxima Jean-Pierre, 40, Bellport, NY
Paul E. Jeffers, 39, New York, NY
Joseph Jenkins, 47, New York, NY
Alan K. Jensen, 49, Wyckoff, NJ
Prem N. Jerath, 57, Edison, NJ
Farah Jeudy, 32, Spring Valley, NY
Hweidar Jian, 42, East Brunswick, NJ
Luis Jimenez, 25, New York, NY
Eliezer Jimenez, 38, New York, NY
Nicholas John, 42, New York, NY
Charles Gregory John, 44, New York, NY
Scott M. Johnson, 26, New York, NY
LaShawana Johnson, 27, New York, NY
William Johnston, 31, North Babylon, NY
Arthur Joseph Jones, 37, Ossining, NY
Donald W. Jones, 43, Fairless Hills, PA
Allison Horstmann Jones, 31, New York, NY
Brian L. Jones, 44, New York, NY
Christopher D. Jones, 53, Huntington, NY
Donald T. Jones, 39, Livingston, NJ
Linda Jones, 50, New York, NY
Mary S. Jones, 72, New York, NY
Andrew Jordan, 35, Remsenburg, NY
Robert Thomas Jordan, 34, Williston, NY
Ingeborg Joseph, 60, Germany
Stephen Joseph, 39, Franklin Park, NJ
Karl Henri Joseph, 25, New York, NY
Albert Joseph, 79
Jane Eileen Josiah, 47, Bellmore, NY
Lt. Anthony Jovic, 39, Massapequa, NY
Angel Luis Juarbe, 35, New York, NY
Karen Susan Juday, 52, New York, NY
The Rev. Mychal Judge, 68, New York, NY
Paul W. Jurgens, 47, Levittown, NY
Thomas Edward Jurgens, 26, Lawrence, NY
Kacinga Kabeya, 63, McKinney, Texas
Shashi Kadaba, 25, Hackensack, NJ
Gavkharoy Kamardinova, 26, New York, NY
Shari Kandell, 27, Wyckoff, NJ
Howard Lee Kane, 40, Hazlet, NJ
Jennifer Lynn Kane, 26, Fair Lawn, NY
Vincent D. Kane, 37, New York, NY
Joon Koo Kang, 34, Riverdale, NJ
Sheldon R. Kanter, 53, Edison, NJ
Deborah H. Kaplan, 45, Paramus, NJ
Alvin Kappelmann, 57, Green Brook, NJ
Charles Karczewski, 34, Union, NJ
William A. Karnes, 37, New York, NY
Douglas G Karpiloff, 53, Mamaroneck, NY
Charles L. Kasper, 54, New York, NY
Andrew Kates, 37, New York, NY
John Katsimatides, 31, East Marion, NY
Sgt. Robert Kaulfers, 49, Kenilworth, NJ
Don Jerome Kauth, 51, Saratoga Springs, NY
Hideya Kawauchi, 36, Fort Lee, NJ
Edward T. Keane, 66, West Caldwell, NJ
Richard M. Keane, 54, Wethersfield, CT
Lisa Kearney-Griffin, 35, Jamaica, NY
Karol Ann Keasler, 42, New York, NY
Paul Hanlon Keating, 38, New York, NY
Leo Russell Keene, 33, Westfield, NJ
Joseph J. Keller, 31, Park Ridge, NJ
Peter Kellerman, 35, New York, NY
Joseph P. Kellett, 37, Riverdale, NY
Frederick H. Kelley, 57, Huntington, NY
Joseph A. Kelly, 40, Oyster Bay, NY
Maurice Patrick Kelly, 41, New York, NY
Thomas W. Kelly, 51, New York, NY
Timothy C. Kelly, 37, Port Washington, NY
William Hill Kelly, 30, New York, NY
James Joseph Kelly, 39, Oceanside, NY
Richard John Kelly, 50, New York, NY
Thomas Michael Kelly, 41, Wyckoff, NJ
Thomas Richard Kelly, 38, Riverhead, NY
Robert C. Kennedy, 55, Toms River, NJ
Thomas J. Kennedy, 36, Islip Terrace, NY
John Keohane, 41, Jersey City, NJ
Lt. Ronald T. Kerwin, 42, Levittown, NY
Howard L. Kestenbaum, 56, Montclair, NJ
Douglas D. Ketcham, 27, New York, NY
Ruth E. Ketler, 42, New York, NY
Boris Khalif, 30, New York, NY

Sarah Khan, 32, New York, NY
Taimour Firaz Khan, 29, New York, NY
Rajesh Khandelwal, 33, South Plainfield, NJ
Olivia Bhowanie Devi Khemraj, Jersey City, NJ
SeiLai Khoo, 38, Jersey City, NJ
Michael Kiefer, 26, Hempstead, NY
Satoshi Kikuchihara, 43, Scarsdale, NY
Andrew Jay-Hoon Kim, 26, Leonia, NJ
Lawrence Don Kim, 31, Blue Bell, PA
Mary Jo Kimelman, 34, New York, NY
Andrew Marshall King, 42, Princeton, NJ
Lucille T. King, 59, Ridgewood, NJ
Robert King, 36, Bellerose Terrace, NY
Lisa M. King-Johnson, 34, New York, NY
Takashi Kinoshita, 46, Rye, NY
Chris Michael Kirby, 21, New York, NY
Howard Kirschbaum, 53, New York, NY
Glenn Davis Kirwin, 40, Scarsdale, NY
Richard J. Klares, 59, Somers, NY
Peter A. Klein, 35, Weehawken, NJ
Alan D. Kleinberg, 39, E. Brunswick, NJ
Karen J. Klitzman, 38, New York, NY
Ronald Philip Kloepfer, 39, Franklin Square, NY
Thomas Patrick Knox, 31, Hoboken, NJ
Andrew Knox, 30, Adelaide, Australia
Yevgeny Knyazev, 46, New York, NY
Rebecca Lee Koborie, 48, Guttenberg, NJ
Deborah Kobus, 36, New York, NY
Gary Edward Koecheler, 57, Harrison, NY
Frank J. Koestner, 48, New York, NY
Ryan Kohart, 26, New York, NY
Vanessa Lynn KolPak, 21, New York, NY
Irina KolPakova, 37, New York, NY
Suzanne Kondratenko, 27, Chicago, ill
Abdoulaye Kone, 37, New York, NY
Bon-seok Koo, 42, River Edge, NJ
Dorota Kopiczko, 26, Nutley, NJ
Scott Kopytko, 32, New York, NY
Bojan Kostic, 34, New York, NY
Danielle Kousoulis, 29, New York, NY
John J. Kren, 52
William Krukowski, 36, New York, NY
Lyudmila Ksido, 46, New York, NY
Shekhar Kumar, 30, New York, NY
Kenneth Kumpel, 42, Cornwall, NY
Frederick Kuo, 53, Great Neck, NY
Patricia Kuras, 42, New York, NY
Nauka Kushitani, 44, New York, NY
Thomas Joseph Kuveikis, 48, Carmel, NY
Victor Kwarkye, 35, New York, NY
Kui Fai Kwok, 31, New York, NY
Angela R. Kyte, 49, Boonton, NJ
Amarnauth Lachhman, 42, Valley Stream, NY
Andrew LaCorte, 61, Jersey City, NJ
Ganesh Ladkat, 27, Somerset, NJ
James P. Ladley, 41, Colts Neck, NJ
Daniel M. van Laere, 46, Glen Rock, NJ
Joseph A. Lafalce, 54, New York, NY
Jeanette LaFond-Menichino, 49, New York, NY
David LaForge, 50, Port Richmond, NY
Michael Patrick LaForte, 39, HolMDel, NJ
Alan Lafrance, 43
Juan Lafuente, 61, Poughkeepsie, NY
Neil K. Lai, 59, E. Windsor, NJ
Vincent A. Laieta, 31, Edison, NJ
William David Lake, 44, New York, NY
Franco Lalama, 45, Nutley, NJ
Chow Kwan Lam, 48, Maywood, NJ
Stephen LaMantia, 38, Darien, CN
Amy Hope Lamonsoff, 29, New York, NY
Robert T. Lane, 28, New York, NY
Brendan M. Lang, 30, Red Bank, NJ
Rosanne P. Lang, 42, Middletown, NJ
Vanessa Langer, 29, Yonkers, NY
Mary Lou Langley, 53, New York, NY
Thomas Langone, 39, Williston Park, NY
Peter J. Langone, 41, Roslyn Heights, NY
Michele B. Lanza, 36, New York, NY
Ruth Sheila Lapin, 53, E. Windsor, NJ
Carol Ann LaPlante, 59, New York, NY
Ingeborg Astrid Desiree Lariby, 42, New York, NY
Robin Larkey, 48, Chatham, NJ
Christopher Randall Larrabee, 26, New York, NY
Hamidou S. Larry, 37, New York, NY
Scott Larsen, 35, New York, NY
John Adam Larson, 37, Colonia, NJ
Gary E. Lasko, 49, Memphis, Tenn
Nicholas C. Lassman, 28, Cliffside Park, NJ
Paul Laszczynski, 49, Paramus, NJ
Jeffrey Latouche, 49, New York, NY

America – Voices Coming Together

Cristina de Laura
Oscar de Laura
Charles Laurencin, 61, New York, NY
Stephen James Lauria, 39, New York, NY
Maria Lavache, 60, New York, NY
Denis F. Lavelle, 42, Yonkers, NY
Jeannine M. LaVerde, 36, New York, NY
Anna A. Laverty, 52, Middletown, NJ
Steven Lawn, 28, West Windsor, NJ
Robert A. Lawrence, 41, Summit, NJ
Nathaniel Lawson, 61, New York, NY
Eugen Lazar, 27, New York, NY
James Patrick Leahy, 38, New York, NY
Lt. Joseph Gerard Leavey, 45, Pelham, NY
Neil Leavy, 34, New York, NY
Leon Lebor, 51, Jersey City, NJ
Kenneth Charles Ledee, 38, Monmouth, NJ
Alan J. Lederman, 43, New York, NY
Elena Ledesma, 36, New York, NY
Alexis Leduc, 45, New York, NY
Hyun-joon (Paul) Lee, 32, New York, NY
Jong-min Lee, 24, New York, NY
Myung-woo Lee, 41, Lyndhurst, NJ
David S. Lee, 37, West Orange, NJ
Linda C. Lee, 34, New York, NY
Gary H. Lee, 62, Lindenhurst, NY
Juanita Lee, 44, New York, NY
Lorraine Lee, 37, New York, NY
Richard Y.C. Lee, 34, Great Neck, NY
Yang Der Lee, 63, New York, NY
Kathryn Blair Lee, 55, New York, NY
Stuart (Soo-Jin) Lee, 30, New York, NY
Stephen Lefkowitz, 50, Belle Harbor, NY
Adriana Legro, 32, New York, NY
Edward J. Lehman, 41, Glen Cove, NY
Eric Andrew Lehrfeld, 32, New York, NY
David Ralph Leistman, 43, Garden City, NY
David Prudencio LeMagne, 27, N. Bergen, NJ
Joseph A. Lenihan, 41, Greenwich, CN
John J. Lennon, 44, Howell, NJ
John Robinson Lenoir, 38, Locust Valley, NY
Jorge Luis Leon, 43, Union City, NJ
Matthew Gerard Leonard, 38, New York, NY
Michael Lepore, 39, New York, NY
Charles Antoine Lesperance, 55
Jeffrey Earle LeVeen, 55, Manhasset, NY
John D. Levi, 50, New York, NY
Neil D. Levin, 47, New York, NY
Alisha Caren Levin, 33, New York, NY
Robert Levine, 56, West Babylon, NY
Robert M. Levine, 66, Edgewater, NJ
Shai Levinhar, 29, New York, NY
Adam J. Lewis, 36, Fairfield, CN
Margaret Susan Lewis, 49, Elizabeth, NJ
Ye Wei Liang, 27, New York, NY
Orasri Liangthanasarn, 26, Bayonne, NJ
Daniel F. Libretti, 43, New York, NY
Ralph M. Licciardi, 30, West Hempstead, NY
Edward Lichtschein, 35, New York, NY
Steven B. Lillianthal, 38, Millburn, NJ
Carlos R. Lillo, 37, Babylon, NY
Craig Damian Lilore, 30, Lyndhurst, NJ
Arnold A. Lim, 28, New York, NY
Darya Lin, 32, Chicago, ill
Wei Rong Lin, 31, Jersey City, NJ
Nickie L. Lindo, 31, New York, NY
Thomas V. Linehan, 39, Montville, NJ
Robert Thomas Linnane, 33, West Hempstead, NY
Alan Linton, 26, Jersey City, NJ
Diane Theresa LiPari, 42, New York, NY
Kenneth P. Lira, 28, Paterson, NJ
Francisco Alberto Liriano, 33, New York, NY
Lorraine Lisi, 44, New York, NY
Paul Lisson, 45, New York, NY
Vincent Litto, 52, New York, NY
Ming-Hao Liu, 41, Livingston, NJ
Nancy Liz, 39, New York, NY
Harold Lizcano, 31, E. Elmhurst, NY
Martin Lizzul, 31, New York, NY
George A. Llanes, 33, New York, NY
Elizabeth Claire Logler, 31, Rockville Centre, NY
Catherine Lisa Loguidice, 30, New York, NY
Jerome Robert Lohez, 30, Jersey City, NJ
Michael W. Lomax, 37, New York, NY
Laura M. Longing, 35, Pearl River, NY
Salvatore P. Lopes, 40, Franklin Square, NY
Luis Lopez, 38, New York, NY
Manuel L. Lopez, 54, Jersey City, NJ
Daniel Lopez, 39, New York, NY
George Lopez, 40, Stroudsburg, PA

Joseph Lostrangio, 48, Langhorne, PA
Chet Louie, 45, New York, NY
Stuart Seid Louis, 43, E. Brunswick, NJ
Joseph Lovero, 60, Jersey City, NJ
Michael W. Lowe, 48, New York, NY
Garry Lozier, 47, Darien, CN
John Peter Lozowsky, 45, New York, NY
Charles Peter Lucania, 34, E. Atlantic Beach, NY
Edward (Ted) H. Luckett, 40, Fair Haven, NJ
Mark G. Ludvigsen, 32, New York, NY
Lee Charles Ludwig, 49, New York, NY
Sean Thomas Lugano, 28, New York, NY
Daniel Lugo, 45, New York, NY
Marie Lukas, 32, New York, NY
William Lum, 45, New York, NY
Michael P. Lunden, 37, New York, NY
Christopher Lunder, 34, Wall, NJ
Anthony LuParello, 62, New York, NY
Gary Lutnick, 36, New York, NY
Linda Luzzicone, 33, New York, NY
Alexander Lygin, 28, New York, NY
James Francis Lynch, 47, Woodbridge, NJ
Michael Lynch, 34, New York, NY
Richard Dennis Lynch, 30, Bedford Hills, NY
Farrell Peter Lynch, 39, Centerport, NY
Louise A. Lynch, 58, Amityville, NY
Michael F. Lynch, 33, New Hyde Park, NY
Michael Francis Lynch, 30, New York, NY
Robert H. Lynch, 44, Cranford, NJ
Sean Patrick Lynch, 36, Morristown, NJ
Sean Lynch, 34, New York, NY
Monica Lyons, 53, New York, NY
Michael J. Lyons, 32, Hawthorne, NY
Patrick Lyons, 34, South Setauket, NY
Robert Francis Mace, 43, New York, NY
Jan Maciejewski, 37, New York, NY
Catherine Fairfax MacRae, 23, New York, NY
Richard B. Madden, 35, Westfield, NJ
Simon Maddison, 40, Florham Park, NJ
Noell Maerz, 29, Long Beach, NY
Jeannieann Maffeo, 40, New York, NY
Joseph Maffeo, 30, New York, NY
Jay Robert Magazine, 48, New York, NY
Brian Magee, 52, Floral Park, NY
Charles Wilson Magee, 51, Wantagh, NY
Joseph Maggitti, 47, Abingdon, MD
Ronald E. Magnuson, 57, Park Ridge, NJ
Daniel L. Maher, 50, Hamilton, NJ
Thomas Anthony Mahon, 37, E. Norwich, NY
William Mahoney, 38, Bohemia, NY
Joseph Maio, 32, Roslyn Harbor, NY
Takashi Makimoto, 49, New York, NY
Abdu Malahi, 37, New York, NY
Debora Maldonado, 47, New York, NY
Myrna T. Maldonado-Agosto, 49, New York, NY
Alfred R. Maler, 39, Convent Station, NJ
Gregory James Malone, 42, Hoboken, NJ
Edward Francis (Teddy) Maloney, 32, Darien, CN.
Joseph E. Maloney, 46, Farmingville, NY
Gene E. Maloy, 41, New York, NY
Christian Maltby, 37, Chatham, NJ
Francisco Miguel Mancini, 26, New York, NY
Joseph Mangano, 53, Jackson, NJ
Sara Elizabeth Manley, 31, New York, NY
Debra M. Mannetta, 31, Islip, NY
Terence J. Manning, 36, Rockville Centre, NY
Marion Victoria Manning, 27, Rochdale, NY
James Maounis, 42, New York, NY
Joseph Ross Marchbanks, 47, Nanuet, NY
Peter Edward Mardikian, 29, New York, NY
Edward Joseph Mardovich, 42, Lloyd Harbor, NY
Lt. Charles Joseph Margiotta, 44, New York, NY
Kenneth Joseph Marino, 40, Monroe, NY
Lester Vincent Marino, 57, MAapequa, NY
Vita Marino, 49, New York, NY
Kevin D. Marlo, 28, New York, NY
Jose J. Marrero, 32, Old Bridge, NJ
John Marshall, 35, Congers, NY
James Martello, 41, Rumson, NJ
Michael A. Marti, 26, Glendale, NY
Lt. Peter Martin, 43, Miller Place, NY
William J. Martin, 35, Rockaway, NJ
Brian E. Martineau, 37, Edison, NJ
Betsy Martinez, 33, New York, NY
Edward J. Martinez, 60, New York, NY
Jose Martinez, 49, HaupPauge, NY
Robert Gabriel Martinez, 24, New York, NY
Lizie Martinez-Calderon, 32, New York, NY
Francis Albert De Martini, 49, New York, NY
Lt. Paul Richard Martini, 37, New York, NY

Joseph A. Mascali, 44, New York, NY
Bernard Mascarenhas, 54, Newmarket, Ont., CD
Stephen F. Masi, 55, New York, NY
Nicholas G. Maa, 65, New York, NY
Patricia A. Maari, 25, Glendale, NY
Michael MaAaroli, 38, New York, NY
Philip W. Mastrandrea, 42, Chatham, NJ
Rudolph Mastrocinque, 43, Kings Park, NY
Joseph Mathai, 49, Arlington, MA
Charles William Mathers, 61, Sea Girt, NJ
William A. Mathesen, 40, Morristown, NJ
Marcello Matricciano, 31, New York, NY
Margaret Elaine Mattic, 51, New York, NY
Robert D. Mattson, 54, Green Pond, NJ
Walter Matuza, 39, New York, NY
Charles A. (Chuck) Mauro, 65, New York, NY
Charles J. Mauro, 38, New York, NY
Dorothy Mauro, 55, New York, NY
Nancy T. Mauro, 51, New York, NY
Tyrone May, 44, Rahway, NJ
Keithroy Maynard, 30, New York, NY
Robert J. Mayo, 46, Morganville, NJ
Kathy Nancy Mazza-Delosh, 46, Farmingdale, NY
Edward Mazzella, 62, Monroe, NY
Jennifer Mazzotta, 23, New York, NY
Kaaria Mbaya, 39, Edison, NJ
James J. McAlary, 42, Spring Lake Heights, NJ
Brian McAleese, 36, Baldwin, NY
Patricia A. McAneney, 50, Pomona, NY
Colin Richard McArthur, 52, Howell, NJ
John McAvoy, 47, New York, NY
Kenneth M. McBrayer, 49, New York, NY
Brendan McCabe, 40, Sayville, NY
Michael J. McCabe, 42, Rumson, NJ
Thomas McCann, 46, ManalaPan, NJ
Robert Garvin McCarthy, 33, Stony Point, NY
Justin McCarthy, 30, Port Washington, NY
Kevin M. McCarthy, 42, Fairfield, CN
Michael Desmond McCarthy, 33, Huntington, NY
Stanley McCaskill, 47, New York, NY
Katie Marie McCloskey, 25, Mount Vernon, NY
Tara McCloud-Gray, 30, New York, NY
Charles Austin McCrann, 55, New York, NY
Tonyell McDay, 25, Colonia, NJ
Matthew T. McDermott, 34, Basking Ridge, NJ
Joseph P. McDonald, 43, Livingston, NJ
Brian G. McDonnell, 38, Wantagh, NY
Michael McDonnell, 34, Red Bank, NJ
John F. McDowell, 33, New York, NY
Eamon J. McEneaney, 46, New Canaan, CN
John Thomas McErlean, 39, Larchmont, NY
Katherine (Katie) McGarry-Noack, 30, Hoboken, NJ
Daniel F. McGinley, 40, Ridgewood, NJ
Mark Ryan McGinly, 26, New York, NY
Lt. William E. McGinn, 43, New York, NY
Thomas H. McGinnis, 41, Oakland, NJ
Michael Gregory McGinty, 42, Foxboro, MA
Scott Martin McGovern, 35, Wyckoff, NJ
Ann McGovern, 68, E. Meadow, NY
William J. McGovern, 49, Smithtown, NY
Stacey S. McGowan, 38, Basking Ridge, NJ
Francis Noel McGuinn, 48, Rye, NY
Patrick J. McGuire, 40, Madison, NJ
Thomas M. McHale, 33, Huntington, NY
Keith McHeffey, 31, Monmouth Beach, NJ
Denis J. McHugh, 36, New York, NY
Ann M. McHugh, 35, New York, NY
Dennis P. McHugh, 34, SParkill, NY
Michael Edward McHugh, 35, Tuckahoe, NY
Robert G. McIlvaine, 26, New York, NY
Donald James McIntyre, 38, New City, NY
Stephanie McKenna, 45, New York, NY
Barry J. McKeon, 47, Yorktown Heights, NY
Evelyn C. McKinnedy, 60, New York, NY
Darryl Leron McKinney, 26, New York, NY
Robert C. McLaughlin, 29, Westchester, NY
George Patrick McLaughlin, 36, Hoboken, NJ
Gavin McMahon, 35, Bayonne, NJ
Robert Dismas McMahon, 35, New York, NY
Edmund M. McNally, 41, Fair Haven, NJ
Daniel McNeal, 29, Towson, MD.
Walter Arthur McNeil, 53, Stroudsburg, Pa
Jaselliny McNish, 37
Christine McNulty, 42, Peterborough, England
Sean Peter McNulty, 30, New York, NY
Robert William McPadden, 30, Pearl River, NY
Terence A. McShane, 37, West Islip, NY
Timothy Patrick McSweeney, 37, New York, NY
Martin E. McWilliams, 35, Kings Park, NY
Rocco A. Medaglia, 49, Melville, NY

112 In Rememberance of the Tragedies of September 11, 2001

Abigail Medina, 46, New York, NY
Ana Iris Medina, 39, New York, NY
Deborah Medwig, 46, Dedham, MA.
William J. Meehan, 49, Darien, CN
Damian Meehan, 32, Glen Rock, NJ
Alok Kumar Mehta, 23, Hempstead, NY
Raymond Meisenheimer, 46, West Babylon, NY
Manuel Emilio Mejia, 54, New York, NY
Eskedar Melaku, 31, New York, NY
Antonio Melendez, 30, New York, NY
Mary Melendez, 44, Stroudsburg, Pa
Yelena Melnichenko, 28, Brooklyn, NY
Stuart Todd Meltzer, 32, Syosset, NY
Diarelia Jovannah Mena, 30, New York, NY
Charles Mendez, 38, Floral Park, NY
Lizette Mendoza, 33, N. Bergen, NJ
Shevonne Mentis, 25, New York, NY
Steve Mercado, 38, New York, NY
Wesley Mercer, 70, New York, NY
Ralph Mercurio, 47, Rockville Centre, NY
Alan H. Merdinger, 47, Allentown, Pa
George C. Merino, 39, New York, NY
Yamel Merino, 24, Yonkers, NY
George Merkouris, 35, Levittown, NY
Deborah Merrick, 45
Raymond J. Metz, 37, Trumbull, CN
Jill A. Metzler, 32, Franklin Square, NY
David Robert Meyer, 57, Glen Rock, NJ
Nurul Huq Miah, 35, New York, NY
William Edward Micciulli, 30, Matawan, NJ
Martin Paul Michelstein, 57, Morristown, NJ
Luis Clodoaldo Revilla Mier, 54
Peter T. Milano, 43, Middletown, NJ
Gregory Milanowycz, 25, Cranford, NJ
Lukasz T. Milewski, 21, New York, NY
Corey Peter Miller, 34, New York, NY
Henry Miller, 52, E. Norwich, NY
Phillip D. Miller, 53, New York, NY
Craig James Miller, 29, VA.
Douglas C. Miller, 34, Port Jervis, NY
Michael Matthew Miller, 39, Englewood, NJ
Robert C. Miller, 55, Hasbrouck Heights, NJ
Robert Alan Miller, 46, Matawan, NJ
Joel Miller, 55, Baldwin, NY
Benjamin Millman, 40, New York, NY
Charles M. Mills, 61, Brentwood, NY
Ronald Keith Milstein, 54, New York, NY
Robert Minara, 54, Carmel, NY
William G. Minardi, 46, Bedford, NY
Louis Joseph Minervino, 54, Middletown, NJ
Thomas Mingione, 34, West Islip, NY
Wilbert Miraille, 29, New York, NY
Domenick Mircovich, 40, Closter, NJ
Rajesh A. Mirpuri, 30, Englewood Cliffs, NJ
Joseph Mistrulli, 47, Wantagh, NY
Susan Miszkowicz, 37, New York, NY
Lt. Paul Thomas Mitchell, 46, New York, NY
Richard Miuccio, 55, New York, NY
Frank V. Moccia, 57, HaupPauge, NY
Capt. Louis Joseph Modafferi, 45, New York, NY
Boyie Mohammed, 50, New York, NY
Lt. Dennis Mojica, 50, New York, NY
Manuel Mojica, 37, Bellmore, NY
Manuel Dejesus Molina, 31, New York, NY
Fernando Jimenez Molina, 21, Oaxaca, Mexico
Kleber Rolando Molina, 44, New York, NY
Carl Molinaro, 32, New York, NY
Justin J. Molisani, 42, Middletown Township, NJ
Brian Patrick Monaghan, 21, New York, NY
Franklin Monahan, 45, Roxbury, NY
John Gerard Monahan, 47, WanaMAa, NJ
Kristen Montanaro, 34, New York, NY
Craig D. Montano, 38, Glen Ridge, NJ
Michael Montesi, 39, Highland Mills, NY
Cheryl Ann Monyak, 43, Greenwich, CN
Capt. Thomas Moody, 45, Stony Brook, NY
Sharon Moore, 37, New York, NY
Krishna Moorthy, 59, Briarcliff Manor, NY
Paula Morales, 42, New York, NY
Abner Morales, 37, New York, NY
Carlos Morales, 29, New York, NY
Luis Morales, 46, New York, NY
John Moran, 43, Rockaway, NY
John Moran, 38, Haslemere, Surrey, England
Kathleen Moran, 42, New York, NY
Lindsay S. Morehouse, 24, New York, NY
George Morell, 47, Mount. Kisco, NY
Vincent S. Morello, 34, New York, NY
Steven P. Morello, 52, Bayonne, NJ
Arturo Alva Moreno, 47, Mexico City, Mexico

Yvette Nicole Moreno, 25, New York, NY
Dorothy Morgan, 47, Hempstead, NY
Richard Morgan, 66, Glen Rock, NJ
Nancy Morgenstern, 32, New York, NY
Sanae Mori, 27, Tokyo, Japan
Blanca Morocho, 26, New York, NY
Leonel Morocho, 36, New York, NY
Dennis G. Moroney, 39, E.chester, NY
Lynne Irene Morris, 22, Monroe, NY
Seth A. Morris, 35, Kinnelon, NJ
Stephen Philip Morris, 31, Ormond Beach, FL.
Christopher M. Morrison, 34, Charlestown, MA
Ferdinand V. Morrone, 63, Lakewood, NJ
William David Moskal, 50, Brecksville, OH
Manuel Da Mota, 43, Valley Stream, NY
Marco Motroni, 57, Fort Lee, NJ
Iouri A. Mouchinski, 55, New York, NY
Jude J. Moussa, 35, New York, NY
Peter C. Moutos, 44, Chatham, NJ
Damion Mowatt, 21, New York, NY
Christopher Mozzillo, 27, New York, NY

> "The true way to soften one's troubles is to solace those of others."
>
> Madame De Maintenon.

Stephen V. Mulderry, 33, New York, NY
Richard Muldowney, 40, Babylon, NY
Michael D. Mullan, 34, New York, NY
Dennis Michael Mulligan, 32, New York, NY
Peter James Mulligan, 28, New York, NY
Michael Joseph Mullin, 27, Hoboken, NJ
James Donald Munhall, 45, Ridgewood, NJ
Nancy Muniz, 45, New York, NY
Francisco Munoz, 29, New York, NY
Carlos Mario Munoz, 43
Theresa (Terry) Munson, 54, New York, NY
Robert M. Murach, 45, Montclair, NJ
Cesar Augusto Murillo, 32, New York, NY
Marc A. Murolo, 28, Maywood, NJ
Edward C. Murphy, 42, Clifton, NJ
James F. Murphy, 30, Garden City, NY
Patrick Sean Murphy, 36, Millburn, NJ
Robert Eddie Murphy, 56, New York, NY
Brian Joseph Murphy, 41, New York, NY
Christopher W. Murphy, 35, E.on, MD
James Thomas Murphy, 35, Middletown, NJ
Kevin James Murphy, 40, Northport, NY
Lt. Raymond E. Murphy, 46, New York, NY
Charles Murphy, 38, New York, NY
Susan D. Murray, 54, Summit, NJ
John Joseph Murray, 32, Hoboken, NJ
John Joseph Murray, 52, Colts Neck, NJ
Valerie Victoria Murray, 65, New York, NY
Richard Todd Myhre, 37, New York, NY
Lt. Robert B. Nagel, 55, New York, NY
Takuya Nakamura, 30, Tuckahoe, NY
Alexander J.R. Napier, 38, Morris Township, NJ
Frank Joseph Naples, 29, Cliffside Park, NJ
John Napolitano, 33, Ronkonkoma, NY
Catherine A. Nardella, 40, Bloomfield, NJ
Mario Nardone, 32, New York, NY
Manika Narula, 22, Kings Park, NY
Narender Nath, 33, Colonia, NJ
Karen S. Navarro, 30, New York, NY
Joseph M. Navas, 44, Paramus, NJ
Francis J. Nazario, 28, Jersey City, NJ
Glenroy Neblett, 42, New York, NY
Marcus R. Neblett, 31, Roslyn Heights, NY
Jerome O. Nedd, 39, New York, NY
Laurence Nedell, 51, Lindenhurst, NY
Luke G. Nee, 44, Stony Point, NY
Pete Negron, 34, Bergenfield, NJ
Ann Nicole Nelson, 30, New York, NY
Peter Allen Nelson, 42, Huntington Station, NY

David William Nelson, 50, New York, NY
James Nelson, 40, Clark, NJ
Michele Ann Nelson, 27, Valley Stream, NY
Oscar Nesbitt, 58, New York, NY
Gerard Terence Nevins, 46, Campbell Hall, NY
Kapinga Ngalula, 58, McKinney, TX
Nancy Yuen Ngo, 36, Harrington Park, NJ
Jody Tepedino Nichilo, 39, New York, NY
Martin Niederer, 23, Hoboken, NJ
Alfonse J. Niedermeyer, 40, Manasquan, NJ
Frank John Niestadt, 55, Ronkonkoma, NY
Gloria Nieves, 48, New York, NY
Juan Nieves, 56, New York, NY
Troy Edward Nilsen, 33, New York, NY
Paul R. Nimbley, 42, Middletown, NJ
John Ballantine Niven, 44, Oyster Bay, NY
Curtis Terrence Noel, 22, Poughkeepsie, NY
Daniel R. Nolan, 44, HoPatcong, NJ
Robert Walter Noonan, 36, Norwalk, CN
Daniela R. Notaro, 25, New York, NY
Brian Novotny, 33, Hoboken, NJ
Soichi Numata, 45, Irvington, NY
Jose R. Nunez, 42, New York, NY
Brian Felix Nunez, 29, New York, NY
Jeffrey Nussbaum, 37, Oceanside, NY
James A. Oakley, 52, Cortlandt Manor, NY
Dennis O'Berg, 28, Babylon, NY
James P. O'Brien, 33, New York, NY
Timothy Michael O'Brien, 40, Brookville, NY
Michael O'Brien, 42, Cedar Knolls, NJ
Scott J. O'Brien, 40, New York, NY
Lt. Daniel O'Callaghan, 42, Smithtown, NY
Richard J. O'CNor, 49, Poughkeepsie, NY
Dennis J. O'CNor, 34, New York, NY
Diana J. O'CNor, 38, E.chester, NY
Keith K. O'CNor, 28, Hoboken, NJ
Amy O'Doherty, 23, New York, NY
Marni Pont O'Doherty, 31, Armonk, NY
Douglas Oelschlager, 36, New York, NY
Takashi Ogawa, 37, Tokyo, Japan
Albert Ogletree, 49, New York, NY
Philip Paul Ognibene, 39, New York, NY
James Andrew O'Grady, 32, Harrington Park, NJ
Joseph J. Ogren, 30, New York, NY
Lt. Thomas O'Hagan, 43, New York, NY
Samuel Oitice, 45, Peekskill, NY
Patrick O'Keefe, 44, Oakdale, NY
Capt. William O'Keefe, 49, New York, NY
Gerald Michael Olcott, 55, New Hyde Park, NY
Gerald O'Leary, 34, Stony Point, NY
Christine Anne Olender, 39, New York, NY
Elsy Carolina Osorio Oliva, 27, New York, NY
Linda Mary Oliva, 44, New York, NY
Edward K. Oliver, 31, Jackson, NJ
Leah E. Oliver, 24, New York, NY
Eric T. Olsen, 41, New York, NY
Jeffrey James Olsen, 31, New York, NY
Steven John Olson, 38, New York, NY
Maureen L. Olson, 50, Rockville Centre, NY
Matthew Timothy O'Mahony, 39, New York, NY
Toshihiro Onda, 39, New York, NY
Seamus L. Oneal, 52, New York, NY
Sean Gordon Corbett O'Neill, 34, Rye, NY
John P. O'Neill, 49, New York, NY
Peter J. O'Neill, 21, Amityville, NY
Michael C. Opperman, 45, Selden, NY
Christopher Orgielewicz, 35, Larchmont, NY
Margaret Orloske, 50, Windsor, CN
Virginia A. Ormiston-Kenworthy, 42, NY, NY
Kevin O'Rourke, 44, Hewlett, NY
Juan Romero Orozco, Acatlan de Osorio, Puebla, Mexico
Ronald Orsini, 59, Hillsdale, NJ
Peter K. Ortale, 37, New York, NY
Emilio (Peter) Ortiz, 38, New York, NY
Pablo Ortiz, 49, New York, NY
David Ortiz, 37, Nanuet, NY
Paul Ortiz, 21, New York, NY
Sonia Ortiz, 58, New York, NY
Alexander Ortiz, 36, Ridgewood, NY
Masaru Ose, 36, Fort Lee, NJ
Robert W. O'Shea, 47, Wall, NJ
Patrick J. O'Shea, 45, Farmingdale, NY
James Robert Ostrowski, 37, Garden City, NY
Timothy O'Sullivan, 68, Albrightsville, PA
Jason Douglas Oswald, 28, New York, NY
Michael Otten, 42, E. Islip, NY
Isidro Ottenwalder, 35, New York, NY
Michael Chung Ou, 53, New York, NY
Todd Joseph Ouida, 25, River Edge, NJ
Jesus Ovalles, 60, New York, NY

America – Voices Coming Together

113

Peter J. Owens, 42, Williston Park, NY
Adianes Oyola, 23, New York, NY
Israel Pabon, 31, New York, NY
Angel M. Pabon, 54, New York, NY
Roland Pacheco, 25, New York, NY
Michael Benjamin Packer, 45, New York, NY
DeePa K. Pakkala, 31, Stewartsville, NJ
Jeffrey Matthew Palazzo, 33, New York, NY
Thomas Anthony Palazzo, 44, Armonk, NY
Richard (Rico) Palazzolo, 39, New York, NY
Orio Joseph Palmer, 45, Valley Stream, NY
Frank A. Palombo, 46, New York, NY
Alan N. Palumbo, 42, New York, NY
Christopher M. Panatier, 36, Rockville Centre, NY
Dominique Pandolfo, 27, Hoboken, NJ
Paul Pansini, 34, New York, NY
John M. Paolillo, 51, Glen Head, NY
Edward J. Papa, 47, Oyster Bay, NY
Salvatore PapaAsso, 34, New York, NY
James N. Papapageorge, 29, Yonkers, NY
Vinod K. Parakat, 34, Sayreville, NJ
Vijayashanker Paramsothy, 23, New York, NY
Nitin Parandkar, 28
Hardai (Casey) Parbhu, 42, New York, NY
James Wendell Parham, 32, New York, NY
Debra (Debbie) Paris, 48, New York, NY
George Paris, 33, New York, NY
Gye-Hyong Park, 28, New York, NY
Philip L. Parker, 53, Skillman, NJ
Michael A. Parkes, 27, New York, NY
Robert Emmett Parks, 47, Middletown, NJ
Hasmukhrai Chuckulal Parmar, 48, Warren, NJ
Robert Parro, 35, Levittown, NY
Diane Marie Moore Parsons, 58, Malta, NY
Leobardo Lopez Pascual, 41, New York, NY
Michael J. Pascuma, 50, MAapequa Park, NY
Jerrold H. Paskins, 56, Anaheim Hills, CA
Horace Robert Passananti, 55, New York, NY
Suzanne H. Passaro, 38, E. Brunswick, NJ
Victor Pastrana, 57, Tlachichuca, Puebla, Mexico
Dipti Patel, 38, New Hyde Park, NY
Manish K. Patel, 29, Edison, NJ
Avnish Ramanbhai Patel, 28, New York, NY
Steven B. Paterson, 40, Ridgewood, NJ
James Matthew Patrick, 30, Norwalk, CN
Manuel Patrocino, 34
Bernard E. Patterson, 46, Upper Brookville, NY
Cira Marie Patti, 40, New York, NY
Robert Edward Pattison, 40, New York, NY
James R. Paul, 58, New York, NY
Patrice Paz, 52, New York, NY
Sharon Cristina Millan Paz, 31, New York, NY
Victor Paz-Gutierrez, 43, New York, NY
Stacey L. Peak, 36, New York, NY
Richard Allen Pearlman, 18, New York, NY
Durrell Pearsall, 34, Wainscott, NY
Thomas E. Pedicini, 30, Hicksville, NY
Todd D. Pelino, 34, Fair Haven, NJ
Michel Adrian Pelletier, 36, Greenwich, CN
Anthony Peluso, 46, New York, NY
Angel Ramon Pena, 45, River vale, NJ
Richard Al Penny, 53, New York, NY
Salvatore F. Pepe, 45, New York, NY
Carl Allen Peralta, 37, New York, NY
Robert David Peraza, 30, New York, NY
Jon A. Perconti, 32, Brick, NJ
Alejo Perez, 66, Union City, NJ
Angela Susan Perez, 35, New York, NY
Angel Perez, 43, Jersey City, NJ
Ivan Perez, 37, New York, NY
Nancy E. Perez, 36, Secaucus, NJ
Anthony Perez, 33, Locust Valley, NY
Joseph John Perroncino, 33, Smithtown, NY
Edward J. Perrotta, 43, Mount Sinai, NY
Lt. Glenn C. Perry, 41, Monroe, NY
Emelda Perry, 52, Elmont, NY
John William Perry, 38, New York, NY
Franklin Allan Pershep, 59, New York, NY
Daniel Pesce, 34, New York, NY
Michael J. Pescherine, 32, New York, NY
Davin Peterson, 25, New York, NY
William Russel Peterson, 46, New York, NY
Mark Petrocelli, 28, New York, NY
Lt. Philip S. Petti, 43, New York, NY
Glen Kerrin Pettit, 30, Oakdale, NY
Dominick Pezzulo, 36, New York, NY
Kaleen E. Pezzuti, 28, Fair Haven, NJ
Lt. Kevin Pfeifer, 42, New York, NY
Tu-Anh Pham, 42, Princeton, NJ
Lt. Kenneth John Phelan, 41, New York, NY

Michael V. San Phillip, 55, Ridgewood, NJ
Eugenia Piantieri, 55, New York, NY
Ludwig John Picarro, 44, Basking Ridge, NJ
Matthew Picerno, 44, Holmdel, NJ
Joseph O. Pick, 40, Hoboken, NJ
Christopher Pickford, 32, New York, NY
Dennis J. Pierce, 54, New York, NY
Joseph A. Della Pietra, 24, New York, NY
Bernard T. Pietronico, 39, Matawan, NJ
Nicholas P. Pietrunti, 38, Belford, NJ
Theodoros Pigis, 60, New York, NY
Susan Ancona Pinto, 44, New York, NY
Joseph Piskadlo, 48, N. Arlington, NJ
Christopher Todd Pitman, 30, New York, NY
Josh Piver, 23, New York, NY
Joseph Plumitallo, 45, ManalaPan, NJ
John M. Pocher, 36, Middletown, NJ
William Howard Pohlmann, 56, Ardsley, NY
Laurence M. Polatsch, 32, New York, NY
Thomas H. Polhemus, 39, Morris Plains, NJ
Steve Pollicino, 48, Plainview, NY
Susan M. Pollio, 45, Long Beach Township, NJ
Joshua Poptean, 37, New York, NY
Giovanna Porras, 24, New York, NY
Anthony Portillo, 48, New York, NY
James Edward Potorti, 52, Princeton, NJ
Daphne Pouletsos, 47, Westwood, NJ
Stephen E. Poulos, 45, Basking Ridge, NJ
Richard Poulos, 55, Levittown, NY
Brandon Jerome Powell, 26, New York, NY
Shawn Edward Powell, 32, New York, NY
Tony Pratt, 43, New York, NY
Gregory M. Preziose, 34, HolMDel, NJ
Wanda Ivelisse Prince, 30, New York, NY
Vincent Princiotta, 39, Orangeburg, NY
Kevin Prior, 28, Bellmore, NY
Everett Martin (Marty) Proctor, 44, New York, NY
Carrie B. Progen, 25, New York, NY
David Lee Pruim, 53, Upper Montclair, NJ
Richard Prunty, 57, Sayville, NY
John F. Puckett, 47, Glen Cove, NY
Robert D. Pugliese, 47, E. Fishkill, NY
Edward F. Pullis, 34, Hazlet, NJ
Patricia Ann Puma, 33, New York, NY
Hemanth Kumar Puttur, 26, White Plains, NY
Edward R. Pykon, 33, Princeton, NJ
Christopher Quackenbush, 44, Manhasset, NY
Lars Peter Qualben, 49, New York, NY
Lincoln Quappe, 38, Sayville, NY
Beth Ann Quigley, 25, New York, NY
Lt. Michael Quilty, 42, New York, NY
Ricardo Quinn, 40, New York, NY
James Francis Quinn, 23, New York, NY
Carol Rabalais, 38, New York, NY
Christopher Peter A. Racaniello, 30, New York, NY
Leonard Ragaglia, 36, New York, NY
Eugene J. Raggio, 55, New York, NY
Laura Marie Ragonese-Snik, 41, Bangor, PA
Michael Ragusa, 29, New York, NY
Peter F. Raimondi, 46, New York, NY
Harry A. Raines, 37, New York, NY
Ehtesham U. Raja, 28, Clifton, NJ
Valsa Raju, 39, Yonkers, NY
Edward Rall, 44, Holbrook, NY
Lukas (Luke) Rambousek, 27, New York, NY
Julio Fernandez Ramirez, 51, New York, NY
Maria Isabel Ramirez, 25, New York, NY
Harry Ramos, 41, Newark, NJ
Vishnoo Ramsaroop, 44, New York, NY
Lorenzo Ramzey, 48, E. Northport, NY
A. Todd Rancke, 42, Summit, NJ
Adam David Rand, 30, Bellmore, NY
Jonathan C. Randall, 42, New York, NY
Srinivasa Shreyas Ranganath, 26, Hackensack, NJ
Anne Rose T. Ransom, 45, Edgewater, NJ
Faina Rapoport, 45, New York, NY
Robert Arthur Rasmussen, 42, Hinsdale, IL
Amenia Rasool, 33, New York, NY
Roger Mark Rasweiler, 53, Flemington, NJ
David James Rathkey, 47, Mountain Lakes, NJ
William Ralph Raub, 38, Saddle River, NJ
Gerard Rauzi, 42, New York, NY
Alexey Razuvaev, 40, New York, NY
Gregory Reda, 33, New Hyde Park, NY
Sarah Prothero Redheffer, 35, London, England
Michele Reed, 26, Ringoes, NJ
Judith A. Reese, 56, Kearny, NJ
Donald J. Regan, 47, Wallkill, NY
Lt. Robert M. Regan, 48, Floral Park, NY
Thomas M. Regan, 43, Cranford, NJ

Christian Regenhard, 28, New York, NY
Howard Reich, 59, New York, NY
Gregg Reidy, 26, HolMDel, NJ
Kevin O. Reilly, 28, New York, NY
James Brian Reilly, 25, New York, NY
Timothy E. Reilly, 40, New York, NY
Joseph Reina, 32, New York, NY
Thomas Barnes Reinig, 48, Bernardsville, NJ
Frank B. Reisman, 41, Princeton, NJ
Joshua Scott Reiss, 23, New York, NY
Karen Renda, 52, New York, NY
John Armand Reo, 28, Larchmont, NY
Richard Rescorla, 62, Morristown, NJ
John Thomas Resta, 40, New York, NY
Sylvia San Pio Resta, 26, New York, NY
Eduvigis (Eddie) Reyes, 37, New York, NY
Bruce A. Reynolds, 41, Columbia, NJ
John Frederick Rhodes, 57, Howell, NJ
Francis S. Riccardelli, 40, Westwood, NJ
Rudolph N. Riccio, 50, New York, NY
AnnMarie (Davi) Riccoboni, 58, New York, NY
David Rice, 31, New York, NY
Eileen Mary Rice, 57, New York, NY
Kenneth F. Rice, 34, Hicksville, NY
Lt. Vernon Allan Richard, 53, Nanuet, NY
Michael Richards, 38, New York, NY
Claude D. Richards, 46, New York, NY
Gregory Richards, 30, New York, NY
Venesha O. Richards, 26, N. Brunswick, NJ
James C. Riches, 29, New York, NY
Alan Jay Richman, 44, New York, NY
John M. Rigo, 48, New York, NY
Theresa (Ginger) Risco, 48, New York, NY
Rose Mary Riso, 55, New York, NY
Moises N. Rivas, 29, New York, NY
Joseph Rivelli, 43, New York, NY
Isaias Rivera, 51, Perth Amboy, NJ
Linda Rivera, 26, New York, NY
Juan William Rivera, 27, New York, NY
Carmen A. Rivera, 33, Westtown, NY
David E. Rivers, 40, New York, NY
Joseph R. Riverso, 34, White Plains, NY
Paul Rizza, 34, Park Ridge, NJ
John Frank Rizzo, 50, New York, NY
Stephen Louis Roach, 36, Verona, NJ
Joseph Roberto, 37, Midland Park, NJ
Michael Edward Roberts, 31, New York, NY
Leo A. Roberts, 44, Wayne, NJ
Michael Roberts, 30, New York, NY
Donald Walter Robertson, 35, Rumson, NJ
Jeffrey Robinson, 38, Monmouth Junction, NJ
Catherina Robinson, 45, New York, NY
Michell Lee Robotham, 32, Kearny, NJ
Donald Robson, 52, Manhasset, NY
Raymond J. Rocha, 29, Malden, MA
Antonio Tome Rocha, 34, E. Hanover, NJ
Laura Rockefeller, 41, New York, NY
John M. Rodak, 39, Mantua, NJ
Antonio Rodrigues, 35, Port Washington, NY
Carmen Milagros Rodriguez, 46, Freehold, NJ
Anthony Rodriguez, 36, New York, NY
Marsha A. Rodriguez, 41, West Paterson, NJ
Richard Rodriguez, 31, Cliffwood, NJ
Gregory E. Rodriguez, 31, White Plains, NY
David B. Rodriguez-Vargas, 44, New York, NY
Matthew Rogan, 37, West Islip, NY
Karlie Barbara Rogers, 25, London, England
Scott Rohner, 22, Hoboken, NJ
Keith Roma, 27, New York, NY
Joseph M. Romagnolo, 37, Coram, NY
Elvin Santiago Romero, 34, Matawan, NJ
Efrain Franco Romero, 57, Hazleton, Pa
James A. Romito, 51, Westwood, NJ
Sean Rooney, 50, Stamford, CT
Eric Thomas Ropiteau, 24, New York, NY
Aida Rosario, 42, Jersey City, NJ
Angela Rosario, 27, New York, NY
Fitzroy St. Rose, 40, New York, NY
Mark H. Rosen, 45, West Islip, NY
Brooke Rosenbaum, 31, Franklin Square, NY
Linda Rosenbaum, 41, Little Falls, NJ
Sheryl Lynn Rosenbaum, 33, Warren, NJ
Mark Louis Rosenberg, 26, Teaneck, NJ
Lloyd D. Rosenberg, 31, Morganville, NJ
Andrew I. Rosenblum, 45, Rockville Centre, NY
Joshua M. Rosenblum, 28, Hoboken, NJ
Joshua A. Rosenthal, 44, New York, NY
Richard David Rosenthal, 50, Fair Lawn, NJ
Daniel Rossetti, 32, Bloomfield, NJ
Norman Rossinow, 39, Cedar Grove, NJ

Nicholas P. Rossomando, 35, New York, NY
Michael Craig Rothberg, 39, Greenwich, CN
Donna Marie Rothenberg, 53, New York, NY
Nick Rowe, 29, Hoboken, NJ
Timothy A. Roy, 36, MAapequa Park, NY
Paul G. Ruback, 50, Newburgh, NY
Ronald J. Ruben, 36, Hoboken, NJ
Joanne Rubino, 45, New York, NY
David Michael Ruddle, 31, New York, NY
Bart Joseph Ruggiere, 32, New York, NY
Susan Ann Ruggiero, 30, Plainview, NY
Adam K. Ruhalter, 40, Plainview, NY
Gilbert Ruiz, 45, New York, NY
Stephen P. Russell, 40, Rockaway Beach, NY
Steven Harris Russin, 32, Mendham, NJ
Lt. Michael Thomas Russo, 44, Nesconset, NY
Wayne Alan Russo, 37, Union, NJ
Edward Ryan, 42, Scarsdale, NY
John J. Ryan, 45, West Windsor, NJ
Jonathan Stephan Ryan, 32, Bayville, NY
Matthew Lancelot Ryan, 54, Seaford, NY
Tatiana Ryjova, 36, South Salem, NY
Christina Sunga Ryook, 25, New York, NY
Thierry Saada, 27, New York, NY
Jason E. Sabbag, 26, New York, NY
Thomas E. Sabella, 44, New York, NY
Scott Saber, 38, New York, NY
Joseph Sacerdote, 48, Freehold, NJ
Mohammad Ali Sadeque, 62, New York, NY
Francis J. Sadocha, 41, Huntington, NY
Jude Elias Safi, 24, New York, NY
Brock Joel Safronoff, 26, New York, NY
Edward Saiya, 49, New York, NY
John Patrick Salamone, 37, N. Caldwell, NJ
Hernando R. Salas, 71, New York, NY
Juan Salas, 35, New York, NY
Esmerlin Salcedo, 36, New York, NY
John Salvatore Salerno, 31, Westfield, NJ
Richard L. Salinardi, 32, Hoboken, NJ
Wayne John Saloman, 43, Seaford, NY
Nolbert Salomon, 33, New York, NY
Catherine Patricia Salter, 37, New York, NY
Frank Salvaterra, 41, Manhasset, NY
Paul R. Salvio, 27, New York, NY
Samuel R. Salvo, 59, Yonkers, NY
Carlos Samaniego, 29, New York, NY
Rena Sam-Dinnoo, 28, New York, NY
James Kenneth Samuel, 29, Hoboken, NJ
Hugo Sanay-Perafiel, 41, New York, NY
Alva Jeffries Sanchez, 41, Hempstead, NY
Erick Sanchez, 43, New York, NY
Jacquelyn P. Sanchez, 23, New York, NY
Eric Sand, 36, Westchester, NY
Stacey Leigh Sanders, 25, New York, NY
Herman Sandler, 57, New York, NY
James Sands, 39, Bricktown, NJ
Ayleen J. Santiago, 40, New York, NY
Kirsten Santiago, 26, New York, NY
Maria Theresa Santillan, 27, Morris Plains, NY
Susan G. Santo, 24, New York, NY
Christopher Santora, 23, New York, NY
John Santore, 49, New York, NY
Mario L. Santoro, 28, New York, NY
Rafael Humberto Santos, 42, New York, NY
Rufino Conrado F. Santos, 37, New York, NY
Kalyan K. Sarkar, 53, Westwood, NJ
Chapelle Sarker, 37, New York, NY
Paul F. Sarle, 38, Babylon, NY
Deepika Kumar Sattaluri, 33, Edison, NJ
Gregory Thomas Saucedo, 31, New York, NY
Susan Sauer, 48, Chicago, IL
Anthony Savas, 72, New York, NY
Vladimir Savinkin, 21, New York, NY
John Sbarbaro, 45, New York, NY
Robert L. Scandole, 36, Pelham Manor, NY
Michelle Scarpitta, 26, New York, NY
Dennis Scauso, 46, Dix Hills, NY
John A. Schardt, 34, New York, NY
John G. Scharf, 29, Manorville, NY
Fred Claude Scheffold, 57, Piermont, NY
Angela Susan Scheinberg, 46, New York, NY
Scott M. Schertzer, 28, Edison, NJ
Sean Schielke, 27, New York, NY
Steven Francis Schlag, 41, Franklin Lakes, NJ
Jon S. Schlissel, 51, Jersey City, NJ
Karen Helene Schmidt, 42, Bellmore, NY
Ian Schneider, 45, Short Hills, NJ
Thomas G. Schoales, 27, Stony Point, NY
Marisa Di Nardo Schorpp, 38, White Plains, NY
Frank G. Schott, 39, MAapequa Park, NY

Gerard P. Schrang, 45, Holbrook, NY
Jeffrey Schreier, 48, New York, NY
John T. Schroeder, 31, Hoboken, NJ
Susan Kennedy Schuler, 55, Allentown, NJ
Edward W. Schunk, 54, Baldwin, NY
Mark E. Schurmeier, 44, McLean, VA
Clarin Shellie Schwartz, 51, New York, NY
John Schwartz, 49, Goshen, CN
Mark Schwartz, 50, West Hempstead, NY
Adriane Victoria Scibetta, 31, New York, NY
Raphael Scorca, 61, Beachwood, NJ
Randolph Scott, 48, Stamford, CT
Christopher J. Scudder, 34, Monsey, NY
Arthur Warren Scullin, 57, New York, NY
Michael Seaman, 41, Manhasset, NY
Margaret Seeliger, 34, New York, NY
Carlos Segarra, 54, New York, NY
Anthony Segarra, 52, New York, NY
Jason Sekzer, 31, New York, NY
Matthew Carmen Sellitto, 23, Morristown, NJ
Howard Selwyn, 47, Hewlett, NY
Larry John Senko, 34, Yardley, PA
Arturo Angelo Sereno, 29, New York, NY
Frankie Serrano, 23, Elizabeth, NJ
Alena Sesinova, 57, New York, NY
Adele Sessa, 36, New York, NY
Sita Nermalla Sewnarine, 37, New York, NY
Karen Lynn Seymour-Dietrich, 40, Millington, NJ
Davis (Deeg) Sezna, 22, New York, NY
Thomas Joseph Sgroi, 45, New York, NY
Jayesh Shah, 38, Edgewater, NJ
Khalid M. Shahid, 35, Union, NJ
Mohammed Shajahan, 41, Spring valley, NY
Gary Shamay, 23, New York, NY
Earl Richard Shanahan, 50, New York, NY
Shiv Shankar, 34, New York, NY
Neil G. Shastri, 25, New York, NY
Kathryn Anne Shatzoff, 37, New York, NY
Barbara A. Shaw, 57, Morris Township, NJ
Jeffrey J. Shaw, 42, Levittown, NY
Robert J. Shay, 27, New York, NY
Daniel James Shea, 37, Pelham Manor, NY
Joseph Patrick Shea, 47, Pelham, NY
Linda Sheehan, 40, New York, NY
Hagay Shefi, 34, Tenafly, NJ
John Anthony Sherry, 34, Rockville Centre, NY
Atsushi Shiratori, 36, New York, NY
Thomas Shubert, 43, New York, NY
Mark Shulman, 44, Old Bridge, NJ
See-Wong Shum, 44, Westfield, NJ
Allan Shwartzstein, 37, ChapPaqua, NY
Johanna Sigmund, 25, Syndmoor, PA
Dianne T. Signer, 32, New York, NY
Gregory Sikorsky, 34, Spring valley, NY
Stephen Gerard Siller, 34, West Brighton, NY
David Silver, 35, New Rochelle, NY
Craig A. Silverstein, 41, Wyckoff, NJ
Nasima H. Simjee, 38, New York, NY
Bruce Edward Simmons, 41, Ridgewood, NJ
Arthur Simon, 57, Thiells, NY
Paul Joseph Simon, 54, New York, NY
Kenneth Alan Simon, 34, Secaucus, NJ
Michael Simon, 40, Harrington Park, NJ
Marianne Simone, 62, New York, NY
Barry Simowitz, 64, New York, NY
Jeff Simpson, 38, Lake Ridge, VA
Roshan R. (Sean) Singh, 21, New York, NY
Khamladai K. (Khami) Singh, 25, New York, NY
Thomas Sinton, 44, Croton-on-hudson, NY
Peter A. Siracuse, 29, New York, NY
Muriel F. Siskopoulos, 60, New York, NY
Joseph M. Sisolak, 35, New York, NY
John P. Skala, 31, Clifton, NJ
Francis J. Skidmore, 58, Mendham, NJ
Toyena Corliss Skinner, 27, Kingston, NJ
Paul A. Skrzypek, 37, New York, NY
Christopher Paul Slattery, 31, New York, NY
Vincent R. Slavin, 41, Belle Harbor, NY
Robert Sliwak, 42, Wantagh, NY
Paul K. Sloan, 26, New York, NY
Stanley S. Smagala, 36, Holbrook, NY
Wendy L. Small, 26, New York, NY
Catherine T. Smith, 44, West Haverstraw, NY
Karl Trumbull Smith, 44, Little Silver, NJ
Sandra Fajardo Smith, 37, New York, NY
Daniel Laurence Smith, 47, Northport, NY
George Eric Smith, 38, West Chester, PA
James G. Smith, 43, Garden City, NY
Joyce Smith, 55, New York, NY
Kevin Smith, 47, Mastic, NY

Leon Smith, 48, New York, NY
Moira Smith, 38, New York, NY
Rosemary A. Smith, 61, New York, NY
Jeffrey Randall Smith, 36, New York, NY
Bonnie S. Smithwick, 54, Quogue, NY
Rochelle Monique Snell, 24, Mount Vernon, NY
Leonard J. Snyder, 35, Cranford, NJ
Astrid Elizabeth Sohan, 32, Freehold, NJ
Sushil Solanki, 35, New York, NY
Ruben Solares, 51, New York, NY
Naomi Leah Solomon, 52, New York, NY
Daniel W. Song, 34, New York, NY
Michael C. Sorresse, 34, Morris Plains, NJ
Fabian Soto, 31, Harrison, NJ
Timothy P. Soulas, 35, Basking Ridge, NJ
Gregory T. SPagnoletti, 32, New York, NY
Donald F. SPampinato, 39, Manhasset, NY
Thomas SParacio, 35, New York, NY
John Anthony SPataro, 32, Mineola, NY
Robert W. Spear, 30, Valley Cottage, NY
Maynard S. Spence, 42, Douglasville, GA
George E. Spencer, 50, West Norwalk, CN
Robert Andrew Spencer, 35, Red Bank, NJ
Mary Rubina Sperando, 39, New York, NY
Frank J. Spinelli, 44, Short Hills, NJ
William E. Spitz, 49, Oceanside, NY
Joseph P. Spor, 35, Yorktown Heights, NY
Klaus Sprockamp, 42, Muhltal, Germany
Saranya Srinuan, 23, New York, NY
Michael F. Stabile, 50, New York, NY
Lawrence T. Stack, 58, Lake Ronkonkoma, NY
Capt. Timothy Stackpole, 42, New York, NY
Richard James Stadelberger, 55, Middletown, NJ
Eric A. Stahlman, 43, HolMDel Township, NJ
Gregory M. Stajk, 46, Long Beach, NY
Corina Stan, 31, Middle Village, NY
Alexandru Liviu Stan, 34, New York, NY
Mary D. Stanley, 53, New York, NY
Joyce Stanton
Patricia Stanton
Anthony M. Starita, 35, Westfield, NJ
Jeffrey Stark, 30, New York, NY
Derek James Statkevicus, 30, Norwalk, CN
Craig William Staub, 30, Basking Ridge, NJ
William V. Steckman, 56, West Hempstead, NY
Eric Thomas Steen, 32, New York, NY
William R. Steiner, 56, New Hope, PA
Alexander Robbins Steinman, 32, Hoboken, NJ
Andrew Stergiopoulos, 23, New York, NY
Andrew Stern, 45, Bellmore, NY
Martha Jane Stevens, 55, New York, NY
Richard H. Stewart, 35, New York, NY
Michael James Stewart, 42, New York, NY
Sanford M. Stoller, 54, New York, NY
Lonny J. Stone, 43, Bellmore, NY
Jimmy Nevill Storey, 58, Katy, TX
Timothy Stout, 42, Dobbs Ferry, NY
Thomas S. Strada, 41, Chatham, NJ
James J. Straine, 36, Oceanport, NJ
Edward W. Straub, 48, Morris Twp, NJ
George Strauch, 53, Avon-by-the-Sea, NJ
Edward T. Strauss, 44, Edison, NJ
Steven R. Strauss, 51, Fresh Meadows, NY
Steven F. Strobert, 33, Ridgewood, NJ
Walwyn W. Stuart, 28, Valley Stream, NY
Benjamin Suarez, 36, New York, NY
David S. Suarez, 24, Princeton, NJ
Ramon Suarez, 45, New York, NY
Yoichi Sugiyama, 34, Fort Lee, NJ
William Christopher Sugra, 30, New York, NY
Daniel Suhr, 37, Nesconset, NY
David Marc Sullins, 30, New York, NY
Lt. Christopher P. Sullivan, 38, MAapequa, NY
Patrick Sullivan, 32, New York, NY
Thomas Sullivan, 38, Kearney, NJ
Hilario Soriano Sumaya, 42, New York, NY
James Joseph Suozzo, 47, HaupPauge, NY
Colleen Supinski, 27, New York, NY
Robert Sutcliffe, 39, Huntington, NY
Selina Sutter, 63, New York, NY
Claudia Suzette Sutton, 34, New York, NY
John F. Swaine, 36, Larchmont, NY
Kristine M. Swearson, 34, New York, NY
Brian Edward Sweeney, 29, Merrick, NY
Kenneth J. Swensen, 40, Chatham, NJ
Thomas F. Swift, 30, Jersey City, NJ
Derek O. Sword, 29, New York, NY
Kevin T. Szocik, 27, Garden City, NY
Gina Sztejnberg, 52, Ridgewood, NJ
Norbert P. Szurkowski, 31, New York, NY

America – Voices Coming Together

115

Harry Taback, 56, New York, NY
Joann Tabeek, 41, New York, NY
Norma C. Taddei, 64, New York, NY
Michael Taddonio, 39, Huntington, NY
Keiichiro Takahashi, 53, Port Washington, NY
Keiji Takahashi, 42, Tenafly, NJ
Phyllis Gail Talbot, 53, New York, NY
Robert R. Talhami, 40, Shrewsbury, NJ
Sean Patrick Tallon, 26, Yonkers, NY
Paul Talty, 40, Wantagh, NY
Maurita Tam, 22, New York, NY
Rachel Tamares, 30, New York, NY
Hector Tamayo, 51, New York, NY
Michael Andrew Tamuccio, 37, Pelham Manor, NY
Kenichiro Tanaka, 52, Rye Brook, NY
Rhondelle Tankard, 31, Devonshire, Bermuda
Michael Anthony Tanner, 44, Secaucus, NJ
Dennis Gerard Taormina, 36, Montville, NJ
Kenneth Joseph Tarantino, 39, Bayonne, NJ
Allan Tarasiewicz, 45, New York, NY
Ronald Tartaro, 39, Bridgewater, NJ
Darryl Taylor, 52, New York, NY
Lorisa Ceylon Taylor, 31, New York, NY
Donnie Brooks Taylor, 40, New York, NY
Michael M. Taylor, 42, New York, NY
Paul A. Tegtmeier, 41, Hyde Park, NY
Yeshavant Moreshwar Tembe, 59, Piscataway, NJ
Anthony Tempesta, 38, Elizabeth, NJ
Dorothy Temple, 52, New York, NY
Stanley L. Temple, 77, New York, NY
David Tengelin, 25, New York, NY
Brian J. Terrenzi, 29, Hicksville, NY
Lisa Marie Terry, 42, Rochester, MI
Goumatie T. Thackurdeen, 35, New York, NY
Harshad Sham Thatte, 30, Norcross, GA
Thomas F. Theurkauf, 44, Stamford, CT
Lesley Anne Thomas, 40, Hoboken, NJ
Nigel Bruce Thompson, 33, New York, NY
Brian T. Thompson, 49, Dix Hills, NY
Clive Thompson, 43, Summit, NJ
Glenn Thompson, 44, New York, NY
Perry Anthony Thompson, 36, Mount Laurel, NJ
Vanavah Alexi Thompson, 26, New York, NY
Capt. William Thompson, 51, New York, NY
Eric Raymond Thorpe, 35, New York, NY
Nichola A. Thorpe, 22, New York, NY
Sal Tieri, 40, Shrewsbury, NJ
John Patrick Tierney, 27, New York, NY
Mary Ellen Tiesi, 38, Jersey City, NJ
William R. Tieste, 54, Basking Ridge, NJ
Kenneth F. Tietjen, 31, Matawan, NJ
Stephen Edward Tighe, 41, Rockville Centre, NY
Scott C. Timmes, 28, Ridgewood, NY
Michael E. Tinley, 56, Dallas, TX
Jennifer M. Tino, 29, Livingston, NJ
Robert Frank TiPaldi, 25, New York, NY
John J. Tipping, 33, Port Jefferson, NY
David Tirado, 26, New York, NY
Hector Luis Tirado, 30, New York, NY
Michelle Titolo, 34, Copiague, NY
John J. Tobin, 47, Kenilworth, NJ
Richard J. Todisco, 61, Wyckoff, NJ
Vladimir Tomasevic, 36, Etobicoke, ON, CAN
Stephen K. Tompsett, 39, Garden City, NY
Thomas Tong, 31, New York, NY
Azucena de la Torre, 50, New York, NY
Luis Eduardo Torres, 31, New York, NY
Doris Torres, 32, New York, NY
Amy E. Toyen, 24, Newton, MA
Christopher M. Traina, 25, Bricktown, NJ
Daniel Patrick Trant, 40, Northport, NY
Abdoul Karim Traore, 41, New York, NY
Walter Travers, 44, Upper Saddle River, NJ
Glenn J. Travers, 53, Tenafly, NJ
Felicia Traylor-Bass, 38, New York, NY
Lisa L. Trerotola, 38, Hazlet, NJ
Karamo Trerra, 40, New York, NY
Michael Trinidad, 33, New York, NY
Francis Joseph Trombino, 68, Clifton, NJ
Gregory J. Trost, 26, New York, NY
William Tselepis, 33, New Providence, NJ
Zhanetta Tsoy, 32, Jersey City, NJ
Michael Patrick Tucker, 41, Rumson, NJ
Lance Richard Tumulty, 32, Bridgewater, NJ
Ching Ping Tung, 44, New York, NY
Simon James Turner, 39, London, England
Donald Joseph Tuzio, 51, Goshen, NY
Robert T. Twomey, 48, New York, NY
Jennifer Tzemis, 26, New York, NY
John G. Ueltzhoeffer, 36, Roselle Park, NJ

Tyler V. Ugolyn, 23, New York, NY
Michael A. Uliano, 42, Aberdeen, NJ
Jonathan J. Uman, 33, Westport, CN
Anil Shivhari Umarkar, 34, Hackensack, NJ
Allen V. Upton, 44, New York, NY
Diane Maria Urban, 50, Malverne, NY
John Damien Vaccacio, 30, New York, NY
Bradley H. Vadas, 37, Westport, CN
William Valcarcel, 54, New York, NY
Mayra Valdes-Rodriguez, 39, New York, NY
Ivan Vale, 27, New York, NY
Felix Antonio Vale, 29, New York, NY
Santos Valentin, 39, New York, NY
Benito Valentin, 33, New York, NY
Manuel Del Valle, 32, New York, NY
Carlton Francis Valvo, 38, New York, NY
Edward Raymond Vanacore, 29, Jersey City, NJ
Jon C. VandeVander, 44, Ridgewood, NJ
Frederick T. Varacchi, 35, Greenwich, CN
GoPalakrishnan Varadhan, 32, New York, NY
David Vargas, 46, New York, NY
Scott C. Vasel, 32, Park Ridge, NJ
Santos Vasquez, 55, New York, NY
Azael Ismael Vasquez, 21, New York, NY
Arcangel Vazquez, 47, New York, NY
Peter Anthony Vega, 36, New York, NY
Sankara S. Velamuri, 63, Avenel, NJ
Jorge Velazquez, 47, Passaic, NJ
Lawrence Veling, 44, New York, NY
Anthony M. Ventura, 41, Middletown, NJ
David Vera, 41, New York, NY
Loretta A. Vero, 51, Nanuet, NY
Christopher Vialonga, 30, Demarest, NJ
Matthew Gilbert Vianna, 23, Manhasset, NY
Robert A. Vicario, 40, Weehawken, NJ
Celeste Torres Victoria, 41, New York, NY
Joanna Vidal, 26, Yonkers, NY
John T. Vigiano, 36, West Islip, NY
Joseph Vincent Vigiano, 34, Medford, NY
Frank J. Vignola, 44, Merrick, NY
Joseph B. Vilardo, 44, Stanhope, NJ
Sergio Villanueva, 33, New York, NY
Chantal Vincelli, 38, New York, NY
Melissa Vincent, 28, Hoboken, NJ
Francine A. Virgilio, 48, New York, NY
Lawrence Virgilio, 38
Joseph G. Visciano, 22, New York, NY
Joshua S. Vitale, 28, Great Neck, NY
Maria Percoco Vola, 37, New York, NY
Lynette D. Vosges, 48, New York, NY
Garo H. Voskerijian, 43, Valley Stream, NY
Alfred Vukosa, 32, New York, NY
Gregory Wachtler, 25, Ramsey, NJ
Gabriela Waisman, 33, New York, NY
Wendy Rosario Wakeford, 40, Freehold, NJ
Courtney Walcott, 37, New York, NY
Victor Wald, 49, New York, NY
Benjamin Walker, 41, Suffern, NY
Glen J. Wall, 38, Rumson, NJ
Peter G. Wallace, 66, Lincoln Park, NJ
Mitchel Scott Wallace, 34, Mineola, NY
Lt. Robert F. Wallace, 43, New York, NY
Roy Michael Wallace, 42, Wyckoff, NJ
Jean Marie Wallendorf, 23, New York, NY
Matthew Blake Wallens, 31, New York, NY
John Wallice, 43, Huntington, NY
Barbara P. Walsh, 59, New York, NY
James Walsh, 37, Scotch Plains, NJ
Jeffrey Patrick Walz, 37, Tuckahoe, NY
Ching H. Wang, 59, New York, NY
Weibin Wang, 41, Orangeburg, NY
Lt. Michael Warchola, 51, Middle Village, NY
Stephen Gordon Ward, 33, Gorham, ME
James A. Waring, 49, New York, NY
Brian G. Warner, 32, Morganville, NJ
Derrick Washington, 33, Calverton, NY
Charles Waters, 44, New York, NY
James Thomas Waters, 39, New York, NY
Capt. Patrick J. Waters, 44, New York, NY
Kenneth Watson, 39, Smithtown, NY
Michael H. Waye, 38, Morganville, NJ
Walter E. Weaver, 30, Centereach, NY
Todd C. Weaver, 30, New York, NY
Nathaniel Webb, 56, Jersey City, NJ
Dinah Webster, 50, Port Washington, NY
Joanne Flora Weil, 39, New York, NY
Steven Weinberg, 41, New City, NY
Michael Weinberg, 34, New York, NY
Scott Jeffrey Weingard, 29, New York, NY
Steven Weinstein, 50, New York, NY

Simon Weiser, 65, New York, NY
David T. Weiss, 50, New York, NY
David M. Weiss, 41, Maybrook, NY
Vincent Michael Wells, 22, Redbridge, ENG
Timothy Matthew Welty, 34, Yonkers, NY
Christian Wemmers, 43, San Francisco, CA
Ssu-Hui (Vanessa) Wen, 23, New York, NY
Oleh D. Wengerchuk, 56, Centerport, NY
Peter M. West, 54, Pottersville, NJ
Whitfield West, 41, New York, NY
Meredith Lynn Whalen, 23, Hoboken, NJ
Eugene Whelan, 31, Rockaway Beach, NY
James Patrick White, 34, Hoboken, NJ
John S. White, 48, New York, NY
Leonard Anthony White, 57, New York, NY
Edward James White, 30, New York, NY
Kenneth W. White, 50, New York, NY
Malissa White, 37, New York, NY
Wayne White, 38, New York, NY
Adam S. White, 26, New York, NY
Leanne Marie Whiteside, 31, New York, NY
Mark Whitford, 31, Salisbury Mills, NY
Michael T. Wholey, 34, Westwood, NJ
Mary Lenz Wieman, 43, Rockville Centre, NY
Jeffrey David Wiener, 33, New York, NY
William J. Wik, 44, Crestwood, NY
Alison Marie Wildman, 30, New York, NY
Lt. Glenn Wilkinson, 46, Bayport, NY
John C. Willett, 29, Jersey City, NJ
Brian Patrick Williams, 29, New York, NY
Crossley Williams, 28, Uniondale, NY
Louie Anthony Williams, 44, New York, NY
David Williams, 34, New York, NY
Deborah Lynn Williams, 35, Hoboken, NJ
Kevin Michael Williams, 24, New York, NY
Louis Calvin Williams, 53, Mandeville, LA
Lt. John Williamson, 46, Warwick, NY
Donna Wilson, 48, Williston Park, NY
Cynthia Wilson, 52, New York, NY
William E. Wilson, 55, New York, NY
David H. Winton, 29, New York, NY
Glenn J. Winuk, 40, New York, NY
Thomas Francis Wise, 43, New York, NY
Frank T. Wisniewski, 54, Basking Ridge, NJ
Alan L. Wisniewski, 47, Howell, NJ
David Wiswall, 54, N. MAapequa, NY
Sigrid Charlotte Wiswe, 41, New York, NY
Michael Wittenstein, 34, Hoboken, NJ
Christopher W. Wodenshek, 35, Ridgewood, NJ
Martin P. Wohlforth, 47, Greenwich, CN
Katherine S. Wolf, 40, New York, NY
Jenny Seu Kueng Low Wong, 25, New York, NY
Yuk Ping Wong, 47, New York, NY
Jennifer Y. Wong, 26, New York, NY
Siu Cheung Wong, 34, Jersey City, NJ
Yin Ping (Steven) Wong, 34, New York, NY
Brent James Woodall, 31, Oradell, NJ
James J. Woods, 26, New York, NY
Patrick Woods, 36, New York, NY
Richard Woodwell, 44, Ho-Ho-Kus, NJ
Capt. David Terence Wooley, 54, Nanuet, NY
John Bentley Works, 36, Darien, CN
Martin Michael Wortley, 29, Park Ridge, NJ
Rodney James Wotton, 36, Middletown, NJ
William Wren, 61, Lynbrook, NY
John Wright, 33, Rockville Centre, NY
Neil R. Wright, 30, Asbury, NJ
Sandra Wright, 57, Langhorne, PA
Jupiter Yambem, 41, Beacon, NY
Suresh Yanamadala, 33, Plainsboro, NJ
Matthew David Yarnell, 26, Jersey City, NJ
Myrna Yaskulka, 59, New York, NY
Shakila Yasmin, 26, New York, NY
Olabisi L. Yee, 38, New York, NY
Edward P. York, 45, Wilton, CN
Kevin Patrick York, 41, Princeton, NJ
Raymond York, 45, Valley Stream, NY
Suzanne Youmans, 60, New York, NY
Jacqueline (Jakki) Young, 37, New York, NY
Barrington L. Young, 35, New York, NY
Elkin Yuen, 32, New York, NY
Joseph Zaccoli, 39, Valley Stream, NY
Adel Agayby Zakhary, 50, N. Arlington, NJ
Arkady Zaltsman, 45, New York, NY
Edwin J. Zambrana, 24, New York, NY
Robert Alan Zampieri, 30, Saddle River, NJ
Mark Zangrilli, 36, Pompton Plains, NJ
Ira Zaslow, 55, N. Woodmere, NY
Kenneth Albert Zelman, 37, Succasunna, NJ
Abraham J. Zelmanowitz, 55, New York, NY

Martin Zempoaltecatl, 22, New York, NY
Zhe (Zack) Zeng, 28, New York, NY
Marc Scott Zeplin, 33, Harrison, NY
Jie Yao Justin Zhao, 27, New York, NY
Ivelin Ziminski, 40, Tarrytown, NY
Michael Joseph Zinzi, 37, Newfoundland, NJ
Charles A. Zion, 54, Greenwich, CN
Julie Lynne Zipper, 44, Paramus, NJ
Salvatore J. Zisa, 45, Hawthorne, NJ
Prokopios Paul Zois, 46, Lynbrook, NY
Joseph J. Zuccala, 54, Croton-on-Hudson, NY
Andrew Steven Zucker, 27, New York, NY

American Airlines Flight 11

from Boston, MA, to Los Angeles, CA, crashed into the north tower of the World Trade Center with 92 people on board.

CREW

Jeffrey Collman, 41, Novato, CA
Sara Low, 28, Batesville, Arkansas
Karen A. Martin, 40, Danvers, MA
1st Of. Thomas McGuinness, 42, Portsmouth, NH
Kathleen Nicosia, 54, Winthrop, MA
John Ogonowski, 52, Dracut, MA
Betty Ong, 45, Andover, MA
Jean Roger, 24, Longmeadow, MA
Dianne Snyder, 42, Westport, MA
Madeline Sweeney, 35, Acton, MA

PASSENGERS

David Angell, 54, Pasadena, CA
Lynn Angell, 45, Pasadena, CA
Seima Aoyama, 48, Culver City, CA
Myra Aronson, 52, Charlestown, MA
Christine Barbuto, 32, Brookline, MA
Carolyn Beug, 48, Los Angeles, CA
Kelly Ann Booms, 24, Brookline, MA
Carol Bouchard, 43, Warwick, RI
Robin Caplan, 33, Westboro, MA
Neilie Casey, 32, Wellesley, MA
Jeffrey Coombs, 42, Abington, MA
Tara Creamer, 30, Worcester, MA
Thelma Cuccinello, 71, Wilmot, NH
Patrick Currivan, 52, Winchester, MA
Brian Dale, 43, Warren, NJ
David DiMeglio, 22, Wakefield, MA
Donald Americo DiTullio, 49, Peabody, MA
Albert Dominguez, 66, Sydney, Australia
Paige Farley-Hackel, 46, Newton, MA
Alex Filipov, 70, Concord, MA
Carol Flyzik, 40, Plaistow, NH
Paul Friedman, 45, Belmont, MA
Karleton D.B. Fyfe, 31, Brookline, MA
Peter Gay, 54, Tewksbury, MA
Linda George, 27, Westboro, MA
Edmund Glazer, 41, Los Angeles, CA
Lisa Fenn Gordenstein, 41, Needham, MA
Andrew Curry Green, 34, Santa Monica, CA
Peter Hashem, 40, Tewksbury, MA
Robert Hayes, 37, from Amesbury, MA
Edward (Ted) R. Hennessy, 35, Belmont, MA
John A. Hofer, 45, Los Angeles, CA
Cora Hidalgo Holland, 52, of Sudbury, MA
Nicholas Humber, 60, of Newton, MA
Waleed Iskandar, 34, London, England
John Charles Jenkins, 45, Cambridge, MA
Charles Edward Jones, 48, Bedford, MA
Barbara Keating, 72, Palm Springs, CA
David Kovalcin, 42, of Hudson, NH
Judy Larocque, 50, Framingham, MA
Natalie Janis Lasden, 46, Peabody, MA
Daniel John Lee, 34, Van Nuys, CA
Daniel C. Lewin, 31, Charlestown, MA
Susan A. MacKay, 44, Westford, MA
Christopher D. Mello, 25, Boston, MA
Jeff Mladenik, 43, Hinsdale, IL
Antonio Jesus Montoya Valdes, 46, E. Boston, MA
Carlos Alberto Montoya, 36, Bellmont, MA.
Laura Lee Morabito, 34, Framingham, MA
Mildred Naiman, 81, Andover, MA
Laurie Ann Neira, 48, Los Angeles, CA

Renee Newell, 37, of Cranston, RI
Jacqueline J. Norton, 61, Lubec, ME
Robert Grant Norton, 85, Lubec, ME
Jane M. Orth, 49, Haverhill, MA
Thomas Pecorelli, 31, of Los Angeles, CA
Berinthia Berenson Perkins, 53, Los Angeles, CA
Sonia Morales Puopolo, 58, of Dover, MA
David E. Retik, 33, Needham, MA
Philip M. Rosenzweig, 47, Acton, MA
Richard Ross, 58, Newton, MA
Jessica Sachs, 22, Billerica, MA
Rahma Salie, 28, Boston, MA
Heather Lee Smith, 30, Boston, MA
Douglas J. Stone, 54, Dover, NH
Xavier Suarez, 41, Chino Hills, CA
Michael Theodoridis, 32, Boston, MA
James Trentini, 65, Everett, MA
Mary Trentini, 67, Everett, MA
Pendyala Vamsikrishna, 30, Los Angeles, CA
Mary Wahlstrom, 78, Kaysville, UT
Kenneth Waldie, 46, Methuen, MA
John Wenckus, 46, Torrance, CA
Candace Lee Williams, 20, Danbury, CN
Christopher Zarba, 47, Hopkinton, MA

American Airlines Flight 77

from Washington to Los Angeles, crashed into the Pentagon with 64 people aboard.

CREW

David M. Charlebois, 39, Washington, D.C
Michele Heidenberger, 57, Chevy Chase, MD
Jennifer Lewis, 38, Culpeper, Virginia
Kenneth Lewis, 49, Culpeper, Virginia
Renee A. May, 39, Baltimore, MD

PASSENGERS

Yeneneh Betru, 35, Burbank, CA
Mary Jane (MJ) Booth, 64, Falls Church, VA
Bernard Curtis Brown, 11, Washington, D.C
Suzanne Calley, 42, San Martin, CA
William Caswell, 54, Silver Spring, MD
Sarah Clark, 65, Columbia, MD
Zandra Cooper, Annandale, VA
Asia Cottom, 11, Washington, DC
James Debeuneure, 58, Upper Marlboro, MD
Rodney Dickens, 11, Washington, DC
Eddie Dillard, Alexandria, VA
Charles Droz, 52, Springfield, VA
Barbara G. Edwards, 58, Las Vegas, NV
Charles S. Falkenberg, 45, University Park, MD
Zoe Falkenberg, 8, University Park, MD
Dana Falkenberg, 3, University Park, MD
James Joe Ferguson, 39, Washington, DC
Wilson "Bud" Flagg, 63, Millwood, VA
Darlene Flagg, 63, Millwood, VA
Richard Gabriel, 54, Great Falls, VA
Ian J. Gray, 55, Columbia, MD
Stanley Hall, 68, Rancho Palos Verdes, CA
Bryan Jack, 48, Alexandria, VA
Steven D. Jacoby, 43, Alexandria, VA
Ann Judge, 49, Great Falls, VA
Chandler Keller, 29, El Segundo, CA
Yvonne Kennedy, 62, Sydney, Australia
Norma Khan, 45, Reston, VA
Karen A. Kincaid, 40, Washington, DC
Dong Lee, 48, Leesburg, VA
Dora Menchaca, 45, of Santa Monica, CA
Christopher Newton, 38, Anaheim, CA
Barbara Olson, 45, Great Falls, VA
Ruben Ornedo, 39, Los Angeles, CA
Robert Penniger, 63, of Poway, CA
Robert R. Ploger, 59, Annandale, VA
Lisa J. Raines, 42, Great Falls, VA
Todd Reuben, 40, Potomac, MD
John Sammartino, 37, Annandale, VA
Diane Simmons, Great Falls, VA
George Simmons, Great Falls, VA
Mari-Rae Sopper, 35, Santa Barbara, CA
Robert Speisman, 47, Irvington, NY
Norma Lang Steuerle, 54, Alexandria, VA
Leonard Taylor, 44, Reston, VA
Hilda E. Taylor, 62, Forestville, MD

Sandra Teague, 31, Fairfax, VA
Leslie A. Whittington, 45, University Park, MD
John D. Yamnicky, 71, Waldorf, MD
Vicki Yancey, 43, Springfield, VA
Shuyin Yang, 61, Beijing, China
Yuguag Zheng, 65, Beijing, China

United Airlines Flight 175

from Boston, MA, to Los Angeles, CA, was the second hijacked plane to strike the World Trade Center, plowing into the south tower. Two pilots, seven flight attendants and 56 Passengers were on board.

CREW

Michael R. Horrocks, 38, Glen Mills, Pa
Amy N. Jarret, 28, N. Smithfield, R.I
Amy R. King, 29, Stafford Springs, CN
Kathryn L. LaBorie, 44, Providence, RI
Alfred Marchand, 44, Alamogordo, NM
Cpt. Victor Saracini, 51, Lower Makefield Twp, PA
Michael C. Tarrou, 38, Stafford Springs, CN
Alicia Nicole Titus, 28, San Francisco, CA

PASSENGERS

Garnet Edward Bailey, 54, Lynnfield, MA
Mark Bavis, 31, West Newton, MA
Graham Andrew Berkeley, 37, Boston, MA
Touri Bolourchi, 69, Beverly Hills, CA
Klaus Bothe, 31, Linkenheim, Germany
Daniel R. Brandhorst, 41, Los Angeles, CA
David Gamboa Brandhorst, 3, Los Angeles, CA
John Brett Cahill, 56, Wellesley, MA
Christoffer Carstanjen, 33, Turner Falls, MA
John (Jay) J. Corcoran, 43, Norwell, MA
Dorothy Alma DeAraujo, 80, Long Beach, CA
Ana Gloria Pocasangre de Barrera, 49, San Salvador, El Salvador
Lisa Frost, 22, Rancho Santa Margarita, CA
Ronald Gamboa, 33, Los Angeles, CA
Lynn Catherine Goodchild, 25, Attleboro, MA
Peter Morgan Goodrich, 33, Sudbury, MA
Douglas A. Gowell, 52, Methuen, MA
The Rev. Francis E. Grogan, 76, of Easton, MA
Carl Max Hammond, 37, Derry, NH
Peter Hanson, 32, Groton, MA
Sue Jue Kim-Hanson, 35, Groton, MA
Christine Lee Hanson, 2, Groton, MA
Gerald F. Hardacre, 61, Carlsbad, CA
Eric Samadikan Hartono, 20, Boston, MA
James E. Hayden, 47, Westford, MA
Herbert W. Homer, 48, Milford, MA.
Robert Adrien Jalbert, 61, Swampscott, MA
Ralph Kershaw, 52, Manchester-by-the-Sea, MA
Heinrich Kimmig, 43, Willstaett, Germany
Brian Kinney, 29, Lowell, MA
Robert George LeBlanc, 70, Lee, NH
Maclovio Lopez, Jr., 41, Norwalk, CA
Marianne MacFarlane, MacFarlane, 34, Revere, MA
Louis Neil Mariani, 59, Derry, NH.
Juliana Valentine McCourt, 4, New London, CN
Ruth Magdalene McCourt, 45, New London, CN
Wolfgang Menzel, 59, Wilhelmshaven, Germany
Shawn M. Nassaney, 25, Pawtucket, R.I
Marie PapPalardo, 53, Paramount, CA
Patrick Quigley, 40, of Wellesley, MA
Frederick Charles Rimmele, 32, Marblehead, MA
James M. Roux, 43, Portland, ME
Jesus Sanchez, 45, Hudson, MA
Mary Kathleen Shearer, 61, Dover, NH
Robert Michael Shearer, 63, Dover, NH
Jane Louise Simpkin, 36, Wayland, MA
Brian D. Sweeney, 38, Barnstable, MA
Timothy Ward, 38, San Diego, CA
William M. Weems, 46, Marblehead, MA

America — Voices Coming Together

UNITED AIRLINES FLIGHT 93
from Newark, New Jersey, to San Francisco, CA, crashed in rural southwest Pennsylvania, with 45 people on board.

CREW

Sandra W. Bradshaw, 38, Greensboro, NC
Jason Dahl, 43, Denver, CO
Wanda Anita Green, 49, Linden, NJ
Leroy Homer, 36, Marlton, NJ
CeeCee Lyles, 33, Fort Myers, FL
Deborah Welsh, 49, New York, NY

PASSENGERS

Todd Beamer, 32, Cranbury, NJ
Alan Beaven, 48, Oakland, CA
Mark K. Bingham, 31, San Francisco, CA
Deora Frances Bodley, 20, San Diego, CA
Marion Britton, 53, New York, NY
Thomas E. Burnett Jr., 38, San Ramon, CA
William Cashman, 57, N. Bergen, NJ
Georgine Rose Corrigan, 56, Honolulu, HI
Patricia Cushing, 69, Bayonne, NJ
Joseph Deluca, 52, Ledgewood, NJ
Patrick Joseph Driscoll, 70, Manalapan, NJ
Edward P. Felt, 41, Matawan, NJ
Jane C. Folger, 73, Bayonne, NJ
Colleen Laura Fraser, 51, Elizabeth, NJ
Andrew Garcia, 62, Portola Valley, CA
Jeremy Glick, 31, Hewlett, NJ
Lauren Grandcolas, 38, San Rafael, CA
Donald F. Greene, 52, Greenwich, CN
Linda Gronlund, 46, Warwick, NY
Richard Guadagno, 38, of Eureka, CA
Toshiya Kuge, 20, Nishimidoriguoska, Japan
Hilda Marcin, 79, Budd Lake, NJ
Nicole Miller, 21, San Jose, CA
Louis J. Nacke, 42, New Hope, PA
Donald Arthur Peterson, 66, Spring Lake, NJ
Jean Hoadley Peterson, 55, Spring Lake, NJ
Waleska Martinez Rivera, 37, Jersey City, NJ
Mark Rothenberg, 52, Scotch Plains, NJ
Christine Snyder, 32, Kailua, HI
John Talignani, 72, New York, NY
Honor Elizabeth Wainio, 27, Watchung, NJ

PENTAGON

Melissa Rose Barnes, 27, Redlands, CA
Master Sgt. Max Beilke, 69, Laurel, MD
Kris Romeo Bishundat, 23, Waldorf, MD
Carrie Blagburn, 48, Temple Hills, MD
Lt. Col. Canfield D. Boone, 54, Clifton, VA
Donna Bowen, 42, Waldorf, MD
Allen Boyle, 30, Fredericksburg, VA
Christopher Lee Burford, 23, Hubert, NC
Daniel Martin Caballero, 21, Houston, TX
Sgt.1st Cl. Jose Calderon-Olmedo, 44, Annandale, VA
Angelene C. Carter, 51, Forrestville, MD
Sharon Carver, 38, Waldorf, MD
John J. Chada, 55, Manassas, VA
Rosa Maria ChaPa, 64, Springfield, VA
Julian Cooper, 39, Springdale, MD
Lt. CMDr. Eric Allen Cranford, 32, Drexel, N.C.
Ada M. Davis, 57, Camp Springs, MD
Capt. Gerald Francis Deconto, 44, Sandwich, MA
Lt. Col. Jerry Don Dickerson, 41, Durant, Miss
Johnnie Doctor, 32, Jacksonville, Fla
Capt. Robert Edward Dolan, 43, Alexandria, VA
CMDr. William Howard Donovan, 44, Nunda, NY
CMDr. Patrick S. Dunn, 39, Springfield, VA
Edward Thomas Earhart, 26, Salt Lick, KY
Lt. CMDr. Robert Randolph Elseth, 37, Vestal, NY
Jamie Lynn Fallon, 23, Woodbridge, VA
Amelia V. Fields, 36, Dumfries, VA
Gerald P. Fisher, 57, Potomac, MD
Matthew Michael Flocco, 21, Newark, DE
Sandra N. Foster, 41, Clinton, MD
Capt. Lawrence Daniel Getzfred, 57, Elgin, NE
Cortz Ghee, 54, Reisterstown, MD
Brenda C. Gibson, 59, Falls Church, VA
Ron Golinski, 60, Columbia, MD
Diane M. Hale-McKinzy, 38, Alexandria, VA
Carolyn B. Halmon, 49, Washington, DC
Sheila Hein, 51, University Park, MD
Ronald John Hemenway, 37, Shawnee, KS
Maj. Wallace Cole Hogan, 40, FL
Jimmie Ira Holley, 54, Lanham, MD
Angela Houtz, 27, La Plata, MD
Brady K. Howell, 26, Arlington, VA
Peggie Hurt, 36, Crewe, VA
Lt. Col. Stephen Neil Hyland, 45, Burke, VA
Robert J. Hymel, 55, Woodbridge, VA
Sgt. Maj. Lacey B. Ivory, 43, Woodbridge, VA
Lt. Col. Dennis M. Johnson, 48, Pt. Edwards, WI
Judith Jones, 53, Woodbridge, VA
Brenda Kegler, 49, Washington, DC
Lt. Michael Scott Lamana, 31, Baton Rouge, LA
David W. Laychak, 40, Manassas, VA
Samantha Lightbourn-Allen, 36, Hillside, MD
Maj. Steve Long, 39, GA
James Lynch, 55, Manassas, VA
Terence M. Lynch, 49, Alexandria, VA
Nehamon Lyons, 30, Mobile, AL
Shelley A. Marshall, 37, Marbury, MD
Teresa Martin, 45, Stafford, VA
Ada L. Mason, 50, Springfield, VA
Lt. Col. Dean E. Mattson, 57, CA
Lt. Gen. Timothy J. Maude, 53, Fort Myer, VA
Robert J. Maxwell, 53, Manassas, VA
Molly McKenzie, 38, Dale City, VA
Patricia E. (Patti) Mickley, 41, Springfield, VA
Maj. Ronald D. Milam, 33, Washington, DC
Gerard (Jerry) P. Moran, 39, Upper Marlboro, MD
Odessa V. Morris, 54, Upper Marlboro, MD
Brian Anthony Moss, 34, Sperry, OK
Ted Moy, 48, Silver Spring, MD
Lt. CMDr. Patrick Murphy, 38, Flossmoor, IL
Khang Nguyen, 41, Fairfax, VA
Michael Allen Noeth, 30, New York, NY
Diana Borrero de Padro, 55, Woodbridge, VA
Spc. Chin Sun Pak, 25, Lawton, OK
Lt. Jonas Martin Panik, 26, Mingoville, PA
Maj. Clifford L. Patterson, 33, Alexandria, VA
Lt. J.G Darin Howard Pontell, 26, Columbia, MD
Scott Powell, 35, Silver Spring, MD
(Retired) Capt. Jack Punches, 51, Clifton, VA
Joseph John Pycior, 39, Carlstadt, NJ
Deborah Ramsaur, 45, Annandale, VA
Rhonda Rasmussen, 44, Woodbridge, VA
Marsha Dianah Ratchford, 34, Prichard, AL
Martha Reszke, 36, Stafford, VA
Cecelia E. Richard, 41, Fort Washington, MD
Edward V. Rowenhorst, 32, Lake Ridge, VA
Judy Rowlett, 44, Woodbridge, VA
Robert E. Russell, 52, Oxon Hill, MD
William R. Ruth, 57, Mount Airy, MD
Charles E. Sabin, 54, Burke, VA
Marjorie C. Salamone, 53, Springfield, VA
Lt. Col. David M. Scales, 44, Cleveland, OH
CMDr. Robert Allan Schlegel, 38, Alexandria, VA
Janice Scott, 46, Springfield, VA
Michael L. Selves, 53, Fairfax, VA
Marian Serva, 47, Stafford, VA
CMDr. Dan Frederic Shanower, 40, Naperville, IL
Antoinette Sherman, 35, Forest Heights, MD
Don Simmons, 58, Dumfries, VA
Cheryle D. Sincock, 53, Dale City, VA
Gregg Harold Smallwood, 44, Overland Park, KS
(Ret.) Lt. Col. Gary F. Smith, 55, Alexandria, VA
Patricia J. Statz, 41, Takoma Park, MD
Edna L. Stephens, 53, Washington, DC
Sgt. Maj. Larry Strickland, 52, Woodbridge, VA
Maj. Kip P. Taylor, 38, McLean, VA
Sandra C. Taylor, 50, Alexandria, VA
Karl W. Teepe, 57, Centreville, VA
Sgt. Tamara Thurman, 25, Brewton, AL
Lt. CMDr. Otis Vincent Tolbert, 38, Lemoore, CA
Willie Q. Troy, 51, Aberdeen, MD
Lt. CMDr. Ronald Vauk, 37, NamPa, ID
Lt. Col. Karen Wagner, 40, Houston, TX
Meta L. Waller, 60, Alexandria, VA
Staff Sgt. Maudlyn A. White, 38, St. Croix, VI
Sandra L. White, 44, Dumfries, VA
Ernest M. Willcher, 62, N. Potomac, MD
Lt. CMDr. David Williams, 32, Newport, OR
Maj. Dwayne Williams, 40, Jacksonville, AL
Marvin R. Woods, 57, Great Mills, MD
Kevin Wayne Yokum, 27, Lake Charles, LA
Donald McArthur Young, 41, Roanoke, VA
Lisa L. Young, 36, Germantown, MD
Edmond Young, 22, Owings, MD

Matthew 5:3-12

[3] Blessed *are* the poor in spirit: for theirs in the kingdom of heaven.

[4] Blessed *are* they that mourn: for they shall be comforted.

[5] Blessed *are* they meek: for they shall inherit the earth.

[6] Blessed *are* they which do hunger and thirst after righteousness: for they shall be filled.

[7] Blessed *are* the merciful: for they shall obtain mercy.

[8] Blessed *are* the pure in heart: for they shall see God.

[9] Blessed *are* the peacemakers: for they shall be called the children of God.

[10] Blessed *are* they which are persecuted for righteousness'sake: for theirs is the kingdom of heaven.

[11] Blessed are ye, when *men* shall revile you, and persecute *you*, and shall say all manner of evil against you falsely, for my sake.

[12] Rejoice, and be exceeding glad: for great *is* your reward in heaven: for so persecuted they the prophets which were before you.

*But I say unto you, Love your enemies,
bless them that curse you,
do good to them that hate you,
and pray for them which despitefully use you,
and persecute you.*
Matthew 5:44